W9-DBL-716

Gentle Dove

The Holy Spirit, God's Greatest Gift

To DR. MiRDA Thank you FOR your years of Compassionate Care.

...as he was praying, heaven was opened and

the Holy Spirit descended on him in bodily form like a

dove.

Douglas Cooper

EPH 1: 17

DOUGLAS COOPER PH.D

1

DEDICATED

To all those who have thirsty hearts
and an unusual hunger
for spiritual knowledge and experience…
and to Shana, my daughter, a gift from God.

Second Edition   2013

CONTENTS

Appendix A: A Spiritual Breathing Exercise

Appendix B: The Holy Spirit as Power Source

Appendix C: Prerequisites for Receiving the Holy Spirit

Appendix D: Guidelines for Spirit-filled Christians

Appendix E: The Laying on of Hands

Appendix F: Mission Statement for Small Groups Seeking the Spirit

Appendix G: The Second Coming / The Coming of the Kingdom

Appendix H: Religion / Spirituality

Appendix I: The Spiritual Disciplines

Appendix J: The Three Great Truths

Appendix K: The Fruits of the Ego

Appendix L: Feelings; A Path to Connection

Appendix M: Consciousness Raisers!

All Scripture quotations are from the *New International Version* unless noted.

PREFACE

After the cross, the most important doctrine in all of Christendom is the doctrine of the baptism or in-filling of the Holy Spirit. Yet, it is the most neglected and misunderstood of Christian beliefs.

The purpose of this book is to demonstrate that the filling of the Spirit is not merely a teaching to believe in but an enlightening, empowering encounter to be experienced each day. It is the throbbing heart of a vital, dynamic Christianity. Its result is the establishment of a precious moment-by-moment intimacy, a constant union with God through Jesus Christ as we learn to become more God-conscious and to practice His loving presence.

This mystical, marvelous gift, won for you and me by the sacrifice of Jesus on the cross as certainly as He won eternal life for us, is available to every believer right now, solely by faith in the One who promised it to us and who commanded us to receive it.

The gift of the filling of the Holy Spirit is the true seal of God on the Christian. It is a "down-payment" on heaven. It is an identifying sign that the kingdom of God is indeed here now, and inside of you and me just as Jesus said it could be. It brings with it the sacred gifts of love, joy, peace, patience, kindness, and forgiveness. It empowers one for a life of loving service to others.

The goal is to move from a traditional doctrinal paradigm as the foundation of one's religious experience to a new, relational-spiritual paradigm which recognizes that connection, moment-by-moment connection, with the Divine through the in-dwelling presence of the Holy Spirit, is everything.

Note to the reader

At the end of each chapter you will find a section of questions and answers. These are based on questions raised by participants in seminars where I have presented the topic of the baptism of the Holy Spirit. These Q and A sessions have always been fascinating and dynamic. They seemed to offer people a chance to raise questions from sincere and open hearts, from people looking for a more intimate connection with God, although a few came from audience members who were good naturedly skeptical. The questions reflected attitudes like: "Well, this just sounds too good to be true", or "You are going to have to prove this to me", or "If this is so important why haven't we heard about it before?" Then, there have been questions from a few who were openly hostile. Behind their anger there always seemed to lurk a deep fear of something. Some walked out of the gatherings shaking their heads.

We have all been programmed not to rock the religious boat, to conform, to maintain the religious stasis, not to question but to blindly trust the assumptions put to us by our parents, our teachers, our pastors, our traditions, our culture and our church. "Give me that old time religion, give me that old time religion. If it's good enough for grandma, it's good enough for me." … goes the old song. Perhaps we should rethink the words to the song before we totally buy into it. Is your grandparent's religion really something that you are willing to settle for? While there is great value in the traditions handed down from the past, the door must never be closed to the progression of truth, the incredible expansion of the light of spiritual knowledge and experience that is available to the awakened person today, the person who is willing to set aside pressure to conform and fear of the new or unknown and boldly open himself or herself to the quest for ongoing spiritual truth and experience.

Paul was not satisfied with the religion of the Old Testament. "The law came through the prophets, but grace and truth came through Jesus Christ," he wrote. Jesus Himself was not content with the religion of Abraham or Moses. He came to move His followers on, into deeper and deeper truth, into a richer and more profound spiritual experience. Time and time again, He said things like, "Moses said to you… but I say to you…" and then He would give a teaching 180 degrees opposite to what Moses taught. (This, by the way, was one of the behaviors that so upset the religious establishment, the religious status quo, that it eventually got Him killed.) This book is about the incredible "I say unto you" Spirit-centered consciousness that Jesus brought into the world as contrasted with the "ye-have-heard-it-said-of-old" way of law and legalism that sadly still pervades much of religion today.

If you had a computer with an operating system 1.0 that was introduced in 1985, I am sure you would be eager to update as quickly as possible to the new, more advanced, state-of-the-art version 10.0! Have you ever considered opening your self to an update of your spiritual experience? Are you willing to thoroughly examine your beliefs and convictions? Could some be outdated? Frighteningly narrow? Limiting? Are you possibly sitting in a self-imposed religious prison? A prison of fear, fear that if you open yourself to something new, something bigger, some new spiritual experience, that if you start to think for yourself you might lose your God or your religion or your friends?

Jesus said He was come to bring, "freedom to the prisoners." He did not mean only those behind physical walls. It is so easy for us to be conformists and adapt to prison life.

Especially life in a religious prison! We have so much company there! It can feel so safe and comfortable! Right after 9/11 I was visiting with a prison inmate. Only partly with tongue-in- cheek, he said… "Boy, I am lucky to be in here! This is the safest spot in the country right now. Nobody can get to me in here. I feel sorry for you out there in the scary outside world!"

If we see ourselves locked into our religion, it might be tempting to settle in to feeling safe and comfortable and to even put a lot of energy into trying to improve and decorate our religious jail cells! You know, better lighting, ventilation, TV, internet access! Perhaps you are in a religious prison without realizing that the door to your cell has been unlocked all the time!

This book invites you to walk through that door into a new kind of spiritual freedom, joy and abundance. It is going to do something you might never have thought of doing or have dared to do before. *It is going to invite you to create your own personalized religious and spiritual life and experience.* You will be asked to find or develop your own distinctive, inimitable spiritual practices that work especially well for you, that are unique to who you are and what you want to become. You are free to do that you know. The Bible encourages you to "work out your *own* salvation." It is up to you to make your spiritual life happen. Your father or mother can't do it for you. Your preacher can't do it for you. Your church can't do it for you. Each one of us simply must, just for ourselves, answer the question, "Who is Christ for me?"

Most of all, this book is for people who regard themselves more as seekers than believers. It is for people who are more committed to encountering and experiencing the Divine than to simply believing in the Divine in a certain way. ("Even the devils believe ... and tremble!")

Could it be that we are now approaching or have even already entered into a time forecast in the distant past? A time of major transition? A time of great spiritual awakening? A time when new dreams will be dreamed? Incredible, never-before-imagined truths revealed? Deeper spiritual levels accessed and experienced? A whole new spiritual paradigm introduced? *This is indeed beginning to happen now as Christian consciousness rises and we move the foundation of our spiritual lives from law to grace, from rules to relationship, from dogma to devotion, from belief to experience.* Think about it...when you go to church, are you expecting to get more information about God or are you expecting an experience with God? *Do you want an explanation or an experience?* Do you want to discuss God or experience Him?

Too many sermons today seem only to be about imparting information, ideas, and doctrines. The goal of a sermon should not be merely to inform or indoctrinate the hearers but to bring them into Divine union! Listeners should be led to experience what Thomas Merton speaks of: "God loves you, is present in you, lives in you, dwells in you, calls you, saves you and offers an understanding and light which are like nothing you ever found in books or heard in sermons."

I dare you to believe for yourself the words of the Master when He promised: "But when the Spirit of truth comes, he will guide you into all truth". (John 16:13) Are you ready to begin to experience more joy, peace and love than you could ever imagine possible? Can you actually accept the fact that the kingdom of heaven begins *now*? Are you aware that you do not have to wait for the Second Coming to begin enjoying and experiencing it! Let the journey begin! Spiritual growth is the most satisfying, richly rewarding experience you can have, and besides that it is a heck-of-a-lot of fun!

Warning to the reader: this is not a book for the spiritually faint of heart. It is intended to help you examine the very foundation of your spirituality.

It is offered with the hope that it will assist you in daring to take the next step in your spiritual growth. (Baby step or quantum leap? That is up to you.) It recognizes that one of the things we all need most is the readiness to learn and experience something new. God is infinite! It is so exciting! Life is a great spiritual adventure! To seek the presence of God is the greatest adventure of all! There is always more of Him to encounter, more of His love and truth to experience! More of His power to tap! Every Christian should be an evolutionist: a spiritual evolutionist! That is because truth is progressive. Revelation is progressive! The light is increasing! The Spirit is able to keep us in a place of constant growth and increasing enlightenment. *Consciousness rising*. That should describe your inner state. Like the man said in Romans 13:11, "...now it is high time to awake out of sleep."

Check this out. Under the guidance of the Holy Spirit the church has made great progress through the centuries. Gentiles, non-Jews, were eventually welcomed into full fellowship. The priesthood of all believers led to the understanding that every Christian is a minister and has direct access to God without a priestly or clergy "intercessor" or interpreter. The Bible, thanks to the blood of heroic martyrs, became available to all in their own language. Salvation by faith alone came to replace people struggling to earn eternal life by their own good behavior. Slavery was finally abolished. Apartheid and segregation came to be recognized for the evil that they were. Mentally ill people have come to be seen as suffering from a biological-based illness rather than being regarded as demon-possessed. Suicide is now understood as a result of the illness of depression and not something that would automatically preclude a person from entering heaven. Divorced people, instead of being shunned have been cared for and supported by the church and offered a second chance at happiness. Women are seen as the spiritual equal of men and in enlightened churches are no longer barred from full ordination. Gay and lesbian people are no longer excluded from Christian fellowship. The foundation of spiritual life is now understood to be a personal, living, moment-by-moment connection with the Divine. That is progress baby!

Sadly, there are still two more-and-more diverging types of Christianity. One is fear-based and focuses on rules, requirements and rewards and religion. It is often coercive and intolerant. The other is love-based, grace-filled and focuses on love, acceptance, mercy, forgiveness, relationships and personal transformation through the indwelling of the Holy Spirit.

This book is dedicated to helping us all move quickly toward the latter. May it open doors to love.

After 25 years in school I finally learned at least one thing: the only way someone can be of help to you is to challenge your ideas. This book will certainly challenge some of your religious assumptions and traditions. It may discomfort you. In some places it will probably make you angry. I hope so. If you are spiritually lethargic, it may wake you up. If you are by some chance still in spiritual kindergarten, it will challenge you to get out of your comfort zone. It will encourage you to stop depending on others and move on to spiritual maturity, to move on to being in charge of your own incredible, exciting, blossoming spiritual destiny! *Religious stagnation or vibrant spiritual growth. Those are really the only two choices.*

I hope that what is in these pages will help you to let go the mooring lines that are holding you to the dock. I want you to get out of the harbor. Leave the safety of the port. Experience the glorious freedom and challenge and risk of the open seas. It was poet Mary Oliver who asked the poignant question of her readers, "Tell me, what is it you plan to do with your one wild and precious life?" It is your one wild and precious spiritual life that I am asking you to take a hard look at. You say, "It sounds like you want me to reform." Not so. Reform is too easy! These are incredible times. I don't want you to be content with reform. I want you to join the revolution! I want you to revolt! Not revolt against the government or church, but I want to encourage your revolt against your own inner world of spiritual entropy, apathy and complacency. I want this book to make you disgusted with your own raging egotism and narcissism. Most of all, I want it to help heal you in your wounded places, to replace your fear with love, your sadness with joy and your loneliness and alienation with fellowship and oneness.

10

It would be so awfully presumptuous of me to even begin to imply such possibilities for you if it were not for the fact that the focus of this book is the most powerful teaching in Scripture. Here is the bottom line, the best summary I can give you of what is at stake in these pages. *The New Testament teaches plain as day that every Christian is to seek and receive the baptism with the Holy Spirit as a definite experience. An experience beyond conversion, beyond the new birth, beyond water baptism, beyond salvation by faith.* The baptism of the Spirit, simply put, is the Spirit of God coming upon a person by that person's full surrender of his or her will to God and specific invitation to the Spirit to live within in a new and powerful and mysterious way. It is a mystical experience. That is, it cannot be comprehended with the intellect or explained with logic or defined by dogma. Paradoxically, it is only in letting go of trying to explain or understand or make a doctrine out of the Holy Spirit that will allow one to experience it.

Sometimes you have to stop trying so hard to be filled with the Spirit and just allow it to happen. *Surrender is always the path to the truly spiritual encounter.* Permission is given to the Spirit to take possession of oneself, of one's time, energy, talent, and money. The seeker will receive a new and passionate love for Jesus Christ, a new personal intimacy with God and a gift or gifts that will empower a unique loving service to others God..

The Holy Spirit is not a topic about which one can easily maintain a disinterested neutrality about. In fact, it carries inherent within this powerful Essence is a potential for radical inner transformation. The deeper, more mystical truths and experiences of Christianity can indeed be very unsettling to someone who has been leading a self-centered or complacent life, a life centered more on acquiring than serving. Here's the big question when it comes to the Holy Spirit: Are you going to ignore it? Do you want to analyze it? Debate it? Or start experiencing it? I don't want to just talk about the Holy Spirit or write about the Holy Spirit. I want you and I to experience the Holy Spirit. Now.

"If you then, being human and evil, know how to give good gifts to your children; how much more shall your heavenly Father give the Holy Spirit to them that ask Him?" (Luke 11:23).

11

INTRODUCTION

I want to save you some time. The following is a summary of what it is like to live your life in the Spirit. If these characteristic appeal to you, fine, then this book is for you because it tells you how to have these attributes more clearly and simply than perhaps anything else you have ever read. If these characteristics are not something you appreciate and hunger for, then simply set the book aside. Maybe you will be ready for it later. It is even possible you will have to suffer more before you will be ready to relate to what is being said here.

The list below is a gift to you from my heart. I hope you accept this gift even if you don't read the rest of the book. It took me 40 years to put the following characteristics together! You can read them in five minutes…or you could take one a day, savor it and meditate on it in your heart and do this for 43 days before you read the rest of the book or something in between. You decide.

I want you to prepare yourself before you start to read this book. Seriously. Please, slow down. Sit somewhere quiet and comfortable. Peaceful. Phones off. Pagers off. No TV, CD, or DVD. No emails or texting or Tweeting. No Googling or Yahooing. No Facebooking or Myspacing or videogames. No iPhones, iPods, or iPads. I wonder, can you really unplug from it all? This will really be a great test! Think of it as an electronic fast! Relax your body. Let go of the tension in your neck, your jaw, your forehead. Become conscious of your breathing. Take a deep breath. Every breath you take is on loan from God! Slow down. Go ahead, take your own pulse. Put a finger lightly on your wrist or on your neck just below your ear. Feel that steady throb. Every heartbeat you have is on loan from God! Thank Him for it right now! Slow down. Stop rushing everywhere you go for goodness sake. You never, ever need to rush anywhere except into the arms of God! Even that most precious gift of all, the gift of consciousness is on loan to you from God! To really appreciate it you must calm yourself and become aware of the rhythm of your breathing and the beat of your heart. Center yourself. Still yourself. Stop your ceaseless activity and your ceaseless thinking! Turn off your monkey-mind! We get all judgmental about other's drinking or drugging or eating addictions, little realizing that our biggest and most damaging addiction is to our continuous, incessant thinking! *For crying out loud, stop thinking for a moment!* Just sit with the stillness and the silence. "Be still, and know that I am God" is one of the most spiritual verses in the Bible. Stillness, silence, these are portals to the Presence! It is in the silence of the soul that God's voice can be heard.

How long will it take us to get it? There is a reality in the universe that can not be understood through thinking. To connect intimately with God, you may need to let your continuous stream of thinking subside. For many, renunciation of thought may be the necessary key to their spiritual awakening. You can't think your way into God's presence! You can only surrender your way in. Stop thinking so much … it's all a mystery anyway! Unexplainable by reason. "That God can be known by the soul in tender personal experience while remaining infinitely aloof from the curious eyes of reason constitutes a paradox best described as darkness to the intellect but sunshine to the heart," said A.W. Tozer.

I know, I know, I am starting to make a bunch of you really uncomfortable. Good. If your religion has been based solely on intellectual comprehension of certain doctrines then I do not apologize for discomforting you. Don't worry. I am not asking you to abandon reason or give up your mind for emotion. But I am asking you to examine ways that this book can teach you to stop letting your mind be central to your spiritual experience and to realize that your mind is to be most of all a beautiful tool in service to enhancing your soul and your personal, continuing practice of the Presence of God. One spiritual teacher asked the penetrating question, "What is the mind for if not to find God?" The mind may begin the process, but the heart is what completes the journey. "If with all your *heart* you truly seek me, you will surely find me", says the Father. Cleverness is not a means of attaining salvation. No one ever has, and no one ever will, think their way to heaven!

Give me a break. Do not try to speed-read this book. Don't even think about rushing through it. (I really have a huge problem with programs that put people on a "Read the Bible through in a Year" goal. Come on, you don't speed read a love letter! You linger over every word, savor it, re-read the parts that move you. And while we are at it...I am sorry but your mom was wrong. Books are to write in! Please, I beg of you, make lots of notes in the margins and on the inside of the covers. Underline and highlight like crazy. Stop, think, ponder, feel, reflect. Question everything. And enjoy. The book is just a tool, written by a fool with good intentions, to help you explore the limitless adventure of God!

CHARACTERISTICS OF THE SPIRIT-FILLED LIFE

1. You become aware that you are loved beyond belief and are valued, cherished. You experience a sense of well-being, a freedom from fear. Love becomes the focus of your life. Where fear has blocked you, love will free you.

2. A sense of awe and wonder is restored. Life becomes re-enchanted. You open your heart to the adventure, wild beauty and every-day miracles around you. You can once again experience passion. Even bliss. A new sense of aliveness! There is a unique exhilaration, a rapturous amazement that comes from living in the Spirit. "Everything is interesting if you just come at it from a place of wonder," wrote Anne Lamott in *Crooked Little Hear*). "Give the mundane it's beautiful due," said John Updike. "Every hour of the day and night is an unspeakably perfect miracle," wrote Walt Whitman.

3. Child-likeness and simplicity are re-discovered. "I tell you the truth, unless you change (unless you are transformed) and become like little children, you will never enter the kingdom of heaven" (Matthew 18:3). A sense of innocence returns. The Spirit-filled person is able to be much more spontaneous, vulnerable, non-defensive and open. There are moments of pure awareness, pure joy. You become more playful! The child within begins to heal if there has been abuse, pain, loss or abandonment in the past. (It is never too late to have a happy childhood!) The Holy Spirit applies the medicine of love to your childhood wounds. You allow God to "re-parent" you. You become more aware of the innocence and sacredness of children and of your own inner child.

4. Self-esteem increases ("if God be for us, who can be against us?"). One begins to feel empowered. You have a very clear sense of "I am." You will not allow anyone to use or abuse you.

5. You realize that the kingdom of God is available to you *now*. You begin to experience this kingdom as within you, with all its bountifulness. This results in a sense of great abundance. You come to feel content with what you have. Material things lose much of their attraction. You enjoy simplicity. You are less "hungry." You even learn to eat your food prayerfully, slowly, mindfully and with gratitude. You learn to stop eating when you have had

15

enough to sustain you. You come understand that your relationship with food is a reflection of your relationship with God. You lose your feeling of desperation as the empty spots in your soul begin to fill up. The world around you seems to be luscious and full. You become grateful. You live in a state of gratitude and thanksgiving. You are constantly finding things to say "thank you" for. As you fall asleep, "I thank you" may be your last thought. As you wake up, "I thank you" may be your first thought. You naturally begin to practice generosity, for you feel like you have been so blessed and you have so much to give.

6. Fear, guilt and toxic shame disappear as motivating forces in your life. Unconditional love and forgiveness are accepted and replace them. You come to experience an incredible inner peace. You move from fearful to fearless!

7. The assurance of eternal life becomes very clear. It is a constant comfort. Fear diminishes. Death loses its power and its terror. He came to "…free those who all their lives were held in slavery by their fear of death," (Hebrews 1:15). The fear of aging and death is either consciously or unconsciously everyone's mother of all fears! It is at the top of the list of everyone's anxieties. But not yours. Not any more. Spirit-filled people don't get older, they just get closer, closer to God, closer to eternity. Those who practice awareness of the presence of God, find that their former horror of death has vanished! They are fearless! Liberated from the fear of death! People who have had their fear of death dealt with are "dangerous" too! You can't stop them because there is nothing left to threaten them with!

8. Unconditional, non-exploitive love becomes the center of life. Loving service to others becomes the purpose of your life. You finally learn that it is not all about you! You learn to let go of your narcissism. You learn to surrender and suspend your ego. By surrendering the self you learn to align yourself with the now and with what is and to stop constantly judging everything and everybody and trying to change everything and everybody! (What a relief!) You learn to practice a radical humility. You understand that the baptism of the Holy Spirit empowers you for your own personal ministry to others. You come to understand that every Spirit-filled Christian is a minister,

an evangelist. It becomes your greatest delight to serve, to practice random acts of love and kindness. You awaken to the incredible preciousness of each person your life touches. You come to see each one as Jesus. You learn to cherish every one.

9. You begin to experience great joy. Joy in the ordinary. Joy in other people. Joy at the incredible beauty of nature. You learn to live in an attitude of gratitude and praise. "His praise will always be on my lips," (Psalm 34:1). You are shocked to discover that happiness is your natural state! You give yourself permission to have fun! Even in church!

10. Serendipitous gifts begin to come your way. (Serendipity: The gift of being given beautiful and valuable things and experiences not sought for or expected.)

11. Synchronicity is experienced. Once you have placed yourself in oneness with God and He is living in you by His Spirit, you are connected everywhere you go and everywhere you are (think broadband, Wi-Fi, DSL, 4G cellular network!) with the same great creative super-intelligent force that created and sustains the world and continues to expand the very dimensions of the unfathomably immense universe. Your limitations can be transcended. The universe will be on your side! "Meaningful coincidences" begin to happen. (A coincidence is God's way of working a miracle anonymously!) Circumstances begin to work for you, not against you. Other people become helpful to you, cooperative. "Chance" encounters that bless and benefit you and others will increase. There will be many more unexpected, helpful occurrences and other remarkable synchronistic events in your life. When the student is ready, the teacher will appear!

12. Synergy is experienced. Synergy: what a surprise! One plus one does not equal two after all. In the real world, the spiritual world, one plus one turns out to equal three. Or six. Or eighteen. The combined efforts of two or more persons have a greater power and effect than the sum of their individual efforts. "Where two or three come together in my name, there am I with them" (Matthew 18:20). You come to covet time for praying and fellowshipping in the Spirit with other Spirit-filled people in small groups. *Small groups are the*

greatest vehicle there is for spiritual growth. They are a place to be authentic, ask questions, explore new ideas, admit our struggles and faults and ask for help. Find one. If you can't find one, start one. .

13. Your life has a feeling of being directed, guided. You learn to let your life be directed by Spirit instead of by ego! Life becomes the simple, day-by-day outworking of the will of God as you are led by the Holy Spirit. Anxiety and worry disappear. You are able to live much more spontaneously, with an incredible sense of freedom.

14. A little girl, on a long flight with her parents, woke up from a nap and asked sleepily, "Are we here yet?" The Spirit, living in, you teaches you how to be here now! After all, now is all you have! Time is altered. Time's passing loses its significance and power over you. You learn to let go of the guilt of the past and any anxiety about the future. The now is sacred space because it is the point where everything is ending and everything is beginning. God, in fact, lives only in the now. He is not the "I was" or the "I shall be." He is the "I am" and you can be too if you learn to be fully present in the moment with Him! You see, the now is the portal to the "I am" that is your soul and thus it is the portal to your deepest connection with God. *Because when you finally manage to still yourself, when you reluctantly drag yourself out of the world of form, out of the world of the seen and into the world of the unseen, when you rein in your busy mind and bring yourself totally into the present, when you surrender, you empty yourself and thus create the space where God can come to meet you and dwell within you by His Holy Spirit.* That is precisely why we say that surrender is the key to the spiritual. People often refer to God as a "Presence," and rightly so, because He is always present in the present moment!

The Spirit can teach you to actually be where you are! You will begin to get it, that you are never "there". You are always here. You will finally learn to stop treating the present moment as some sort of irritating obstacle to get past so that you can get on to some other moment that you imagine will be somehow better or more important or more exciting. When you are willing to renounce your attachment to the past and your concern about the future, when you realize that this present moment is all you have, that it is your life, you will become grounded in the now and learn to be so grateful for it. You will be able to embrace each moment as a priceless gift from God. It truly is a gift. That is why they call it "the present"! Open your present! We are to find love and joy in our journey. We don't have to wait for God's treasures until we get to our final destination.

A great peace fills you up from the inside as you learn to encounter God in His temple, your surrendered heart, in this powerful way. To ignore and not be fully present in the now is to actually deny life, because life and relationship only exist in the now. Life is now. Salvation is now. There is no past. It is gone. No single human being has ever lived one minute in the future! It does not exist. There is no future. It has not yet arrived. *There is no such thing as tomorrow! Life is now. To try and live either in the future or in the past is a form of madness.* The past and the future are only thought forms. They do not exist.

The Spirit living in you is finally able to reveal to you the sacredness and profoundness of the now. You come to realize that it is always now! That, in fact, now is all there is. Life, your very being, exists only in this moment. You stop living for the next moment or next hour or next day, and live in this very moment. You focus on, enjoy and celebrate what you are doing and who you are with in the present moment instead of trying to hurry on to something else your ego tells you will be more interesting, gratifying or entertaining. If you miss the now, you miss life. You miss love because life and love happen only in the now.

One of the most dramatic gifts the in-filling of the Holy Spirit brings is to guide you to be mindful, fully present with yourself, with God and with other people in the now. The most loving gift you can give another is your full presence with them in the now. Jesus Christ had the amazing gift of being able to be fully and totally present with another person. People who encountered the Master experienced what Paul Tillich called "the eternal now." He could give Himself so fully to another man or woman it was as if time stood still for them inside the gift of His total, loving attentiveness. The most sacred gift you can give God is your fully surrendered presence with Him in the now. The now is a sacred piece of time because God is in it. God hangs out in the now. God lives in the eternal extension of the now. He is a constant extension of the now. That is in fact what eternity is. That is why Jehovah in the Hebrew Scriptures could thunder, "I am that I am." He always has been. He always will be, and most of all, *He is.* That is why Jesus could gently say, "Before Abraham was, I am." If you want to connect and fellowship intimately with Him, you have to be present and conscious right this moment. You have to be in touch with your soul, your heart, your "I amness." Because that is all you have. Really. There is just now. And you. And God. Connected. Intimately.

15. The providence and protection and guidance of the angels become more evident in your life. "Are they not all ministering spirits, sent to minister for them who will be the heirs of salvation?" (Hebrews 1:24). In a very real sense, angels are the "modems" through which we connect with the realms of the Spirit. They are not the light, but they are the light-bearers, they are our personal bond to the heavenly realms, to the deeper most progressive truths and insights and spiritual experiences for us today.

16. To the Spirit-filled person, thought finally stops being central. You are no longer possessed by thought or identified solely by your thoughts. You get it that you are not your feelings and you are not your thoughts; that indeed, on a deeper level of heart, of soul, the true you, the "I am" has the ability to step back and observe both the feelings and the thoughts and not allow your identity or behavior to be determined by either. When you become the observer, from the deeper place of your soul, you no longer need to be the victim of what your mind is thinking or what your emotions are feeling. God has given you this kind of remarkable power of choice so at the soul level, at that deep center of yourself that we call the heart, the "I am" that is truly the part of you most directly created in the image of God, there lives and thrives the true essence of you, much more so than your thoughts or emotions are you.

Remember, *"the I am" is a much deeper and more sacred level of you than the "I" or the "myself" or the ego.* When you learn to access this powerful part of yourself, you become aware of a greater reality that is beyond factual knowledge, beyond beliefs, beyond theology, beyond the intellect, beyond ordinary reason, yes even beyond thinking and feeling. You learn to move from believing-in to knowing. *You learn to move from thinking to being.* You learn to turn off the busyness of your mind (your monkey mind, your rambunctious puppy mind!), and to stop thinking so compulsively. You realize that you are something more than just your mind, something much more than the thoughts you think. You learn to spend less time and energy thinking and more time practicing the Presence of God, being aware and conscious of a sacred sense of Presence within you, within your heart, your soul, each moment. You learn to move quickly from mind to beyond mind, from thinking to God-awareness and God-consciousness. Silence and stillness, learning to be fully present in the now, surrender, these are the portals to this sacred place. Yes, your mind and your emotions and your ego are still important pieces of your self-hood. But when you have surrendered them all to the Holy Spirit, they are transformed from spiritual impediments to useful tools to implement your spiritual journey and your work of loving service in the world. When you surrender your ego, when you come into conscious awareness of God, when you come into alert presence of His I amness and His being, love will arise up in you. You will enter into the kingdom of heaven in that very moment as Jesus promised you could.

17. There is a lasting change in your self-perception and in your sense of reality. You get a new kind of clarity. Through your connection with the Holy Spirit you will experience increasing insights, revelations and expanded awareness. You will have flashes of inner knowing. You will get perspective. You begin to see the "the big picture" of things. Those who see the bigger picture of things are called "visionaries" because they have a larger vision of life and truth than others. Traditional success begins to fade in value. Your definition of success shifts radically. You no longer define yourself in the traditional ways. At a certain level of spiritual maturity, desire for anything external begins to disappear. You realize that you are not what you possess. You are not your stuff! You are not your career, your job or your education. Your focus comes to be on cooperation with others, not competition with them. You will come to understand that you were created to serve.

18. As your spiritual foundation comes to be based on a personal, intimate connection with the Father, you will be released from the control and the hold that external forms and traditions and institutions have had on you. As you move from being "under law" to being "in Spirit," you will come to feel a deep sense of inner peace.

You begin to experience a great sense of tranquility. Sometimes it feels like you are floating in a sea of peace. You begin to understand what Paul was talking about when he described the profound "peace of God which passeth all understanding." "The eternal God is my dwelling place, and underneath are the everlasting arms" (Deuteronomy 33:27). This will allow you to begin to let go of your anger and rage. Did I mention that you will become less agitated in traffic?

19. You discover that you can learn something from everyone. Even the people you disagree with. Even those who do not believe the way you do. *The need to always be right finally disappears!*

20. You stop being judgmental, both of others and yourself. Judgmental exclusivity is replaced with compassionate pluralism. You release yourself from the debilitating need to always be right. You become tolerant. You hold no hatred in your heart for anyone. You don't carry a grudge against anybody. You realize that to judge another is to blaspheme God for that is assuming His role. It is a role that can only be His for only He has all the information to do it intelligently. When you let go of judgment, acceptance of others becomes natural. You become open-minded. You receive the gift of flexibility. You realize that there will be people in the kingdom of heaven who do not belong to your church! Who do not believe the way you do!

21. You stop talking so much. You may not receive the gift of tongues but you do receive "the gift of ears." You learn to listen with ears of love to both what is being said and what is not being said. You become fully present with each person you are with. "Let your conversation be "yes" and "no" said Jesus. "Let your words be thoughtful, few, and true" the Amish teach in their *Rules of a Godly Life*. You will learn to express only love and truth in what you say. When you do speak, your tongue will be dipped in love!

22. You are comfortable with silence. Stillness is treasured and practiced. Aloneness no longer frightens you. You are in good company when you are alone. Solitude can be enjoyed. "Be still and know that I am God" begins to be a big part of your spiritual practice. You learn to access stillness quickly through simple breathing, relaxing and focusing exercises.

23. You learn to be vulnerable, to be honest about your brokenness. You do not need to pretend anymore. You do not need a mask. You do not have to hide behind your money or your education or your appearance. You no longer need to hide your weaknesses or faults. You don't need to use any kind of deception any more. You become consistently honest. You can ask for help. You realize your dependence on others. Friends are cherished. Fellowship and community are sought and treasured. You lose the illusion that you are somehow separate from others, separate from God. Oneness with others and with the divine becomes the central focus of your life. You are able to have deeper and richer relationships than you have ever had before. By learning to keep your heart open, you will reach new levels of sharing and intimacy. You will eventually find yourself a part of a closely connected community, a small group of loving, growing people with whom you can enjoy praying and learning and fellowshipping and serving in ways you never imagined possible.

24. You come to value and respect the earth and its resources. You realize you are a steward of life on this planet. You find nature to be a potent source of spirituality. Your heart will come to be full of gratitude as you open your eyes to the simple beauties of God's creation that surround you.

25. Your wisdom increases. You learn the difference between wisdom and knowledge. Sudden, unexpected flashes of insight, flashes of inner knowing, into people and situations occur. Your perspective is hugely increased. Things begin to fit together unexpectedly. You begin to see how all knowledge and all truth is inter-related. "I am the light of the world; the one who follows Me will not walk in darkness but will have the light of life" (John 8:12 RSV).

26. The Spirit-filled person takes delight in the power of story and myth and ritual. You allow these things a valued place in your life. You share your own story often.

27. Your addictions and attachments begin to lose their power over you. Connection with the Spirit far exceeds in satisfaction and fulfillment the sensory pleasures we often associate with happiness. You still enjoy the physical pleasures of life, but you stop relying on them to fulfill your deeper longings.

28. You find tremendous nourishment insight and energy in books. Certain books will "mysteriously" appear at just the right time to give you the guidance and confirmation you need in your spiritual life.

29. You listen to music frequently and with deep appreciation. Your soul is touched deeply by it. Sometimes it may move you to tears. (If you lose music, you lose your soul.) You learn that music is a portal to the presence of God.

30. You come to learn the incredible *power of choice* for creating and sustaining your spiritual life. *You come to understand that connection with God is everything.* You begin each day by making a choice for, and setting your will to, that connection, *regardless of your feelings.* As a result, you become more fully conscious: God conscious and other-conscious. The vast reserves of your unconscious become easier to tap. You become more intuitive. Your creativity is unleashed. (To be connected to the Spirit is to be "in the Spirit" to be "in-spirit, is to be inspired says Wayne Dyer) The creativity you receive from the Spirit will take you to new levels of personal and spiritual growth that you never imagined possible. You may become more aware of the meaning of some of your dreams. You may awake in the night with exciting, creative ideas and insights that "come out of nowhere." The Spirit will awaken in you a new yearning for beauty, for intimacy and for adventure!

31. You become more sensitive. You are more aware of and touched more deeply by the pain and suffering of others. Your emotions are closer to the surface. You cry more, both inside and outside. (Men cry more than most people think, they just cry inside instead of outside.)

32. You finally learn how to be patient. You are more flexible and spontaneous. You no longer rush about. "Hurry" becomes a nasty word. You at last come to understand that often, what is,is. Stuck in traffic? Going to get all

worked up are you? Think again. You have just been given a golden opportunity to accept what is and to use the moment to practice the presence of God. You can start by thinking about what you are most grateful for. Gratitude … another instant portal to connection with God.

33. You laugh more. You come to see laughter as a spiritual gift. You understand that laughter is the physical expression of joy. Joy and laughter are the great gifts of living in the presence of God! You realize that holiness and humor are not mutually exclusive! You learn that after prayer, laughter is the next most powerful way of forming community, connection and closeness between people. You give yourself permission to play. You discover that the kingdom of God is a party! When you live life in the key of love, joy and laughter become part of the music of your life. Dallas Willard says that we dishonor God as much by fearing and avoiding pleasure as we do by dependence upon it or living for it. Spirit-filled Christians have much to celebrate! Scripture tells us there is a time to laugh and a time to dance. The Holy Spirit seeks out the places where there is laughter.

34. You live in a state of forgiveness toward others. In fact you practice "before-giveness." You may feel anger at someone if they mistreat you or another but you refuse to hold a grudge and you absolutely refuse to hate anyone. You are willing to forgive someone even before they wrong you or even before they apologize if that is what will bring healing. *You come to understand that someone's bad behavior is always a cry for help, a cry for love.* Their bad behavior is a symptom of their woundedness. They are not wrong as much as they are wounded. They are not depraved but dysfunctional. They are afraid. Their fear may show itself in anger or inappropriate and even illegal actions but you do not let this cause you to reject them. You continue to offer love and forgiveness, knowing that forgiveness is the only path out of hell, the only path to healing.

35. Pain, sadness, suffering and illness are still present in your life. However, they are acknowledged, not denied. You learn not to try to escape your legitimate suffering. You learn to surrender it, to allow it to be transcended into a kind of glory, a kind of grace that draws you ever deeper into oneness

with God. You come to know that through surrender, your pain and fear can be transformed into serenity. "We cannot lose once we realize that all that happens to us has been designed to teach us holiness" wrote Scott Peck. "All things work together for good to them that love God" (Romans 8:28).

36. You come to hold your physical body in the highest regard. Exercise and learning to eat healthily in moderation becomes an important part of your life. Your diet will change and you will learn to eat your food slowly, mindfully and with gratitude. You will learn to consider it a kind of sacrament. You will come to see the powerful link between food and spirituality, to see food not as your problem but as your spiritual teacher.

37. You come to experience incredible productivity, success and unlimited abundance in your life, spiritually, emotionally and physically. "God is able to provide you with every blessing in abundance" (2 Corinthians 9:7-9). You no longer come from a place of shortage or scarcity or deprivation. An endless stream of abundance flows from God. When you place yourself in oneness with Him, when you practice His presence moment by moment, you place yourself in that stream. "Seek ye first the kingdom of heaven and all these other things will be added unto you." "But seek first his kingdom and his righteousness, and all these things will be given to you as well" (Matthew 6:33) .

38. The Spirit brings you to understand the truth about God. He is not vengeful, threatening, frightening or punishing. He loves even the wicked. Unconditionally. You see Jesus as the ultimate expression of the Father. You see that in Jesus Christ, God offers full self-disclosure! You finally come to understand above all else, that *God is Christ-like!*

39. Your foundational spiritual beliefs become very simple:

1. God is love. 2. Jesus saves. 3. The Holy Spirit wants to fill you right now.

40. You receive the gift of the Holy Spirit's baptism as a down-payment on heaven.
You understand that this sacred gift is the true seal of the living God upon the Christian right now. "Having believed, you were marked in him with a seal, the promised Holy Spirit, who is a deposit guaranteeing our inheritance…"

(Ephesians 1:13, 14). "Do not grieve the Holy Spirit of God, with whom you were sealed for the day of redemption" (Ephesians 4:30).

41. You wouldn't think of starting your day without making the *choice* to connect to God, to claim your gift of salvation and your personal in-filling of the Holy Spirit. You finally get it that connection with the Divine, God awareness, the practice of the Presence is everything.

No consciousness without connection becomes your motto. In other words when you first wake up and become conscious each morning, you immediately make the choice to submit, surrender and connect to your Abba. *Constant conscious communion with your Father becomes your goal.* You learn to cultivate a sense of God's presence with you every moment.

42. Prayer becomes a joy to you. Not a duty. Your private prayer time becomes a source of great comfort and serenity and centeredness. You are eagerly drawn to opportunities to pray with others. You come to understand that prayer is so much more than just making requests. You learn to still yourself while in prayer, to empty yourself and do nothing but listen with an open heart to the instruction, guidance, support and love your Father has for you for that day. You come to understand that prayer is the conduit through which power from heaven is brought to earth. Best of all, you learn that prayer is a way of loving others. Where prayer and reading the Scriptures once bored you and may have been done only out of a sense of duty or obligation, these activities now become a source of daily anticipation, excitement and joy

43. You come to understand that *you* are a priest. You know that you have access to the Holy of Holies, the very presence of God, without the need for anyone on earth intervening for you. You realize that *every Christian is a minister!* The Holy Spirit provides you with an anointing of power and gift or gifts to equip you for a unique, rewarding and exciting place of service in the world. Your life becomes centered around doing acts of loving service for others.

CHAPTER 1:

THE WIND BENEATH OUR WINGS

But we who would be born again indeed
Must wake our souls unnumbered times a day
And urge ourselves to live with holy greed.
Now open our bosoms to the wind's free play,
And now, with patience forceful, hard, lie still
Submiss and ready to the making will,
Athirst and empty, for God's breath to fill.
George McDonald, *Diary of an Old Soul*

The wind blows wherever it pleases.
You hear its sound,
but you cannot tell where it comes from
or where it is going.
So it is with everyone born of the Spirit.
John 3:8 NIV

But those who hope in the Lord
will renew their strength.
They will soar on wings like eagles
they will run and not grow weary
they will walk and not be faint.
—Isaiah 40:31, NIV

The scream was terrifying. One of the most frightening things I had ever heard. And it came from my own wife. I was working upstairs in our cabin on an isolated beach in Alaska's Bristol Bay. It was mid-summer and our family had come back there as we did every year to fish commercially with nets for salmon. In this remote area the only access was by boat or airplane. I kept my plane tied down in the tall grass near the cabin and used the gravel beach in front as an airstrip when the tide was out.

Our neighboring fisherman with a cabin to the north also had a plane there. Before I had gone up to work in the loft I had seen him with a passenger taxi by on their way to the end of the beach in preparation for takeoff.

Little wonder that my wife had screamed. She had just witnessed the airplane stagger through the air in front of our cabin, veer out over the bay, and fall nose-first into the water in a tremendous fountain of spray, flip upside down and begin to sink!

Engines do not make an airplane fly. I have been witness to that fact twice in my life when the engine quit very inconveniently and unexpectedly in the single engine plane I was flying. My passengers and I did not fall out of the sky. We were able to glide to a safe landing.

In fact, not even wings make a plane fly. An airplane sitting still on the ground on a calm day has wings but it can not get a foot higher off the ground than your Toyota can! The miracle of flight occurs only when air is made to move over and beneath a wing. This is what generates the invisible but powerful force called lift. It is lift alone which allows a plane to take to the air, stay up there and travel forward.

The plane that crashed in front of our house that day had an engine that was running perfectly well. It had strong and solid wings. Yet it came falling out of the sky. Why? Because there was not enough wind beneath its wings. The pilot had taken off with the wind blowing on his tail, or the wind had switched on him in mid-takeoff. He had gotten airborne at the end of the short takeoff area and flown a hundred yards, but with the wind coming from behind, part of the lift that comes from air flowing over the wings of the plane was cancelled out. There was no longer enough lift to sustain flight. The aircraft plunged into the cold and swift-flowing tidal water.

Fortunately, my boat was parked nearby. I scrambled out of the cabin and dashed to it. Just as I was getting the motor started a head appeared out of the water near where the plane had gone down. All that was left sticking out of the water was the upside down tail wheel. The survivor clung to that. Everything

29

was being swept out toward the open sea on the brisk seven-knot tidal current. By the time I caught up with the drifting wreckage I had begun to despair for the other occupant, but just as I slowed the boat to approach the one person in the water, another head popped up!

Two men had a near-death experience and a beautiful flying machine was ruined that day, all for the want of just the least little gust of air coming in the right direction.

EVERYONE WAS SPIRIT-FILLED

There was a time when everyone on earth was filled with the Holy Spirit. Both of them! From the very beginning the Spirit of God was active in this world. The first chapter of the first book of the Bible speaks of the Spirit being present at the first day of creation, moving "upon the face of the waters" when the earth was still formless and empty, with nothing but darkness over the surface of the deep (Genesis 1: 1, 2).

On the sixth day of creation God performed His crowning act: "God created man in his own image, in the image of God he created him; male and female he created them" (Genesis 1:27). When the Father did this, He "formed man of the dust of the ground and breathed into his nostrils the breath of life: and man became a living soul" (Genesis 2:7).

THE BREATH OF SPIRITUAL LIFE

Breath and wind have always been a symbol in the Scriptures of the Holy Spirit. In fact, the Spirit's very name in Hebrew is *ruach*, a noun which has the meaning of wind. (Note: the gender of the Hebrew word is feminine, conveying the female, comforting, nurturing, mothering nature of this life-enhancing member of the Godhead. Could it be that one reason the church has ignored or resisted the doctrine of the Holy Spirit through the centuries is because it seems to be such a struggle for Christians to acknowledge the feminine component of the character and personality of God?) A related Jewish word was *nephesh*, which means breath. This came to be translated as "soul" or "spirit." It referred to the non-physical part of a man or woman and came to be seen as the very breath or presence of God dwelling within us, calling us to life not only physically but spiritually.

In the New Testament Greek the word for Spirit is *pneuma*. It comes from the root word *pneu* which is translated into English as wind, or breeze. *Pneuma* means breath. This is the word the gospel writer used to convey what Jesus meant when He spoke, as He often did, of the Holy Spirit.

In German, the word for breathing, atmen, comes from the very old Sanskrit word Atman, which meant the indwelling divine spirit, or God within.

The very act of breathing, by the way, can become a sacred experience. It is a reminder of God's act of creating you of His enduring love for you, and His presence continually dwelling with you by His Spirit. Just slowing down and becoming aware of your breathing in and out can have a very stilling and calming effect. It can make you more conscious of the Spirit and of the presence of God. It can help you to stop your endless cycle of thinking and bring you to be in the present moment, the now, which is the only place where God is. (See the spiritual breathing exercise in Appendix A.)

How amazing to think that in this precious gift from Jesus, the Holy Spirit, what we have is the very out-breathing of God to fill us up with His inmost life, making it possible for this glorious, eternal magnificent being to live in a personal way in you and me! C.A. Torrey says: "How solemn and how awesome and yet unspeakably glorious life becomes when we realize this." 1. Job understood it long ago: "The Spirit of God has made me, and the breath of the Almighty gave me life" (Job 33:4).

The Bible promises to you and me that our strength will be renewed, that we may soar on wings like eagles. If you will seek the experience of the filling of the Holy Spirit, with the wind of the Spirit under your wings, you will be able to soar to heights in your spiritual life that you never imagined possible. Remember one thing…the only limits on your spiritual growth are self-imposed!

The breath that God breathed into man at creation gave him so much more than physical, biological life. It also gave him spiritual life. It transformed man from a lump of clay, or from being merely a living creature like the animals that had been created before him, into something entirely different, something extraordinarily splendid and very much like the Being who had made him.

The Navajo have a fascinating story that I find relevant and touching. It has been handed down through time and it resonates to some degree with the Christian concept of the Spirit as a holy wind that "bloweth where it listeth". This teaching has power to create and transform spiritual life. "The Spirit of God has made me: the breath of the Almighty gives me life" (Job 33:4).

"Deep in the red-rock, breeze-chiseled country of the American Southwest, live a people whose religion may be more steeped in wind than any other in the world. The Navajo believe humans are brought to life by the Holy Wind that leaves whorls on the tips of our fingers and toes, whispers words of advice in our ears, and dictates the number of days we spend on earth.
The Navajo teach that a holy breeze known as Little Wind or Wind's Child gives people breath and helps them stand erect. A person's posture, balance, and ability all are gifts of the winds dwelling within him. When a child is conceived, it takes a wind from its mother and another from its father. At birth, with its first breath, the child receives yet another wind, sent from the Holy Ones to guide his or her life. Each individual's temperament turns not on upbringing or on any misfiring within his neurological circuitry, but on which winds, the good or the evil, he allows to guide him as he moves through life. This ties individuals strongly to the natural world, for a person's thoughts and actions-indeed, his very mind-belong not to him but to the holy air. "The wind within us stands from our mouths downward," a Navajo elder once said. "We breathe by it. We live by it. It moves all parts, even our hearts." 2.

With one single breath, with that incredible act, God shared a personal, vital, vulnerable part of Himself with His creation. He "breathed into his nostrils the breath of life: and man became a living soul.!" Soul is that incredible, mysterious (and sadly often ignored) part of us that is created most in the image of God. It is our place of "I amness." It is the sacred space within us where God may dwell. Here is the thing: you have a body. You have a mind. You have emotions. *But you are a soul!* Our soul has the unique ability to become an observer, to step back and helpfully observe with deep awareness our actions and thoughts and even how our mind is working. Soul can be a governor on our run-away thoughts and emotions. Soul is that unique part of us that is relational. Soul is all about connectedness. Oneness. It is about the capacity for oneness with each other and with God on a deep level. Soul is love's home within us. Soul is all about the capacity to love. To love deeply and unconditionally and non-exploitatively.

THE LIMITATIONS OF THE MIND

Notice the Navajo story does not say that at his creation, "man became a mind." When will we ever get it? We are not our mind! So often we allow ourselves to be possessed by our own mind/ego, entrapped by our constant, compulsive thinking. Our culture today worships the intellect. It values people more for what they know than for who they really are. In many cases, employers hire people for their "brains." Most people today are compulsive thinkers. They can not quit. *Our greatest addiction of all may be our addiction to constant non-stop thinking!* It was Brother Lawrence who said, "thinking often spoils everything"! People can not sleep at night because they can not shut off their thinking. They can not seem to quiet their minds. People can not stop and really listen to someone else because they are so caught up in thinking their own thoughts. The trouble with compulsively thinking all the time is that many of our thought patterns are based on fear, guilt, anger, jealousy, selfishness and neediness. Men and women can not encounter the presence of God in the present moment, the sacred now, because they are so busy thinking about the past or planning for the future. *Many have never learned how to still their minds so they can experience their souls.*

You may know people who practice fasting from food as a spiritual discipline. (By the way, spiritual disciplines are very important. They show us *how* we can surrender to God and connect with Him. They are kind of like spiritual megavitamins for your spiritual health! Okay, maybe like spiritual antibiotics too! Dallas Willard says that to practice them is to take our lives seriously and "to suppose that the following of Christ was at least as big a challenge as playing the violin or jogging." (See Appendix I at the back of the book which lists some of the disciplines.)

Fasting from food can be helpful but I am suggesting you consider a deeper level of fasting, one that is far more challenging. Experiment with fasting from words and even from thoughts! This is a kind of true spiritual fast that can open you to connection and communion with God as nothing else. It can bring you into an awareness of God that can not be attained by study alone. It may be your path to some of the hidden spiritual mysteries that the Holy Spirit wants to lead you into. If you can learn to access this higher level of spiritual consciousness as the Holy Spirit fills and molds you, the words of Jesus will be fulfilled for you when He promised that the Spirit would guide you into the deepest truths and the most sacred spiritual experience and intimacy with the Father (John 16:13). When Descartes said,"I think, therefore I am," he had it all wrong! Your sacred "I amness", comes from a place far deeper than your thoughts. You are not your mind. You are not your feelings, though these are important parts of who you are. Maybe this will help, think of it this way... you have a body. You have emotions. You have a mind. You *are* a soul! Your soul is the temple of your "I am."

We all know the sad limitations of our bodies. No body gets off this planet alive! Our bodies begin to deteriorate the moment we are born. But... rejoice! Your body is not you! It is only form. Science has shown us that our mind, as wonderful and amazing as it is, is also a physical, electrical entity, a kind of elaborate computer circuit board! It will also fade and disappear as we age and die. But...rejoice, for you are not your mind! It too, even the thoughts it produces are only form. The real you goes far beyond your body and even your mind. The real you, your essence, the real center of your "I amness" is what is called the heart, or soul, or spirit. That is the part of you made most in the image of God.

GOD HAS YOU ON BACKUP!

The Bible says that when a person dies, "then shall the dust return to the earth as it was: and the spirit shall return to God who gave it" (Ecclesiastes 12:7). Notice that when Jesus died, He cried out, "Father into your hands, I

34

commit my spirit" (Luke 23:46). His dead body still hung on the cross. His mind was stilled and His deepest essence returned to its home in the presence of God. Here's the thing... who you and I truly are, our soul, the part of us created uniquely in the image of God, the center of our being comes into this world as a gift from the Creator God. When our lives are over, our souls do not disappear for ever. They are too precious for that. The most important part of you, the deepest you, the real you, your "I amness" is not lost. Think of it this way...God has you on backup! In the great computer of His in the sky, you are in permanent un-erasable memory! Some believe that the soul continues on in consciousness immediately after death. I and others believe that the soul can not experience consciousness without a body and mind. This means that the soul does not become conscious until the resurrection when it is united with a re-created body. *Either way* you believe about life after death, the important point is that your soul, the part of you that is really you, the part that really counts, your "I amness" exists in all its fullness and completeness after your death! It is guarded and cherished by your heavenly Father! Kept in the hollow of His hand! Don't worry, God has got you all totally backed up on His big old hard drive in heaven! The Bible promises that in the life to come, we will be fully restored, so much so that we shall know fully and that we shall be fully known (1 Corinthians 13:12). We will receive the gift of consciousness again after death. We will be restored in relationship with our loved ones again! Jesus proclaimed with the greatest assurance, "He who believes in me will live, even though he dies; and whoever lives and believes in me will never die" (John 11:25).

Let us pay attention, beginning right now, to our soul. Let us become conscious of our "I amness". Let us nourish and feed and grow our souls for that is who we really are and that is the only part of us that will endure! Our hearts are truly the most important thing about us. If we do not nourish our hearts, if we "lose heart" then we have lost everything that is essential. Jesus Christ did not come to try and educate people's intellects, but to engage and nourish and transform and capture their hearts. A. W. Tozer said that we are truly wise only when we follow the insight of the enraptured heart rather than the more cautious reasonings of the theological mind.

All things high and holy and especially good in life come from beyond the body, beyond the mind, beyond the intellect, even from beyond the emotions. These are part of us, but they are not our essence. It is only the life of the heart that truly counts. Love, joy, peace, faith, relationships are eternal and all generate in the soul, from within the heart, from within that God-shaped space the Creator placed inside every man and woman. It is His best gift to us, that piece of Himself. Saint-Exupery expressed it so poignantly: "Only with the heart can one see rightly. What is essential is invisible to the eye." *Remember, you can not think your way to heaven. You only enter into the kingdom by the way of the surrendered heart.* The deep mysteries and personal experience of the presence of God will never come to us in any profound way in the midst of argument, theological discussion or religious theorizing.

MADE IN HIS IMAGE

God was full of joy at His accomplishment! Human beings provided a unique way to display His glory in the universe. His character, His presence of divine love could now have a physical expression in a physical world! While there were many high and holy purposes for the creation of human beings, men and women were also made because God simply wanted them and needed them! His great heart needed someone like Himself with whom he could enjoy fellowship. Someone to love. Someone who had the capacity to love Him back. Someone who was created with the remarkable but risky attribute called the power of choice, so that when His child did chose to love, that love had depth and meaning.

We scarcely begin to understand the incredible value of the priceless gift of the power of choice, of free will, that God allows us to have. He literally sent His Son to die on the cross for us so that we would have the freedom, the option, to reject Him if we so choose! He so valued our ability to freely choose our own way that He died for us rather than take that option away. Can you believe that our freedom is so important to God that He would rather see us be free than force us to be saved?

The sacred, God-gifted power of choice is still the foundation of our being. It is at the heart of our very identity. It empowers us. It allows us. It is with this incredible gift that we alone determine our destiny now and eternally. You are always only one choice, one thought, away from God. One thought away from Spirit connection. One thought away from love and peace. Make a choice... change your path, change your life. Today. If you wish, if you choose.

So you see, at our creation God had given Himself a present! Because He empowered us with freedom of choice, He now had someone with whom He could share genuine fellowship. Someone who could walk with Him in the Garden. He had someone to laugh with! Living souls. Made in His image. His children. Because they had freedom of choice, when they did respond to Him, the love had value, depth and deep and precious meaning.

During the creation process God acknowledged that it was not good for man to be alone. God knew this from His own first-hand experience. Indeed, it must have been out of the joy of companionship with His new child that the Father choose to share the immense pleasure He receives from intimate relationship by creating woman to be an equal companion to man. It is not good for man to be alone. It is not good for God to be alone!

CREATED TO CONTAIN SOMEONE

Man and woman were formed by God for one primary purpose, to be the dwelling place of the Holy Spirit so that they could fellowship intimately with Him. You see, to God, everything is about relationship. Communication. Connection. Oneness with those He loves. That is why He created our first parents with this unique capacity, this God-shaped vacuum in their heart so they would be naturally drawn toward a close relationship with Him. Then He blew His presence into that empty spot and filled it with the marvelous indwelling of the Spirit. Putting Himself inside His children. Becoming one with them.

Allowing them the phenomenal experience of becoming, as the Bible promises, "partakers of the Divine nature." He came to dwell within His own. That in fact was the highest and best purpose of the creation of humankind. This is what made us something more than extra-intelligent animals. *We were not created to be somebody but to contain Someone!* To fellowship with Someone! We can say just as surely as Adam and Eve: "The Spirit of God has made me; the breath of the Almighty gives me life"! (Job 33:4).

You don't have to go into fits and paroxysms of struggle to figure out what your purpose in life is, by the way. It is simple; *you were created to be a temple for the Holy Spirit on this earth, an expression in flesh and blood of the love and truth of the heavenly Father.* Just as Jesus was.

Most people think the great tragedy of Eden was the couple being driven from their beautiful Garden and becoming susceptible eventually to physical death after they made their poor choices. While sad enough, those consequences pale in comparison to the true catastrophe. What happened was far more a spiritual calamity than a physical one.

What the Psalmist most dreaded when he plaintively prayed, "do not cast me from your presence or take your holy spirit from me" (Psalms 51:11), became a terrible reality for our first parents.

The ultimate tragedy befell the human race. Because of the separation caused by turning away from Him, God could no longer indwell people with his Holy Spirit. The marvelous Spirit, symbolized in the Bible by two powerful elements, wind and fire was gone. The room, the cathedral, the Holy Place in the heart of man designed by the Creator to contain the Divine Presence was now empty. When Adam and Eve lost the Presence of their Father, they lost everything. Their God-consciousness was replaced by self-consciousness, by ego. Immediately they felt naked and became defensive and afraid. In an instant their lives moved from love to fear.

In California's Napa Valley where I live, there is a phenomenon that occurs early every sunny morning. The roar of powerful gas burners igniting can be heard echoing across the vineyards as huge, strikingly colored balloons prepare for ascent. As the hot air from the flames rises up and is trapped in the craft's envelope, a powerful lifting force is created. The balloons tug at their restraining ropes like hounds eager to be off on a chase. With the passengers aboard the wicker baskets, the ground crew releases the restraints and the colorful craft soar up and away into the blue skies where the gentle breezes coming off the nearby bay gently drift them over the rolling countryside as the excited sight-seers enjoy spectacular views. Their stimulating flight is sustained only by an invisible column of hot air. No engines. No wings. Fire and air.

The balloons have an excellent safety record, partly because of their simplicity. But danger can still be present. If a pilot runs out of fuel or an igniter refuses to perform, there is no more fire. The supporting air loses its heat, the lift disappears, and the balloon begins an uncontrolled descent.

LOSS OF INTIMACY

Without the lift of the indwelling Spirit, man and woman tumbled into the "fall", and, a terrible fall it was. A fall from consciousness. A fall from grace. A fall from intimacy with the Father. Adam and Eve no longer lived in a state of enlightenment. Oneness with the Divine Being was gone. They were not the only ones to suffer. The great heart of God was touched with loneliness. He became "homesick" for His children. Yes, He lost as much or more than anyone. He has suffered the most from the results of sin and separation.

Some theologians say that a physical body plus the physical breath of life is what makes a "living soul." That is not so. What makes a "living soul" is the physical body, plus the physical breath of life plus the spiritual breath of life. When our parents lost the indwelling of the Spirit, they lost also their very souls. They lost the intimate connection, the intimate oneness with the Father which gave them their sense of purpose, of being, of wholeness. They lost their identity.

Moral degeneration, environmental degradation, disease, slavery, bloodshed, war, pain, death, all arose over time as natural consequences of this great tragedy. Humanity was no longer a temple of God. Men and women were no longer His expression of love in the physical world, no longer the residence of the Holy Spirit. Without the wind of the Spirit beneath their wings, without the uplifting fire in their hearts, without the God-presence in their souls, humanity entered a downward spiral into the depths of

----

Q AND A

Q. Are you really saying one reason God created people is because He needed them?

A. Yes. God needs people. Some anonymous feminist coined that appalling phrase, "a woman needs a man like a fish needs a bicycle." I refuse to comment on that. But I want you to know that God needs people like a bicyclist needs a bicycle. Like Lance Armstrong needs his wheels. An important part of God is realized, fulfilled, nourished, by His connection to His people.

There are three great Christian truths. Theologically, everything else is just commentary. Let's get them out front right away. 1. God is love. 2. Jesus saves. 3. The Holy Spirit wants to live in you right now.   At this point we are concerned with truth #1. Love can not exist in a vacuum. Neither can God. Love is compelled to share, to create, to reach out. It exists only in relationship with someone else. Even God needs someone with whom to share a relationship in order for His great heart of love is to be filled. Indeed, God formed us for Himself. The *Shorter Catechism* of the Anglican church asks the poignant question, "What is the chief End of Man." The answer given is that; "man's chief end is to glorify God and enjoy Him forever." Yes, the amazing truth is that you and I can minister to God! God is passionately longing for our presence! We can succor the Almighty! We can bring Him joy! "I will rejoice over Jerusalem, and take delight in my people" (Isaiah 65:19). "The Lord takes pleasure in His people" (Psalm 149:4). TEV St. Augustine said, "God thirsts to be thirsted after." You and I can cherish God! *The Spirit-filled Christian is constantly being drawn toward self-forgetting adoration and worship and praise of the Father.*

FOOTNOTES CHAPTER 1:

1.Torrey, R.A., *The Person & Work of the Holy Spirit* Whitaker House, New Kensington, PA: 1996, p. 42.

2. DeBlieu, Jan, Wind: How the *Flow of Air has Shaped Life, Myth and the Land*.

CHAPTER 2:

HE DID WHAT!?
He breathed on them and said,
"Receive the Holy Spirit"
John 20:22 NIV

I was just stretching my legs. After driving for several hours I had just pulled off the freeway into one of the trendy little Southern California beach towns. I was walking leisurely down the sidewalk on a pleasantly sunny afternoon, pausing to look in the shop windows. Suddenly, out on the street just a few feet behind me, there was the harsh sound of the squeal of tires on pavement followed by the crash of metal against metal. I spun around to see, much to my horror, a human figure being flung through the air.

A heavy luxury car had slammed into the back of a motorcycle rider who had been waiting for a stoplight to change. The impact had catapulted the man out of his seat. Arcing up and over the handlebars, his body came down flat on the concrete, his helmeted head striking first with a horrible crack as loud as a pistol shot. To this day, I can not forget that haunting sound.

Since he lay in the middle of a busy street some of us immediately formed a protective circle around him to stop traffic. He was a tall, handsome man, probably in his late forties, gray hair, neatly trimmed salt-and-pepper beard. He had black leathers on. His helmet was silver. He lay absolutely still, head turned slightly to one side, eyes closed. I remember someone hollering out that they were calling an ambulance. Then it seemed as if everything froze in place for a time. No one moved. No one said anything. It seemed like several minutes went by, but it was probably more a matter of seconds. Then a woman broke through the crowd that had gathered on the sidewalk. She came on through our little protective circle and quickly knelt down by the biker. With what seemed to be practiced hands she checked for his pulse and leaned over his face apparently to see if he was still breathing. At once she began mouth-to-mouth resuscitation. Taking a deep inhalation she leaned over the stranger's mouth and blew her own breath into his lungs. A policeman on foot appeared and the woman indicated that he should begin compression on the unconscious man's chest. Perhaps she was a doctor or a nurse, so confident were her actions. The ambulance came in a few minutes. The paramedics took over, the biker beginning to stir as they loaded him aboard. The woman slipped away back into the crowd where she had come from.

It was the very first thing Jesus did with His disciples after He had risen. It was only a few hours since He had come forth from the grave. His followers were gathered fearfully behind locked doors when He came in among them, for the first time since His death. What amazement, what jubilation must have filled them as He showed them His wounded hands and side. The Bible says they were "overjoyed"!

As soon as He had established who He was and that He was very much alive, Jesus did an incredible thing. He duplicated an action He had taken only once, millenniums before. "…Jesus said, 'Peace be with you! As the Father has sent me, I am sending you.' And with that, he breathed on them and said, 'Receive the Holy Spirit'". (John 20:21,22). Please notice that Jesus did not do this before the cross. As Andrew Murray wrote, "Our Lord had to die before He could baptize with the Holy Spirit." 1. Just as God's wind had blown life into men's dead, dry bones in the book of Ezekiel, so now Jesus' amazing gift of the Spirit energized and invigorated the discouraged, lifeless and hopeless disciples. This is exactly what He wants to do with dead bones of our religion today!

For the second time in history God breathed on someone! This time He not only performed the gentle, simple act but clearly stated what it represented. Now, at last, for the first time since the Fall, men and women could once again have the very living Presence of God within them! No wonder Jesus was so excited about this! So eager to do it. Little wonder it was practically the first thing He did after His resurrection. It was in fact one of the most significant things He ever did on this earth. And now, incredibly, He is waiting to blow His Holy breath into you and me!

A GIFT FROM THE CROSS

43

Of course, it was the cross that made it all possible. Glory of glories, miracle of miracles, through what Christ accomplished for us on Calvary the way was once again open for the Holy Spirit to dwell inside of people! Jesus tore down the barriers that had been separating men and women from God. The curtain blocking off entrance to the Holy of Holies in the Jerusalem sanctuary had been ripped apart by the eager hands of God the moment Christ died. The Shekinah glory, the burning fiery presence of the Holy Spirit was once again available to everyone! Jesus had bridged the gap. He paid the price. Hooray! We can get our souls back! Intimacy with Divinity! Fellowship with the Father! The kingdom of heaven within! All these treasures restored. Now! The love. The joy. The peace. These treasures come from the gentle breath of Jesus blowing spiritual life into you and me. Restoring us. Enlightening us. Bringing us back to consciousness, spiritual consciousness. Bringing us back to walk again in the Garden with our God. The fellowship of Eden restored at last!

Here's the deal. In the Old Testament God was portrayed as an external, somewhat distant deity, "up" in heaven and known by some intimidating names, *Jehovah, Yahweh, Eloheim*. In the New Testament there was a great shift. He became Immanuel, God *with* us. God incarnate! God in human flesh! God in Jesus Christ! But wait! There was something even more! Now, praise God, *He has become God in us, by the Holy Spirit!* The circle has been completed. We may be restored to full intimacy, fellowship and connection with our Abba!

The same imperative command that Jesus gave His followers right after the resurrection is just as much for us, His disciples today. It is very simple. "Receive the Holy Spirit".

We do not have to earn it. It is a gift. We only have to open our heart and accept it.

We do not have to understand it. In fact it can not be understood or explained, it can only be accepted and experienced, surrendered to. Surrender is your most powerful spiritual tool. It is paradoxical. It is the easiest thing you could ever do. And the hardest. But when you surrender, a whole new dimension of consciousness opens up to you. Total surrender is crucial because it is not how much of the Spirit *we* have. It is how much the Spirit has of *us*.

Notice that Jesus had a reason for making the Holy Spirit available to His disciples. He said "as the Father has sent me, so I am sending you." He gave them their challenge. Then He breathed on them and empowered them for the task. And what an assignment it was! He was commissioning them to take on the same role God had given to Him when the Father sent Him into the world. Now, His followers were to assume nothing less than the very mission of Christ. They were to become the representatives of God's truth, God's character, God's extravagant love. The Father was making Himself dependent on men and women to restore and advance His kingdom on earth.

WITH, OR IN?

The Holy Spirit has been present in the world since creation. He has always worked WITH people in an attempt draw them closer to God. The startling, dramatic truth of the gospel however, is that since the cross, a whole new dimension of spirituality has been opened up to everyone who wants it. The Holy Spirit is now able to dwell IN you and me!

Jesus distinguished clearly between the Spirit working with someone and the Spirit being in a person. I can't believe how we have missed this important point for so long. He made one of the most exciting and encouraging promises of His ministry when He said, "Whoever believes in me, as the Scripture has said, streams of living water will flow from within him." By this he meant the Spirit, whom those who believed in him were LATER to receive. Up to that time the Spirit had NOT been given, since Jesus had not yet been glorified". (John 7:38,39 emphasis added)

Just before His death the Savior comforted His disciples with these fascinating words: "I will ask the Father, and he will give you another Counselor to be with you forever, the Spirit of truth. The world cannot accept him, because it neither sees him nor knows him. But you know him, for he lives WITH you and will be IN you". John 14:16,17 emphasis added)

45

The whole purpose of this book is to have its readers move from having the Holy Spirit working WITH them to surrendering themselves and allowing the Spirit to live IN them. I want you to have not only the precious assurance of your salvation, but also the wonderful certainty that you allowed the Master to breathe on you! I want you to know that you are now baptized with the Holy Spirit. If someone asks you if you are "filled with the Spirit" I don't want you to hem and haw and peep and mutter and give some kind of spiritually wimpish reply like… "well, I am not a Pentecostal"or "I hope to be filled with the Spirit when the Latter Rain falls". I want you to be able to say, "Yes, by God's grace, I am filled with the Spirit!" Such a clear testimony will bring great joy to the heart of the One who died to make it possible for you!

Q and A:

Q. Why did Jesus wait until after He was resurrected to breathe on His disciples and tell them to receive the gift of the indwelling Spirit?

A. The Holy Spirit indwelling a person's heart was not possible for every believer until Jesus' sacrifice had been completed. His blood had to be shed first. This eliminated the barrier between men and women and their God. This wonderful gift of the baptism of the Spirit is, along with salvation, part of the hard-won bounty from the battle at the cross. *It is vital to understand that at Calvary, Jesus not only won eternal life for you and me, but also the right to be restored to oneness and intimacy with the Father through the presence of the Holy Spirit.* That is why the Lord could teach that the "kingdom of heaven is here now" and "the kingdom of heaven is within you". Spiritual life, life eternal, is not something that begins on the other side of death. It is a quality of life that begins NOW. It is immediately accessible to anyone who opens their heart to God and chooses to be filled with the Holy Spirit.

To acknowledge salvation and disregard the gift of the Spirit is to accept only half of the gospel! Sadly, there are many Christians who have only a half-gospel. They have the head part but not the heart part. They may have the belief part down. They may have the "truth" but that is insufficient without the Spirit. God pleads with us to worship Him *"in spirit and in truth"*. Some of us have been way too long on truth and way too short on Spirit! Go ahead, cut off one prong from an electric plug-in. Stick the plug in the wall and see how much power you get! We need the full gospel to receive spiritual healing and spiritual power. To reject or ignore Jesus' command to "Receive the Spirit" is a kind of blasphemy against the sacrifice that made it possible. It leaves us un-fulfilled and disempowered.

Q. You say that people could not be filled with the Spirit until after Jesus' death. What about Moses and David and Elijah and John the Baptist?

A. There were occasions when certain individuals in the Bible were especially touched and empowered by the Spirit to perform special tasks. Other examples would be Saul, Samuel, Sampson, Gideon, Elisha, Daniel, and Mary. A personal and transforming empowering by the Spirit for every believer did not become available until after the cross.

Q. You scare me when you use terms like "enlightened" and "consciousness." Those sound awfully "New Age" or Buddhist to me. Isn't it dangerous to dabble with Eastern religions?

A. Buddha did not have an exclusive on the use of the word "enlightened." Christians should be the most enlightened people on earth. They have a Master who was the most enlightened man in history. He said He was "the Light of the world" and He told us to let our light shine. Enlightenment is a very simple thing. It is not something you must struggle for a lifetime to achieve. Enlightenment is the gift that comes to you when you cry "Jesus, breathe on me!" It is yours when you surrender to the filling of the Holy Spirit and become God-conscious, conscious of the loving, sustaining presence of God within you moment by moment.

Whenever you come to be aware and experience that the light of God is continually surrounding you, the love of God is continually enfolding you, that wherever you are, God is, then you will have achieved enlightenment. The true test of your enlightenment will be seen in how much of the energy of your life is then directed toward doing acts of loving service for other people. Tolstoy said it so simply in the conclusion of his outstanding book, *The Kingdom of God is Within You:* "The sole meaning of life is to serve humanity…" 2.

FOOTNOTES CHAPTER 2:

1. Murray, Andrew, *The Blood of the Cross*. (Whitaker House, Springdale, PA: 1981) p.13.

2. Tolstoy, Leo, *The Kingdom of God is Within You.(* University of Nebraska Press, Lincoln NB, 1984), p.368.

CHAPTER 3:

TEAR DOWN THIS WALL!

And when Jesus had cried out again in a loud voice,

He gave up his spirit.

At that moment the curtain of the temple was torn in two from top to bottom.

Matthew 27:50, 1

One of the greatest speeches of the twentieth century was almost not given. Except for the courage of two men, it would have gone unheard and the incredibly significant events it triggered may never have occurred!

In June of 1987 President Ronald Reagan was invited to Berlin, Germany, to speak on the occasion of that city's 750th anniversary. One of his speechwriters, Peter Robinson, was given the task of preparing the draft of a thirty-minute speech for him.

Recognizing that the divided city of Berlin was the spot in the world where the Cold War, the conflict between the communist world and the West, was most intense and visible, Robinson understood how critically important the president's speech could be. The writer had been warned by diplomats in the U.S. State Department to be cautious about what went into the speech. They urged him to be sophisticated, not to let Reagan bash the Soviets. They told him not to even mention the Berlin Wall, insisting that the people of Berlin had gotten used to it. They told him the speech would be heard by radio throughout much of East Germany, and maybe even as far away as Moscow. They urged him to be careful not to offend anyone.

In Berlin with the White House advance team a month before the president's trip, Robinson met with a group of West Berliners over dinner. "Is it true that you have gotten used to the Wall", he asked them? People stopped eating. There was a long silence. Then one man spoke up, "My sister lives twenty miles away but I have not been allowed to see her in two decades. Do you think I can get used to that?" Another man quickly jumped in with the comment that on his way to work every morning he had to walk by a guard tower where an East German soldier with a rifle and binoculars stared down at him." He speaks the same language I speak, He shares the same history. But one of us is an animal, and the other is a zookeeper, and I am never quite certain which is which." Then abruptly, the hostess broke in. She made a fist of one hand and slammed it into the palm of the other. Then she said, "If this man Gorbachev is serious with his talk of *glasnost* and *perestroika*, he can prove it. He can get rid of this Wall!

Back in Washington D.C., Robinson took that woman's dramatic comment and made it the central part of the speech he was preparing for the president. Reviewing the first draft, Reagan said that he liked the speech, "especially the passage about tearing down the Berlin Wall." But when the draft was circulated to the State Department and the National Security Council three weeks before it was to be delivered, the response was contempt and vehemence for what Robinson had written. For three weeks, bureaucrats fought the speech. They argued that it was crude and unduly provocative. They submitted seven alternative drafts in an attempt to discredit or change the original. In all seven, the call for the Wall to be torn down was deleted. The president resisted every attempt to water down the speech. But even on the morning that Air Force One left for Berlin, the State Department made a last effort to block the speech by forwarding yet another draft. Tom Griscom, the director of communications chose not to take it to the forward cabin. Air Force One landed and hours later President Reagan was standing before the Brandenburg Gate, where he delivered what has become one of the most famous speeches of the 20th Century.

"There is one sign the Soviets can make that would be unmistakable, that would advance dramatically the cause of freedom and peace. General Secretary Gorbachev, if you seek peace, if you seek prosperity for the Soviet Union and Eastern Europe, if you seek liberalization: Come here to this gate! Mr. Gorbachev, open this gate! Mr. Gorbachev, tear down this wall!"

THE WALL COMES DOWN

Two-and-a-half years later the wall was gone. The barrier between East and West, the barrier between tyranny and freedom ripped apart by the hands of the very people who had been so oppressed by it

Shortly after the fall of the Berlin Wall, the reforms of openness and restructuring which Mikhail Gorbachev had introduced led to unexpected and unprecedented cries for freedom and independence among the people of the Soviet Republic. Incredibly in February of 1990, the Central Committee of the Soviet Communist Party agreed to give up its monopoly of power. Individual republics like Lithuania and Estonia declared independence. A directly elected president of the Republic of Russia came to office, Boris Yeltsin. In November of 1991 he issued a decree banning the Communist Party. December 8, 1991, the leaders of the now independent republics met to issue a declaration that the Soviet Union was ended. On December 26th the Supreme Soviet had voted to dissolve itself and had terminated all institutions and ceased all operations. Communism received a death blow. Now, even the formidable Iron Curtain had fallen!

Two of the greatest miracles of the 20th. Century occurred within months of each other, all without a single shot being fired! People around the globe were astounded by these incredible, unexpected events. Government leaders and politicians are still scratching their heads, trying to figure out how this could have happened. Historians are still grappling with how to explain it.

COMMUNISM'S FAILURE

In 1960, Nikita Khrushchev, Premier of the former Soviet Union, gave one of the most quoted speeches of his career. He spoke from the October Palace in Kiev, Ukraine. He adamantly declared, "In 25 years, all religion will be stamped out in the Soviet Union." Then, sarcastically he said, "We will keep one priest as a relic so future generations will know what they look like." In the year 2004, forty-four years after Khrushchev's boastful statement, a Christian evangelist walked onto the stage of the same auditorium, filled with 1,800 people, their Bibles open, eager to hear the Word of God.

When communism turned its back on religion, when it emphasized material security over spirituality, when it placed the value of the state over the value and the rights of the individual person, it doomed itself to creating atheistic, addiction-ridden, and eventually bankrupt societies.

Communism's inability to eradicate the God-given spiritual instinct and nature must rank among the great failures of history. It was, more than anything else, a hunger for spirituality that brought the Iron Curtain and the Berlin wall down. Official atheism created a hunger that could be ignored no longer.

Sensing the moral bankruptcy that communism has caused, in one of the most incredible statements of the twentieth century, Mikhail Gorbachev admitted:

We have changed our attitude on some matters, such as religion, for example, which admittedly we used to treat in a simplistic manner... Now we do not only proceed from the assumption that no one should interfere in matters of individual conscience, we also say that the moral values which religion generated and embodied for centuries can help in the work of renewal in our country too.

He went on to envision the Soviet Union transforming into: "...*A commonwealth of sovereign democratic states, based on spiritual values, pluralism, religious tolerance and mutual understanding.*"(Italics supplied) 1. A few months after his remarks, incredibly, the Soviet parliament passed a law guaranteeing a broad range of religious and spiritual rights. It prohibited the state from interfering in church affairs and at last got the government out of the business of propagating atheism. Only after history has moved further along will we begin to understand and truly appreciate the courage, vision and yes, inspiration of Mikhail Gorbachev who almost single-handedly transformed and revolutionized what was one of the world's greatest empires.

Commenting on these incredible events, Don Feder of the *Boston Herald* wrote;

"It's as if the 73-year old horror of communism was not more than a divine object lesson. We were taken to the brink of the abyss and bade to look in, to see the fate that awaited mankind in a Godless world." 2.

In his speech at the Berlin wall, Ronald Reagan also said, "...this Wall will fall. For it cannot withstand faith; it cannot withstand truth. The wall cannot withstand freedom." In these words there is great hope for those of us living in the new and frightening era of terrorism. Here is the reassurance, borne out by the incredible recent history we have been examining of a great, comforting truth... God will let no evil triumph in the end.

Imagine how many troops on both sides would have been killed if the West would have attempted to take down the Berlin Wall by force! Imagine the civilian casualties, imagine the devastating economic impact. To have attempted the removal of the Iron Curtain by force could only have brought on a nuclear World War III.

What military might could not do with force, the power of freedom, the power of truth, the power of the spiritual inevitably accomplished. Though it is sadly underappreciated, the successful, bloodless ending of the Cold War was the greatest liberation of mankind, the greatest victory for freedom in the history of the world. (Since the cross)

"Not by might nor by power, but by my Spirit, says the Lord Almighty"(Zechariah 4:6).

Spiritual power will always win out over coercion or force. 3.

The British Empire was one of the most powerful military entities on earth. Yet it could not withstand the simple, non-violent spiritual energy of one little man, Mahatma Gandhi, who almost single-handedly brought freedom and autonomy to India. He, in turn, was a huge inspiration to Martin Luther King Jr. Dr. King, following Gandhi's example, with non-violent protest and prayer was able to successfully lead a Civil Rights Movement that transformed the face of America. His peaceful methods allowed us to avoid what could have been a blood-bath, an internal terrorist uprising that would have made 9/11 pale by comparison, or even another civil war.

ANOTHER CURTAIN THAT FELL

Religious "Iron Curtains", religious "Berlin Walls" must come down before freedom and spirituality can flourish. At the death of the Savior, the hand of God Himself ripped down the curtain that blocked access into the Holy of Holies in the Jewish temple. It was the place where the personal presence of God dwelt, the abiding place of the essence and power of spirituality. Religious institutions have been struggling for two thousand years to hang that curtain back up!

The truth is, Jesus came to overthrow the traditional, patriarchal religion of His day. He went to church to cause a riot more than once! He disrupted, boycotted and blockaded the economic activities in the temple in Jerusalem! He told the highest church administrators that they were rotten inside and called them some very insulting names! To top it off, by His death He unleashed the mysterious power of a pair of unseen hands which ripped in half the curtain in the Holy of Holies in the temple.

The Holy of Holies was the heart and center of the Jewish religion and in one fell swoop Jesus opened it up to the world. Spirituality was let loose in the world by this magnificent act! No longer would there be a distinction between the sacred and the secular. Religion would no longer be able to isolate itself, segregate itself, set itself apart and above the rest of the world. Thanks to Jesus Christ, everything in the world has become sacred. All of life, spiritual. If you think there are differences between the sacred and the secular, it is because you have created them.

In a very real sense, the torn curtain, that remarkable, dramatic and mystical event, was the death knell of traditional religion. It was the end of legalism. No more did people need to try to achieve salvation by their good behavior and their religious practices, by works.

Jesus opened up the sacred presence of God, the abiding place of the Shekinah to every person in the world. All had direct access through Him to the person of God. *Religion was finished. The new spirituality had begun! Jesus Christ awakened the sleeping giant of spirituality.* He triggered a spiritual chain reaction that can never be stopped. As hard as religion might try, the powerful genie of spirituality can never be stuffed back in the bottle. It can not be crammed back into the Most Holy Place. The Holy Spirit is loose in the world! Loose in human hearts!

Of royal colors was that veil. "Blue and purple, and scarlet, and fine twined linen of cunning work" (Exodus 26:31). This thick curtain separated the most Holy Place of the Jerusalem temple from the other compartments. In it the Ark of the Covenant was housed. Upon it was the mercy seat and here, between the golden wings of the protecting cherubim, shone the symbol of the very Presence of God Himself. "The glory of the Lord filled the tabernacle" (Exodus 40:34).

With force greater than a thunderbolt, with unexplained power from far beyond the human spectrum, a pair of unseen hands eagerly ripped apart the curtain in the temple! With shock and terror, the hitherto complacent priests saw their sacred Holy of Holies exposed to the world. How astounding that this was God's very first act upon the death of His Son!

And when Jesus had cried out again in a loud voice, he gave up his spirit.
At that moment the curtain of the temple was torn in two from top to bottom. The earth shook and the rocks split (Matthew 27:50-51). God could not stand to delay even a second before performing this astonishing act! He had waited for centuries to do this thing! Notice that the veil was not torn from the bottom to the top as a man might do it. It was ripped from top to bottom as only Divine power could do it. A silent explosion of Divine energy!

No more barriers to God! The intimacy of the fellowship in Eden restored! Freedom from bondage at last! By His death, Christ had gained for mankind the right to direct access to the very presence of God! He had won for us the right to the Spirit-filled life!

It was one of the most significant moments in human history. God opened up His temple, He opened up His heart, and He said to every Jew, every Gentile, every man, woman and child, "Come on in"! Now, we are all invited into the Most Holy Place. It is not just a private reserve for the priests any more. We in fact all may become priests. We can all chose to "come boldly to His throne of grace" (Hebrews 4:16 NKJV).

While the cross has come to symbolize the significance of that great hour, a more enlightened Christendom might come to ponder with equal solemnity and holy awe the emblem of a torn curtain. With all our steeples and bells and naves and founts, in our stained-glass renderings of doves and fish and pomegranates and lilies, there should be room for the simple significant symbol of the rent veil. It is after all a reminder of the most precious truth; every man and woman and child now has the right to direct access to the very presence and personality of God through the indwelling Holy Spirit. *Stop and ponder for a moment the incredible fact that God dwells in you!*

The distance, the distortions about God have been banished by the cross. We may all know and experience Him intimately. He no longer dwells in distant tabernacles in the desert. The fiery glory of the Shekinah has been released from its temple bonds. The King James version says that when Jesus died, "He gave up the ghost." Well that He surely did. He gave up the ghost so that we could have the Ghost! The Holy Spirit!

"Therefore, brothers, since we have confidence to enter the Most Holy Place by the blood of Jesus, by a new and living way opened for us through the curtain, that is his body, and since we have a great priest over the house of God, let us draw near to God" (Hebrews 10:19-23).

Sacred mysterious mixture of fire and light! The Shekinah glory! Symbol of the fiery presence of the Holy Spirit! The Spirit of love, released at last by the torn curtain; willing now, eager, after the cross, to make its home in you and me! "Do you not know that your body is a temple of the Holy Spirit, who is in you, whom you have received from God? (1 Corinthians 6:19).

Stop reading for a moment. Here is a little exercise for you. Put the book down and touch your finger tips to both sides of your head above your ears. What is that part of your anatomy called? Your temples, right? (Sorry, couldn't resist.)

Guess what. You are either a temple of love or a temple of fear and anger. The choice is yours. And you get to choose every morning.

Through what Christ has done for us, you and I can now live every moment of our lives in the presence of Divinity! We can make the practice of

God's presence the central fact of our lives. We may enter into a sacred oneness with Him. No longer does the Shekinah glory reflect against the wall of some remote desert sanctuary. God no longer dwells in temples. There are not more walls or curtains holding Him in. He dwells in people. By His Spirit. "And in him you too are being built together to become a dwelling in which God lives by his Spirit" (Ephesians 2:22). We can live every day as if we are the very temple of God on earth! Our mind is His altar, our heart His sanctuary!

When the incredible, mysterious gift of the filling of the Holy Spirit becomes a reality for you, once you have chosen to ask for it and accept it, you can then say with Paul, "I no longer live, but Christ lives in me" (Galatians 2:20).

Supreme privilege. Ultimate opportunity. To be the citadel of God on earth. To give the Creator an expression in flesh and blood in our time!

Q&A:

Q. Do any of the other religions of the world teach anything like the doctrine of the filling of the Holy Spirit?

A. First of all Christianity is not a religion. It is a relationship. It is not a belief-system, it is a love affair! Religions focus on man's efforts to please or placate a god or gods. They are about man looking for god. Christianity is about a God who comes looking for His children. Looking for them in the Garden. Looking for them at Bethlehem. Looking for them at Calvary. Looking for them at Pentecost. Jesus is the good shepherd who goes out in the dark and stormy night to find the one lost sheep. He is the eager father of the prodigal, running down the road to embrace his lost son. No one ever painted a more beautiful picture of what God is like than did Jesus with that incredible story. It has been called the greatest short story in the history of literature. His account of the prodigal son eliminates more bad theology about God and what He is really like than does anything else ever written. "But while he was still a long way off, his father saw him and was filled with compassion for him; he ran to his son, threw his arms around him and kissed him" (Luke 15:20). Imagine it! A God who runs toward us!

No other religion in the world presents a seeking God, one who is willing to make Himself vulnerable enough to enter into the human dimension, to enter into the hearts of His people with His Spirit, to live there and to empower them to become the expression of His presence and personality on this earth. The Father says of His children, "you will be called 'Sought After'" (Isaiah 62:12). No other religion in the world has a God who cared enough to come into the enemy's camp, not on not a seek-and-destroy mission but on a seek-and -save mission! In fact He came "undercover"! Wrapped up in swaddling clothes as a babe! He came to this world *incognito!* Phillip Yancey reminds us that the incarnation was a daring raid into enemy territory. No, sorry, no other religion has a god that has even come close to pulling off anything like that!

Q. You seem to think the tearing of the curtain was something really important. Why is that and if it is true, why didn't my church teach me about it? How could I have missed something so profound?

A. The torn curtain is so significant because it symbolizes the barriers coming down between men and women and God. It indicated that paradigm shift from religion to personal spirituality. A fantastic new intimacy with God became available at that moment. Through what happened on the cross, the way was now opened for the restoration of the kind of fellowship and closeness with the Father which Adam and Eve enjoyed in Eden. The Holy Spirit was available to be *with* people before the cross. Now the Holy Spirit was available to be *in* the believer. This is a crucial, earth-shaking distinction!

Why haven't you been taught about it before? Anything related to the indwelling of the Holy Spirit seems to have been mysteriously overlooked or ignored in the teachings of many Christian churches. Perhaps you missed it because, like those who tried to worship in the temple in the time of Jesus, you were distracted by the money-changing! Materialism can be such a trap! Today, so much energy goes into acquiring and maintaining our many possessions and our demanding, high-energy life-style that we give ourselves little time or opportunity to practice the presence of God.

Another problem might be that your church focused so much on the ritual of the Old Testament sanctuary and its services that you have missed the heart of the matter. Some have made little wooden models of the sanctuary and lectured on its symbols and measured its courts but managed to ignore the meaning of the Shekinah, the illuminating presence of the Holy Spirit that the whole temple was built to house! For others, an emphasis on a supposed "investigative judgment" (a teaching wholly unsupported by Scripture) or the apocalyptic end-time myths or distorted teaching like the rapture have been the distractions that have kept them focused more on fear and guilt and judgment. These depressing, low-energy, fear-inducing religious negatives kept them away from the more profound, positive truths, such as the love and the joy and the peace that are the beginnings of heaven on earth right now for the person who invites in the presence of the Holy Spirit. Here's the deal; God is not your judge … He is your healer!

I am afraid that some Christians are kept from a personal, satisfying relationship with the Holy Spirit because they substitute the Bible in place of the Spirit! They try to take the Bible as literally word-for-word inspired for one thing. They end up venerating the book and not the Author. They do not realize that the Bible is the signpost, not the journey. If the traveler stops to worship the signpost, he will not get very far!

Others allow more modern spiritual writers or teachers or prophets to take the place of the personal guidance and instruction of the Holy Spirit. (For example, for Mormons, it may be the extra-biblical writings of Joseph Smith. For Seventh-day Adventists, the writing of Ellen G. White, for Catholics, the proclamations of the Holy See) While the Spirit can and often does work through such means, they are fallible and they are no substitute for the personal direction the Holy Spirit longs to give each individual.

And here is a tricky one… the law. Some substitute the law for the Spirit. They put their energy into trying to keep the law, little realizing that it is causing them to neglect a personal, passionate encounter with the Holy Spirit. Some traditionalists define their religion by carefully keeping the law. They try to rely on the law as their guide instead of the Spirit as their Guide! The law is good for calling us to a high standard of behavior, but it is insufficient in helping us achieve good behavior. Only the Spirit can empower us to live lives above reproach. The Bible promises: "...live by the Spirit and you will not gratify the desires of the sinful nature." Then it goes on to say something even more startling: "But if you are led by the Spirit, you are not under law" (Galatians 5:16-18). We are to live and discern the will of God first and foremost by our daily, moment-by-moment connection with the Holy Spirit. Nothing must be allowed to substitute for that. Not our church, not our religion, not the law, not our doctrines. "But when he, the Spirit of truth comes, *he will guide you into all truth*" (John 6:13 emphasis added).

For some, there has always been the risk of becoming a "courtyard Christian". Courtyard Christians hang around and try to worship or socialize in the outer courts of the temple but seem oblivious of their right to move on into the Holy of Holies, into the presence of the living God. Before the curtain was torn, even the most faithful believers could not enter the Most Holy Place. They had to be content with the offerings they could present in the courtyard of the temple. After the cross, many continued to busy themselves with the same old rituals, but the cross changed everything. It moves us from distant religious spectators to participants who are intimately involved in our own personal spirituality. Sadly, because of apathy or fear, there are many who still hang back in the courtyard of the temple. They seem to be in some kind of religious trance that prevents them from moving on in to the Holy of Holies. So many don't seem to get it: Christianity is a highly radical and revolutionary force. It is about so much more than receiving eternal life someday in the future. The baptism of the Spirit is about an extraordinary life of adventure and challenge and intimacy with God that begins right now. It is a striking way to live. It calls you to a revolutionary life sincerely and aggressively devoted to loving God, loving people, and to living ethically and morally. It is simply put, a life of radical, costly discipleship.

How far would a group of Germans get if they were to show up with a cement mixer and try to rebuild the Berlin Wall? There are those misguided religious souls who struggle to replace the curtain in the sanctuary that God ripped apart! The intimacy is just too threatening; the freedom just too intimidating. They don't want the Holy Spirit wandering loose in the world or in the church, or in their hearts, threatening to upset their comfort level, their beliefs or the established order of things.

FOOTNOTES CHAPTER 3:

1. Gorbachev, Michael, Interview, *The New York Times*.

2. Fedor, Don, quoted in *The Boston Herald*, May 1991.

3. Hawkins, David R. M.D., Ph.D. *Power vs. Force*. (Hay House, Inc, Carlsbad, CA: 2002), p.76, 77.

CHAPTER 4:
ARE YOU CONNECTED?

Set your minds on things above…
not on earthly things.
Put to death greed." Colossians 3:5

Your sole business in life is to attain god-realization. All else is useless and
worthless.
—Sivananda

The Beechcraft Bonanza lifted off into the clear blue California sky and pointed its nose northward. It promised to be a pleasant afternoon flight from the Central Valley to Portland, Oregon. The doctor was going to attend some medical meetings. He was bringing along his wife and two small children. Every one on board enjoyed the spectacular views. Once they reached altitude they could see the snow-capped Sierra Nevada mountains on their right, and in the distance off to their left were the sparkling waters of the Pacific Ocean. The flight went smoothly enough until, approaching the town of Red Bluff and the mountain range that lay ahead, they could see a heavy build-up of towering clouds in front of them. This did not concern the doctor since he was instrument-rated. He called Air Traffic Control on the radio and received a clearance to switch from visual to instrument flight rules. He was assigned an altitude and heading and proceeded on his way. Eventually, the airplane penetrated the billowing white clouds. The pilot could no longer see anything beyond his wingtips. Still, the flight progressed smoothly.

About 30 minutes later, ATC called the Bonanza. The airplane was approaching the mountains and the controller wanted to instruct the pilot to climb to a higher altitude so he would have plenty of clearance over the peaks. There was no answer. The controller noted that radar still showed the plane where it was supposed to be and on course. He waited a few moments and called again: "Bonanza 3275 Victor, turn left to heading 320, climb and maintain

8000." No response. Now, with the aircraft getting ever-closer to the rising slopes, the controller became alarmed. "75 Victor, 75 Victor, do you copy?" Hoping the pilot could still hear him even if he could not transmit back, the controller frantically said, "Bonanza 3275 Victor, begin an immediate climb to 8000 feet, you are approaching mountainous terrain." There was still only silence. Despite more desperate calls, no response ever came from the airplane. The controller watched in horror as the blip on his screen approached the mountains and then disappeared from his screen.

The aircraft's wreckage was found the next day at the 5500-foot level of a 5900-foot peak. There were no survivors. A subsequent investigation by the National Transportation Safety Board showed that there had been no mechanical failure with the airframe or the engine. The investigators did discover that the volume had been turned way down on the airplane's VHF communications receiver. The volume was turned way up on the AM radio receiver which was tuned to a popular music station.

The doctor missed out on life-saving guidance because he had become distracted. He was unaware, not fully conscious of his situation and as a result he was not able to hear the voice that could have saved him and his family. Was the doctor a bad man? No. Was he a stupid or ignorant man? No. He was simply distracted.

In his book, *The Purpose Driven Life*, Rick Warren writes:

It is human nature to get distracted by minor issues. We play Trivial Pursuit with our lives. Henry David Thoreau observed that people live lives of 'quiet desperation,' but today a better description is aimless distraction. 1.

The Holy Spirit is the voice of Jesus in the world today. The Bible says, "For as many are led by the Spirit of God, these are the sons of God" (Romans 8:14). He wants to speak His love and His guidance into your heart. He eagerly anticipates communicating His life-saving and life-enhancing truth to you. But He can't. Not if you have your energy and attention focused on something else. He is too much of a gentleman to force Himself on you. He speaks with a still, small voice. A voice easily drowned out by the cacophony of modern, 21st-century life. Sometimes His voice is simply the persistent voice of your conscience or your intuition. Other times He will speak to you through the Bible or some other spiritual book. Sometimes He communicates through your good friends or through a worship service or through the beauty of His splendid creation. There are unlimited ways He can touch your heart and soul, but only if you are not distracted. Only if you are aware. Only if you are God-conscious. If you do get distracted and lose your connection with God, you lose your connection with kindness, gentleness, compassion and wisdom.

Practicing the presence of God, maintaining your connection moment by moment with the source of Divine power is absolutely essential. In fact, it is everything. It is the beating heart of spirituality. *The only hope for the world today is enough people learning to practice the presence of God.* God is eager to bathe your whole life in His presence! Practicing God's presence means that you are constantly making a choice to be in conscious union with Him. This union is the only source of our strength. It is the only source of love. One humble person, connected in this way with the Father can become a force for light and love and harmony to thousands of people in the world! This is what Jesus meant when He said, "You are the light of the world." The whole idea of the Spirit-filled life is to allow the love of God to operate in our consciousness. As this happens, we become that love.

Every time you think God's name, your cells will fall more deeply into Divine alignment. Surrender you body to love, seeing your only function on this earth as being love's hands, feet, words, and actions. … With every breath you take, you will thrill to breathe in God's Spirit. Your entire body will awaken to a new and almost startling aliveness. You will live in Him, as He lives in you. 2.

There is a lot of talk about consciousness today, but the ultimate consciousness is the simple consciousness of the presence of the Holy in your soul. Whatever has your attention has you, it is your master. What you love, you will become. That is why it is essential to learn to establish perpetual communion with the Father, the source of love and light. Frank Laubach wrote, "Oh, this thing of keeping in constant touch with God, of making him the object of my thought and the companion of my conversations, is the most amazing thing I ever ran across."3.

It is all too easy to get so caught up in our busyness and our own thinking that we fail to keep an on-going connection with God. It is not uncommon for us to fall "asleep" spiritually and ignore His presence as we go through our day. Here are some simple, helpful, spiritual "alarms" you can use to wake you up and bring you back into God-consciousness.

1. Tape a little note to your bathroom mirror, the bottom of your computer screen and the dashboard of your car that says: "Help me to live in your presence."

2. Every time the phone rings, before you answer it, say this little prayer: "Father, help me to be love to the person on the other end of the line."

3. Every time you flip on a light switch say: "Abba, may the power of your Spirit bring light and love into the world through me!"

4. When you put the key in the ignition of your car, before you turn it on, stop. You are about to start a fire that will provide incredible energy and power. Ask for the power and presence of God to be ignited in you.

5. Most of us download something on our computers or phones many times a day. Next time you are waiting those few seconds to download your current e-mail or Facebook updates or the latest news headlines or stock quotes, let God know that you want His love and peace and gentleness down-loaded into your soul!

CONNECTION IS EVERYTHING

If you are in connection with your source, with your Divine power, He can access you. You put yourself in a position to hear His still small voice when you are connected. If you are truly God-conscious, God-connected. you will learn to be acutely aware of the very presence of God at all times. Then you will be able to be aware of the slightest little nudge from the Holy Spirit! You will have a kind of guidance you would not otherwise have. You will have a wisdom deeper than your own. As Wayne Dyer says: "When you are in spirit, you are inspired!" You become very creative when you are in-spirit because you are connected to the same abundant source which fires the furnace of the sun, which grows every living thing on earth and is expanding the universe continually on into the immeasurable cosmos! That creativity will give you a wonderful fresh and unique perspective on life.

When you are in the Spirit you can see the Big Picture. You are able to think, not just outside the box, but outside the circle, outside your organization, outside your religion. Whole new vistas of thought and possibility will open up to you. Perhaps you will even become irresistible! Of the Spirit-filled disciple Stephen, it was said, "And they were not able to resist the wisdom and the spirit by which he spoke" (Acts 6:10).

There are after all, two ways to be abnormal. One is to be below normal, the other to be above normal. Francis Chan has said that something is wrong when our lives make sense to unbelievers! Sometimes, living the Spirit-filled life may mean doing what others see as crazy! Billy Graham said that, for the Christian, to be filled with the Spirit is not an option. It is a necessity. It is indispensable; it is the normal Christian life. Anything less, he said, is sub-normal! Our Lord Jesus was definitely not normal! His Spirit is calling every one of us to live very radically, to live *beyond normal*, like He did. I would like to see every one of you readers become abnormal mystics who help to turn the world upside down! *Why be normal? Normal is highly overrated!* I want you to be somersaulting into the inconceivable every day! I want your lives to be re-enchanted! I want you to be overwhelmed every day with a sense of awe and wonder. I want you to find yourself on a great, spiritual adventure as you journey toward the sacred! But none of this can happen for any of us if we are distracted. Tragically, it is usually our distractions that cause us to neglect our soul, to become oblivious. Spiritually oblivious. So get ready, here they come. Some blocks to the Spirit-filled life.

TWENTY-FIRST CENTURY IDOLATRY
The folks who spend their days
In buying cars and clothes and rings,
Don't seem to know that empty lives
Are just as empty, filled with things.
—Anonymous

Materialism is one of the most dangerous distractions of our age. It's been said that a materialist is somebody who spends more than they make on stuff they don't need to impress people they don't even like! Americans need to face the truth: our economy and our very culture is being relentlessly driven by pathological consumerism. Meanwhile, of the seven billion people in the world, over half of them struggle to survive on less than $2 a day. Another way to put it is if one hundred people represent the entire world's population, fifty-three of them would be earning less than $2 a day. Every year, 40 million people die of starvation and diseases that are preventable. Of the 125,000 people who die needlessly around the world every day, 40,000 are children.

The need to accumulate, to acquire belongings, to make the credit card payments on the ones we have, this grasps the energy and attention of the majority of people in our society. So many are caught up in the work-spend cycle that it has become the norm. Someone has said there is truly an epidemic of affluenza in the land! Focused on always acquiring more, we forget to be grateful for what we have. Television and the advertising industry fuel an ever-growing lust for more and more. The lifestyles and the possessions of the rich and famous intrigue us. The hedonistic spending of "celebrities" is flaunted as a proof of their "success" and held up as some kind of standard at which to aim for. It should be a cause of great consternation and concern to us that with less than 5% percent of the world's population, our country consumes almost a third of all the world's goods and energy. In the book, *The Day America Told the Truth*, the writers interviewed average Americans and ask them what they thought would best fulfill their potential as humans. The two top responses? 1. To be rich 2. To be thin. 3.

"Too many Americans view expensive purchases as 'shortcuts to well-being', says Martin Seligman, a psychologist a the University of Pennsylvania. In a *Time* magazine report titled "The Real Truth About Money", studies by Ruut Veenhoven, a sociologist at Erasmus University in Rotterdam, were reported as showing that once a person's income exceeds $10,000 or so a year, money and happiness decouple and cease to have much to do with each other. *Time* reports:

Over the past two decades, in fact an increasing body of social-science and psychological research has shown that there is no significant relationship between how much money a person earns and whether he or she feels good about life…Edward Diener, a psychologist at the University of Illinois, interviewed members of the Forbes 400, the richest Americans. He found the Forbes 400 were only a tiny bit happier than people as a whole. 4.

When asked once about how much money it takes for one to be happy, the wise old John D. Rockefeller replied, "Just a little bit more!"

In our capitalistic society, it is particularly easy to allow money to seduce you away from what is truly important, truly valuable. An unprejudiced writer from abroad gave this report after touring the United States for nine months. "I know of no country, indeed, where the love of money has taken a stronger hold on the affections of men…" The writer was Alexis de Tocqueville and the year was 1831! What would he say about us now, now that we are the richest nation on earth?

Marcus Borg calls the "dominant values" of society, "achievement, affluence and appearance". 5.

There is still no greater threat, no greater distraction to the spiritual life for almost everyone than money. Jesus put it bluntly and clearly when He said, "You cannot serve both God and money" (Luke 6:13). In *The Purpose Driven Life*, Pastor Rick Warren says: "To become a real servant you are going to have to settle the issue of money….Living for ministry and living for money are two mutually exclusive goals. Money has the greatest potential to replace God in your life. More people are sidetracked from serving by materialism than by anything else. They say, 'After I achieve my financial goals, I'm going to serve God.' That is a foolish decision they will regret for eternity" 6.

Think about it for a moment, if you dare. You want to know how you are doing spiritually? You don't need to go to a retreat to find out. Take a look at your check register! The most accurate reflection of your values and beliefs is going to be found in your checkbook. How you spend your money is a direct, unarguable expression about how you truly feel about things, how important they are to you and what your priorities really are.

Eckhart Tolle in his book *A New Earth*, talks about "the fiction of ownership:

The ego tends to equate having with Being: I have, therefore I am. And the more I have, the more I am…if you live in a culture that to a large extent equates self-worth with how much and what you have, if you cannot look through this collective delusion, you will be condemned to chasing after things for the rest of your life in the vain hope of finding your worth and completion of your sense of self there. 7.

TOYS

I was waiting for someone in the parking lot of a shopping mall in trendy Marin County, California recently. Marin has the highest per capita income anywhere in California after Beverly Hills. (It also is reported to have the highest divorce rate, suicide rate and the highest per-capita use of anti-depressants of anywhere in the country.) As I was sitting there, a beautiful, sparkling red BMW convertible with the top down pulled into the empty spot beside me. A striking blonde with designer dark glasses perched on top of her head got out and walked quickly toward the mall. She appeared to be a woman who had not yet gotten the victory over shopping! I got out of my car to stretch my legs and look at the vehicle next to me. Walking around behind it, I saw a bumper sticker that read, "IF YOU THINK MONEY CAN'T BUY HAPPINESS, THEN YOU DON'T KNOW WHERE TO SHOP!"

Soulless, wanton spending can be such a trap, such a spiritual distraction. Author Chris Blake says, "When I enter a shopping mall, I feel that I'm on the enemy's ground. You might think I am overreacting, but I think more people pay allegiance to Satan through materialism than through Satanism, atheism and terrorism combined." 8.

What kind of a message about the meaning and purpose of life are we sending our children when they see our hunger for the material? It starts early. You mommies can begin programming your daughters to be "material girls" early on nowadays. You can buy your baby daughter a cute little onesie that says BORN TO SHOP. There are sweet little pink purses across the front.

Remember, right after 9/11 when the country was in crises. The stock market was slumping, hotels were stuck with empty rooms and airlines were flying with empty seats. (I was on one of the first flights out of the San Francisco Bay area to Honolulu the first day airlines were allowed to fly after

9/11. There were eight of us on board the giant Boeing 757.) The whole economy was taking a major hit. Our president came on the television to offer his advice to all citizens on how to cope with the crises. Did he call for saving and sacrifice to face the challenges ahead? No. "Go shopping!" he proclaimed! Save some money? Prepare for difficult times to come? No. Go shopping! Not to go shopping would be well... unpatriotic!

"Go shopping" seems to be the ultimate panacea for Americans. Feeling depressed? Hey, for a quick pick-me- up, just go shopping. The economy starting to crumble? Is Depression 2.0 knocking at the door? No problem. We can fix it if enough people will just get out their credit cards and "go shopping." Americans carry more than one billion credit cards!

The blonde's bumper sticker reminded me of the time I was traveling on the freeway and passed a gigantic motor home. It had a motorcycle mounted in a rack on the front. There was a satellite dish on top and the RV was towing a twin-engine cabin cruiser. There was a bumper sticker on it that said, "HE WHO HAS THE MOST TOYS WHEN HE DIES WINS!"

There are those who give the advice that you are a fool if you die leaving any money on the table. You should just live it up while you can. After all, they say, there are no pockets in a shroud.

The late Steve Fossett, a 66-year-old retired trader in soybean futures, seemed to be vying for the winner's title in the toy accumulation race until he lost his life while flying his airplane over the eastern Sierras. According to *Newsweek* magazine (November 14, 2005) under the roof of his southern California mansion he kept both a $205,000 Ferrari 465GT and a $234,000 Aston Martin Vanquish, both of which can hit 186 mph. When he decided he wanted to travel really fast, he could jump in his $17 million Citation X personal jet. For a slower pace, he could relax aboard his $5.5 million catamaran or just float away in his $500,000 custom-made hot-air balloon! Now, his toys sit forlornly in their garages.

Paul Allen, Microsoft cofounder, has outdone Fossett when it comes to toys that float. His new yacht, the 413-foot Octopus, cost more than $250 million and includes a helipad, music studio and pool. When Larry Ellison, CEO of Oracle, found out about Allen's boat, he ordered builders to stretch his under-construction yacht, Rising Sun from 420 to 452 feet in order to keep well ahead of Allen.

For the toy collectors who can't decide to go by land or sea, there is now available the latest in amphibious luxury. For $1.2 million they can buy a full-size motor home that can be driven off the road into a lake to become an RV yacht!

I can't cast too many stones at some of these toy-collectors because a few years ago I stopped to count up how many gasoline engines I owned. It was frightening. I had a chain saw, a generator, a lawnmower, four snow machines, eight outboard motors, six cars or pick up trucks, three motorcycles, two inboard boat engines, two engines on one airplane and one on the other. I stopped counting when I got to 32 gasoline engines! Now, its true that some of these were used for business, but still, can you imagine how much time, energy and money the care and feeding and maintenance of that many engines takes! It is practically a full-time job! Not to mention the barrels of gas it costs to run them!

The insanity of uncontrolled consumption has certainly clouded the spiritual vision of us all. Karl Marx made an infamous comment about religion being the opiate of the masses. He got it wrong. Stuff is the opiate of the masses in this century! We all seem to be addicted to more, more, more. It is the ego that is always hungry, hungry for more. It is constantly compelling us to compare ourselves with others and with what they have. Cars, homes, clothes, for example, designer label clothes, are used in our society as identity enhancers. Does anyone get it, that eventually the point comes when more is less, when more is counter-productive and destructive and dysfunctional. Why do economists seem to think that the economy is failing if it is not growing at a four or five percent or more rate every year? Shouldn't just maintaining the economy where it is for awhile be a more financially healthy goal? Doesn't someone need to tell these people that when something is continuously growing it is called cancer? Don't they know that when you put too much new wine even in new wineskins, the skins will burst? (That's called a bubble popping, ever hear of that term before?!) Greed threatens our world more than any other force.

The great lie of the advertising industry is that we need more in order to be happy. Wasn't it in the Sermon on the Mount that Jesus said, "Living well is the best revenge?" Woops! Wait a minute, that message was propaganda delivered to your brain courtesy of the liquor industry!

Socrates said, "He is nearest to God who needs the fewest things". "Buddha said… "detach, detach!" The path to enlightenment and the way to end personal suffering was to let go of attachments, he advised. Thoreau, said, "simplify, simplify." Another wise man said, "Want what you have." Because so many of us have already crossed over the line our modern rallying cry might be, "de-accumulate, de-accumulate!" It is time we gave up our attachments to so many possessions and began to journey more lightly through the world. Here's the thing; the farther you go with God, the less you can take with you!

This book is a call to all of us to wake up, grow up and stop playing with our toys! Stop our anxious, desperate grasping! To finally realize that it is through giving that we truly live, not through acquiring.

SOUL HUNGER

Every person has a place in them that is hungry for God. We were created to contain His Spirit. Until we have connected with our Source we will always have a longing, a craving, an emptiness within. We will desperately try to fill that empty spot with something. If we do not find the original we will search hungrily among the counterfeits. Materialism, alcohol, food, illicit sex, these have been called "soul cocaine." These things can give people just a tiny little drop of what they imagine to be transcendence. When we see others struggling with their weaknesses or addictions, we should give up our awful judging and condemnation and see the person's dysfunctional behavior as a cry for help. *The people we judge as "wrong" are not so much wrong as they are wounded. They are not so much depraved as they are dysfunctional. What we see as their bad behavior is actually a cry for help, a call for love.*

It was G.K. Chesterton who said, "Everyman who knocks on the door of a brothel is looking for God." When we see addictions in ourselves we should be aware that they reveal to us the places where our heart has not been fully surrendered to and captured by the love of God. Addictions of any kind can create a subtle kind of false transcendence. C.S. Lewis wrote in *The Weight of Glory*, "We are half-hearted creatures, fooling about with drink and sex and ambition when infinite joy is offered us."

As a pastor and counselor, one of the saddest and profoundly disconcerting and frustrating problems I have had to face with clients are marital affairs. They can come to have such incredible power over the spouse that has been unfaithful. Logic is handily dismissed. Appeals to reason are quickly rejected. The most intricate justifications for the behavior are created with the greatest ingenuity. One common justification that I often hear from religious people is: "Oh, when Susy and I read the Bible and pray together, we feel really close to God. I just don't feel that with my wife." Implying of course that this clearly justifies the affair and gives God's blessing to the relationship. One of the most provocative and almost frightening descriptions of the incredibley destructive power of addiction, particularly as applied to an adulterous affair, appears in the book *The Sacred Romance:*

And this is the power of addiction. Whatever the object of our addiction is, it attaches itself to our intense desire for eternal and intimate communion with God and each other in the midst of Paradise—the desire that Jesus himself placed in us before the beginning of the world. Nothing less than this kind of un-fallen communion will ever satisfy our desire or allow it to drink freely without imprisoning it and us. Once we allow our heart to drink water from these less-than-eternal wells …it overpowers our will and becomes, as Jonathan Edwards said, "like a viper, hissing and spitting at God" and us if we try to restrain it. 9.

We needy creatures really only have two choices as the foundation for our life…addiction and adultery or God, personal connection with God. The Father created us for intimacy with Him and nothing, absolutely nothing else will suffice. C.S. Lewis said, "If I find in myself desires which nothing in this world can satisfy, the only logical explanation is that I was made for another world".

THE TYRANNY OF THINGS

It was the wisest Teacher of all who said, "Take heed and beware of coveteousness: a man's life consisteth not of the abundance of things which he possesseth" (Luke 12:15 KJV).   When a young, wealthy, well-educated man asked the Master what he needed to do to have the Spirit-filled life, to enter into the kingdom of God, he was told simply to sell everything he had, give his possessions to the poor and come and follow Jesus (Luke 18:22 KJV). Shaking his head sadly at such a preposterous suggestion, the young fellow walked away. Alas, he walked away in to obscurity. Oh what might have been! He could have become a model to the world for unselfish giving to this day. He could have been remembered right along with the widow who gave her mite. He might have become the thirteenth disciple! He might have written the fifth gospel! His name might have been permanently etched in history as one who helped to transform the world. But his many possessions distracted him. His story brings you and me face to face with the key issue of life: are we going to live for ourselves or for God? Jesus was right; you simply cannot live for both God and money. So ask yourself, are you primarily a capitalist or a Christian? What would your financial planner think if you told him you were a committed servant of someone who said, "Do not store up treasures for yourself on earth…Do not be anxious about tomorrow"? I am not saying it is this way for everyone, because it is not, but for some of us, it may come down to this: would you rather have your stuff or would you rather have the Spirit?

There is nothing wrong with having the things that make your life function comfortably and effectively, and it is the responsibility of each of us to provide adequately for our future so that we will not be a burden on someone else, but the bottom line is this, money or possessions must never be allowed to distract us from the Spirit-filled life. It is a great puzzle to me that though we come into this world with nothing and we leave it with nothing, much of our life is devoted to the intense preoccupation with acquiring things in the little time we are here. Last I heard, they still don't allow U-Haul trailers through the pearly gates.

The call of the Christ is a call away from the world of form. The world of form is not merely things or possessions. It can also be relationships, situations we get ourselves into, circumstances, even thoughts and feelings. All of these can be blocks and distractions that prevent us from fully surrendering, emptying ourselves and creating the space where the Holy Spirit can come in to our soul, to our "I am" and make there His tabernacle.

Pure Christian spirituality is a very radical thing in this world. It calls into question every area of life and living. If your Christianity does not affect your lifestyle and the way you handle your pocketbook there is something sadly lacking with it. Christianity is in fact subversive of traditional religion, traditional politics and traditional economics which are based on greed, on constantly getting and spending and acquiring more and more.

Thomas Linacre was an Englishman who lived from 1460-1524. As a Christian, he was very excited when one of the first translations of the New Testament in his own language was made available to him. But he was shocked by what he read. He said, "Either this is not the gospel, or we are not Christians."

The Master taught economics based on generosity. Christ called into question the traditional ways that people live their lives, religiously, socially and economically. Malcolm Muggeridge warned: "The only ultimate disaster that can befall us is to feel at home here in this world."

When will we ever get it? We are not our stuff! As Anna Quindlen has written:
"Stuff is not salvation." She worries about Americans who have the acquisition habits of a 7-year old with their desires untethered from need or the ability to pay. She says bluntly that our addiction to consumption has become so out of control that it qualifies as a sickness. 10.   Never value yourself by the things you have or de-value yourself because of the things you do not have. Your value does not come from your valuables! The most important things in life are not things!

It is as St. Exupery wrote: "It is only with the heart that one can see rightly. What is essential is invisible to the eye." Two-thousand years before,

Paul got it right too when he said: "We fix our eyes not on what is seen, but on what is unseen. For what is seen is temporary, but what is unseen is eternal" (2 Corinthians 4:18). Money can't buy happiness because the things that are really important in life are not sold in stores!

God made us to be human beings, not human havings! Our sense of perspective is so vastly different than God's. There is a story of a man who was praying one day. He said, "God" God responded, "Yes?" The fellow said, "Can I ask a question?" "Go right ahead" said God. "God, what is a million years to you?" God said, "A million years to me is only a second." Then the man asks him, "God, what is a million dollars to you?" God said, "A million dollars to me is as a penny." So the man said, "God, can I have a penny?" And God said, "Sure!... Just a second."

I like Peter Gomes' simple definition of wealth: "Wealth is not what you have: wealth is what you have been given that enables you to give to others." 11.

Philanthropy has come to be associated with big organizations or institutions but it is interesting that the word "philanthropy," when broken down from its original source, means simply "love to mankind". The purpose of life is not to be found in competing or consuming but in contributing. There are basically three ways to live your life. You can be a human being, a human having or a human doing. You get to choose. Are you going to chase money or meaning?

Most people today define wealth and success far differently than God does. God cares most about what we are becoming, not about what we have. He cares more about what we are than what we do. Are we becoming more filled with his Spirit every day? More in-spirit. More "inspired"? Are we growing into greater awareness of and closeness with our Father? More conscious of His presence? Are we becoming more kind and compassionate? Are we becoming love?

Q&A:

Q. Are you trying to make us feel guilty for having money?

A. No. Well….maybe. A little. The real problem is not "having money." The problems begin when the money has you. In the interest of full disclosure, I should probably tell you that I have a skewed perception of money. In the small, remote Alaska village I grew up in during the 1950's, there was no money. At least not in everyday life. That was because there was no place to spend it. There were no stores. There was no bank. (There were no roads or cars, or TV or phones or electricity either.) No one had a mortgage. Or car payments, or utility bills. It was a subsistence life-style in many ways with a portion of our food coming from the land, including our frequent salmon dinners and mooseburger lunches! I was not interested in an allowance and did not receive one because I would not have been able to do anything with it. Money held no interest for me in those formative years. To this day, sometimes to my detriment I am sure, I would still rather not concern myself about money. When I do try to focus on it, I can feel its allure and pull and power. I can see how very easy it would be to become obsessed with it.

I now understand that I still do not have any money or possessions. What I do have is not my own at all, but placed in trust with me. I am simply entrusted with the stewardship of it, to use it under the Spirit's guidance to sustain my family and minister to the needs of others.

FOOTNOTES CHAPTER 4:

1. Warren, Rick, *The Purpose Driven Life*. (Zondervan, Grand Rapids: 2002), p.32.

2. Williamson, Marianne, *A Course in Weight Loss*. (Hay House, Carlsbad, California: 2010) p.241

3. Patterson, James, *The Day America Told the Truth*. (Prentice Hall Press:1991).

4. Easterbrook, Gregg *"The Real Truth about Money"*, *Time Magazine*, January 17, 2005
p. A33.

5. Borg, Marcus J., *Meeting Jesus Again for the First Time.* (Harper San Francisco, 1994),   p. 87.

6. Warren, Rick, *The Purpose Driven Life.* (Zondervan, Grand Rapids: 2002), p. 267.

7. Tolle, Eckhart, *A New Earth.*(Dutton, New York: 2005), p.45.

8. Blake, Chris, *Swimming Against the Current.* (Pacific Press, Nampa, Idaho, 2007), p.60.

9. Curtis, Brent and Eldredge, John, *The Sacred Romance.* (Thomas Nelson, 1997), p. 133.

10. Quindlen, Anna, *Newsweek* Magazine. (December 22, 2008), p.64.

11. Gomes, Peter J., *The Good Book.* (William Morrow, New York, 1996), p.309.

CHAPTER 5:

MORE DISTRACTIONS!

The telling question of a person's life is their relationship to the infinite
-- Carl Jung

There are other more subtle distractions to spiritual connection, to living the Spirit-filled life, than possessions. Frenzied activity, everlasting busyness, is at the center of many empty and distracted lives. A life caught up in frantic activity, a life centered on constantly struggling for more status and achievement can be a huge barrier to leading a Spirit-filled, God-centered life, even when what is being done is a good thing or even a religious thing. The Bible says to "be still and know that I am God." But so many people are incapable of being still anymore. Incapable of being silent. And that is a very great tragedy, for in their distraction, they have made themselves oblivious to the spiritual. That still small voice of comfort and intuition and conscience is overwhelmed by the cacophony of life. When we are not tuned in to God's frequency, we lose our guidance. We lose our sense of purpose. We lose our blessing. Not because God does not want to give us these gifts, but because we can not hear Him because we are distracted. Could God be trying to speak to you every day and the awful rush and business and noisiness of your life is blocking Him? Some religious people seem to think that the mysteries of God will be revealed in the clamor of theological discussion, debate or theorizing. Not usually.

When a man meets a stranger, perhaps someone sitting next to him on an airplane, often the first question he puts to him after the introductions are over, is, "What do you do?" The answer comes back, "Oh, I am a contractor" or "I am a lawyer" or "I am a fireman." It is as if we seem to think that we are what we do. As if one's occupation was the absolute most significant thing about a person. But when will we get it? We are not our occupation! We are not what we do for a living! It was John Eagan who said, "Define yourself radically as one beloved by God. This is the true self. Every other identity is an illusion."

The greatest measure of who you are and of your success is not your job title or the size of your bank account or your stock portfolio or how many cool possessions you have or how successful your career is. *The real measure of your success is how close you are to God.* What degree of oneness you enjoy with your God. How connected you are with the Father. How filled you are with the Spirit. Carl Jung said: "The telling question of a person's life is their relationship to the infinite." The spiritual teacher Sivananda said, "Your sole business in life is to attain God-realization. All else is useless and worthless." Think these statements are too radical? Think again. It is the very essence of life. As the Bible says, "Seek ye first the kingdom of heaven." What Sivananda calls God-consciousness, I call the filling of the Holy Spirit. It is out of this experience that the kingdom comes into our hearts and transforms us from selfish, grasping, egocentric, materialistic creatures into beings who realize the purpose of their existence is to live out in human flesh the grace and love and compassion of God on this earth. It starts with our spouse our children, our neighbors. *The Holy Spirit is such a treasure because He is able to gift us with the supernatural ability to love all others unconditionally.* The Bible says to "Honor all men." Only the Spirit can help us see that every human being we meet is absolutely precious, a beloved child of God. He teaches us that every man and woman and child we encounter is worthy of being treated as staggeringly valuable. You have heard the word "Namaste" that is used as a greeting in some countries. It is both a "hello" and a blessing all in one. Did you know that it means, "I greet what is holy in you. I honor you as a child of God."? Wouldn't it be wonderful if we could give up our "hey's" and our "hi's" and our harrrrr ya?, as they say down south, and start acknowledging each other when we meet with, "I honor you as a child of God"? *We are to honor the Christ in each other*!

As Dr. Greg Smalley says, "Life goes much better when we treat each other as priceless treasures." A friend of mine told me recently that when she was just a little girl, she came to realize that her father cherished her. "And that" she said, "has made all the difference in my life." Does your child know that you cherish her? Do you know that little children sometime spell love T-I-M-E?

WHAT REALLY MATTERS

There was once an old Lancashire woman who was listening to a group of her friends discussing the remarkable success of the new minister in their village. Some praised his heart-stirring sermons. Others spoke of his kindness and warmth and his ability to treat equally both the poor and the wealthy in the congregation. There was a general agreement among the parishioners that the pastor must be very talented and well-educated. "Nay," broke in the old woman. "I will tell you what it is. Your man is very thick with the Almighty!"

When my daughter Shana was in the sixth grade she received a challenging homework assignment one day. She was given biographical sketches of several important people and told to make up an epitaph that could go on their tombstone and describe their life in one sentence. While she was working on this, my eleven-year-old looked up from the table at me and earnestly asked me, "Daddy, what would you like written on your tombstone?"

Tough question! If my college and seminary professors had posed a few more like it, I might have framed my diplomas and hung them on the wall instead of filing them away in a cardboard box with my lawn mower warranty!

Some of the traditional etchings on headstones ran through my mind --- "devoted husband, loving father" ---"here lies the biggest fool in the cemetery". I have heard of some pretty funny epitaphs too; I have always liked the one that says, "Here lies an atheist. All dressed up. And no place to go." There is one down in a Georgia cemetery that says, "I told you I was sick." And a very sincere one in a Burlington, Vermont graveyard: "She lived with her husband fifty years. And died in the confident hope of a better life"!

Perhaps the best thing that could be written about any of us would come close to the words used by the wise old English woman to describe the pastor: "He was very thick with the Almighty." Or maybe, "He walked with God." Or "He was one with God." Oneness. Life is absolutely all about oneness. Oneness with God, oneness with the self, oneness with each other.

I think one of the best definitions of sin is: *anything that diminishes or distorts or destroys oneness*. Sin occurs when oneness becomes otherness. Me versus them. Competition instead of cooperation. The kingdom of God is here on earth now in our ability to realize our oneness with each other and with God. Sin is "turning to our own way" (Isaiah) Sin, to put it simply, is selfishness. The very essence of sin is self-will. It happens when we place ego, ourselves, at the center of our life instead of Jesus. Sin is any deviation from unconditional love. Sin is anything that cuts us off from practicing the presence of God.

To put it in the simplest terms, *the whole purpose of the spiritual life is union with God*. Jesus' touching prayer just before His death says it all: "My prayer is…that all of them may be one, Father, just as you are in me and I am in you. May they also be one that the world may believe that you have sent me. I have given them the glory that you gave me, that they might be one as we are one. I in them and you in me." He also said, "Abide in me as I abide in you" and "I am the vine you are the branches" (John 17:20-23). You can't get much tighter with someone than that! The oneness spills over from our relationship with God to the sacred oneness we can have with each other. Paul got it. He wrote: "There is neither Jew nor Gentile, neither slave nor free, neither male nor female, for you are all one in Christ Jesus" (Galatians 3:28). Connecting deeply to other people is a path to connecting to the Divine.

DANGEROUS DISTRACTIONS

There are even more subtle and deadly distractions from the spiritual life than possessions or busyness. Beware of addictions. Never underestimate their power. Some addictions to alcohol, drugs, sex or food for example are so powerful that they can shut off all hope of establishing a connection with God if left unacknowledged and untreated.

Then there is the more recent and subtle addiction to continual electronic distraction. This has become an incredibly powerful trap for many people. It used to be just radio. Then there was TV. It has been calculated that by the age of 20, the average American has seen one million commercials!

Before you knew it VHS players came along. You could watch all the movies you wanted right at home. Now we have DVD and Blue ray players, MP3 and iPods, iPhones and iPads. Laptops and notebooks and tablets, cell phones and email, the Internet, text-messaging, Blackberries and podcasts, blogs, tivo, wii, Facebook, Twitter and on and on. Now there are new ways to be electronically distracted on the horizon such as having a video and TV screen built in to the lenses of your glasses and your computer, and a cell phone built into your clothing. Video games seem to be especially addictive for young males. Recently an Alabama man was sentenced to death. His defense team had argued that his obsession with the video game "Grand Theft Auto" had affected his mind and led him to kill two police officers.

I live near the campus of a Christian college. At the end of last quarter, several students had to be asked to leave. They had been spending so much time playing video games, staying up all night and frequently missing classes the next day. As a result they were failing all their coursework.

CNN reports that some gamers in South Korea have developed such all-consuming addictions that they camp out at Internet cafes for hours and sometimes, even days on end, playing video games and living on instant-cup noodles and cigarettes, barely sleeping and seldom washing. One man died after nearly 50 straight hours of playing online computer games. The report says Korea has 17 million gamers, some 35 percent of the entire population, and that many of them are obsessed with the activity. A recent startling survey showed that the average American Christian spent ten minutes a day in prayer and four hours a day watching TV!

Ironically, such addictions are usually misguided attempts to find spiritual connection. It is no accident, as Carl Jung said of one of his patients: "His craving for alcohol was the equivalent, on a low level, of the spiritual thirst of our being for wholeness; expressed in medieval language, the union with God…. Alcohol in Latin is "spiritus" and you use the same word for the highest religious experience as well as for the most depraving poison. The helpful formula therefore is: *spiritus contra spiritum*". 1.

83

People long for spiritual life, for a connection to the Divine. When they do not find the genuine article they seek it among many different distractive and destructive counterfeits. These counterfeits can end up blocking them from true spirituality. As Jung implied, the only way they can recover is to realize their helplessness, and surrender themselves into the loving arms of their heavenly Father. In His wisdom God offers "self control" as one of the fruits of the Spirit. When will we ever get it? As Kate Moss so famously said, "There is nothing that tastes as good as skinny feels!" In other words, there is no indulgence that is as satisfying as a clear conscience and a guilt-free heart. This wisdom has become painfully clear over the last few years to men like Bill Clinton, John Edwards, Tiger Woods, Herman Cain, and the former governors of New York and South Carolina.

PAIN FROM THE PAST

Another incredibly powerful block to spiritual connection comes from persistently hanging on to the pain and guilt and the wounds of one's past. Let's say that you were a child who was abused, verbally, physically or sexually. Or maybe as a young adult you went through a terrible divorce from an unfaithful or abusive spouse. Or perhaps you were unfairly fired from your job because you spurned your boss' sexual advances or because you reported a superior's lack of ethics. Maybe your church let you down, rejected you or judged you harshly and unfairly. Or maybe you did something yourself that was very selfish and abusive and hurtful to another person. Maybe you served in Iraq or Afghanistan and you ended up doing or supporting the doing of some truly awful things. If clung to and not forgiven, healed or released, the accumulated pain or guilt from such experiences in the past can form a negative energy field in you that will effectively keep you so distracted from the positive that you will be unable to connect with the higher world of Spirit. Your role as the victim, as the abused or the abuser will keep drawing you back into your past, into your body of pain and guilt.

There is a huge counterfeit emotional payoff in being "the victim." Some people make a whole life, a whole career, out of this role and are locked in the drama of their past. They get such a pay-off from clinging to this dysfunctional state that they refuse to surrender it. This blocks their spiritual growth. It prevents them from moving on to health and healing, to love and light. Their life creates incredible amounts of chaos and suffering for themselves and others around them.

Sadly, some who do not find release from the anger and pain of a wounded or abusive past will themselves go on to become perpetrators. One thing is certain, if you do not find healing, you will either be a victim or a victimizer. Maybe both. But the good news is, this does not have to be so. The abuse, the violence, the addiction, the dysfunction of any kind can stop with you. You do not have to pass it on to the next generation through your children. You have a choice. *You can be a transmitter or a transformer!*

Even Jesus had to offer forgiveness to his abusers, His persecutors, before He could move on with the Divine plan for His life! Jesus was forgiveness personified. When He said, "Father forgive them for they know not what they do," it was not only a gift He was giving to those who harmed Him. It was an assertion that He was not going to allow Himself to be the victim of His torturers. It was a release that made it possible for Him to eventually move on beyond the darkness and the pain. Without offering that gift of forgiveness, He would not have been prepared for His own resurrection that was to come. When you forgive someone, you let go of your role of being a victim. You let go of your fear, your anger. You also let go of the past. Unforgiveness is a kind of prison. It creates towering walls that keep love out. It locks you up in emotional chains. Unforgiveness will trap you in the past quicker than anything else. Only when you forgive and release the past are you prepared to enter into the sacred presence of God, something which is possible only when you are present in the now.

Like Jesus, you too, may have to let some things go in order to facilitate your resurrection, your new birth, in order to start a new life of oneness and connection with God through the Spirit. As Mary Ann Williamson has written, "Forgiveness is the only path out of hell." Mark Twain said, "Forgiveness is the fragrance the violet bestows on the heel that crushes it." It is a sobering thought that we can not be any closer to God than we can be to the person we like the least! So forgive. Send the person who harmed you only love. Release them to God. *The Holy Spirit can not long dwell in an unforgiving heart.*

God absolutely loves to forgive! He longs to forgive. He aches to forgive! It is one of His favorite things to do. It brings Him great pleasure! God lives in an attitude of forgiveness. It is part of His very nature and character. What's more, He is not a begrudging forgiver. He is a cheerful forgiver! It delights Him to forgive. *Isn't it amazing that you can't possibly out-sin God's forgiveness?* Your prayer for forgiveness is one prayer you can be assured will be answered instantly. How then could we, who have been forgiven so much, fail to offer forgiveness to anyone?

We absolutely must allow ourselves to be released from our lower energies of anger, blame, revenge, guilt, shame and fear. If you persist in allowing your ego to hold on to any of these states, if you allow your sense of victimhood or your woundedness to be the focus of your life, you will not be able to access the power and presence of the Holy Spirit. These negatives must be surrendered to God so that you can be released from them. A break in a relationship between two people creates a hole the devil can crawl right through!

As a Spirit-filled child of God you can transcend your past. You are set free! You are bound by nothing! You do not need to be enslaved by your fear or your anger any longer. Always remember, anger and fear are powerful energies waiting to be transformed. You must allow the light of God's restoring presence in to all the dark spots inside you. You must come to see where there is a lack of love in your life and be willing to address it. We have no idea how powerful the light of love really is. For example, one positive, light-filled, love-filled thought can cancel out hundreds of negative thoughts! The light the Spirit brings to you has the power to transform darkness into glory, to utterly change your anger and fear into love. We can not do this for ourselves. We can only surrender our hearts to someone who can. The Bible says that our Lord was wounded for our transgressions, our lapses, our offenses and with His stripes we are healed. Your goal then, is to be able to detach yourself from all that is not

God. Then you will be surrendered. Then you will be empty. Then you will be ready for the great adventure of the filling of His Spirit!

Q&A:

Q. Are you implying that if I am filled with the Holy Spirit I will always be protected from accidents or illness?

A. No. God's gifts are spiritual. This includes the precious gift of salvation, eternal life. The filling of the Spirit is given to us for spiritual purposes. This is the realm God works in. This is where His promises apply. He offers no guarantees of prosperity or physical safety or freedom from pain and illness for believers. Spirit-filled Christians get sick and die and have accidents and tragedies in their lives every day. They are as susceptible to the risks of cancer, flu pandemics, hurricanes, earthquakes and tsunamis as anyone else. However, the promise is that the Spirit will bring wisdom. I do believe that when we stop letting ourselves be distracted and become aware and connected to our source of truth and power, a spin-off benefit is that we may at times better our odds of avoiding circumstances or situations that could be harmful to us.

I get so sick and tired of people "blaming the victim." There is a twisted theology that has persisted since the time of Jesus (Master, who did sin, this man or his parents, that he was born blind?). It implies that anyone who has an accident or some other tragedy in his or her life, anyone who develops a physical or especially a mental illness is somehow lacking in his or her Christian experience or has fallen into some kind of sin and is being punished. When a popular conference president from my church was tragically killed in a head-on car crash a few years ago, there were murmurings among a few pious members that this man must have had some sin in his life. They speculated that he was having a secret affair, since God allowed the accident to happen! Of course, Jesus' answer to the above question of who sinned and caused the calamity, was simply "neither." Neither the behavior of the man or his parents caused the blindness.

Q. You point out all the distractions that can block the Spirit filling me. I feel like I am surrounded by them. How can I ever get rid of these things that are such a big part of modern life?

A. You can't. The distractions you face, your pain from the past, the addictions you may have are more powerful than you are. If you try to fight them, if you struggle to overcome them, guess who usually wins? Struggling against these things usually results in your getting sucked right back down into the whirlpool. Your only hope is to surrender. It is the greatest of all paradoxes, but surrender is the only path to power and to healing. (By His stripes we are healed!) Your only part in overcoming the distractions of life and in receiving the filling of the Spirit is to admit your powerlessness and helplessness. You chose to let go of your struggle and make the conscious decision to respond to the one who said, "Come to me, all you who are weary and burdened, and I will give you rest" (Matt. 11:28). You can not beat back the darkness in your life by your own efforts. You can not chase the darkness out of a room with a broom. But you can turn on the light. You can open the door to the one who stands there and knocks and let in the light. Some people make receiving the gift of the Spirit seem like such a complicated process. It is not. A child can do it. You simply need to ask for it. Choose it. Surrender to it and then *allow* it. People need to learn to simply relax in the Spirit and let it flow into them and through them unimpeded. The Spirit-filled life is not attained by trying. It is attained by abiding. It is not achieved. It is received. It does not come through struggle but through surrender. It is a gift. Just like salvation.

FOOTNOTES CHAPTER 5

1, Jung, C. G., letter to Bill W., *AA Grapevine*, 1968 p. 12

CHAPTER 6

THE PERILS OF FUNDAMENTALISM: BIBLIOLATRY AND OTHER CRIMES

Fundamentalism is not the only valid form of faith, and to say it is, is the great lie of our time.
—Andrew Sullivan

There is the story of the preacher in the days of the late nineteenth-century who was appalled when many of the females in his congregation were caught up in trying out a contemporary new hairstyle. It involved taking their long tresses and wrapping them up on the crown of their head in a fancy top-knot. Convinced that this new fashion was a tool of the devil destined to lead his flock morally astray he devoted an entire sermon to condemning this abomination. Taking to the pulpit one Sunday he loudly trumpeted to his flock that God had even led him to a text in the Bible that would prove the error of their ways. He held up the Holy book, pointing at a text with his finger and conveniently leaving out the words in Matthew 24:17, "Let him which is on the house…" he thundered, "Here it is right here, TOP NOT COME DOWN!"

Here is a startling fact we all have to learn how to deal with better; God did not write the Bible. People did. The Bible writer's were inspired in the ideas and principles they presented however, not all of their views can be removed from their original social and historical context and plopped down in the an altogether different context in the modern world of the 21st century and be expected to give us an inerrant revelation today. Fundamentalists would consider this view of Scripture heretical. Fundamentalists certainly take their scriptures literally. They believe in the absolute inerrancy of their holy writings. Their scriptures take precedence over everything else including people and their needs. Fundamentalist Muslims take the Koran this way. Fundamentalists Christians consider every word of scripture to be the infallible word of God to be taken literally. Here is the great tragedy; fundamentalism is the spawning ground of many an atheist.

Inerrancy is inspiration distorted, corrupted. Literalism can lead to such practices as capital punishment, the stoning to death of adulterers and homosexuals, all males required to wear beards, all women keeping their heads covered in church, no woman being allowed to speak in church, handling poisonous snakes in church and yes, right in the same category with snake-handling, the equally appalling practice ... are you ready for this ... of no woman being allowed to become an ordained pastor!

Sorry, this will make you grit you teeth but here goes... autocastrations have been the result of some zealots taking the Bible literally. Matthew 19:12 KJV refers to "eunuchs which were so born from their mother's womb: and there are some eunuchs, which were made eunuchs of men: and there be eunuchs which have made themselves eunuchs for the kingdom of heaven's sake." There have been sincere fundamentalist Bible-obsessed young men who combined this text with also taking literally the verse that says, "And if thy right hand offend thee, cut it off and caste it from thee: for it is profitable for thee that one of thy members should perish, and not thy whole body should be cast into hell." Matthew 5:30 KJV

A young man in Australia in 1985 decided to join the last group of eunuchs the Bible mentions. It wasn't like he was someone whose sexual behavior was out of control. He was already someone who was more celibate then some priests. He had never had a sexual relationship with another person. He may not have had time to, because he spent most of his free time in his room reading the Bible from cover to cover, over and over again. Occasionally however, he would give in to his impulses and relieve his sexual tension by masturbating. Alarmed that this practice would ban him from heaven, he used his considerable experiencing castrating bulls on the family farm. He used a razor to open his scrotum. He cut out his testicles. Then he flushed them down the toilet. Afterward, he expressed no regret for his deed. He also refused his doctor's offer of testosterone replacement therapy.

It's one thing when a person's fundamentalist stance does them harm. Quite another when the innocent are made to suffer because of it. In Oregon City Oregon not long ago, a 15-month old girl died needlessly. Medical examiners said she could have certainly been saved by simple treatment with antibiotics. The girl's parents however, were members of Followers of Christ Church. This fundamentalist church takes the Bible literally. They believe that it instructs them to heal the sick only through anointing. Former members report that those in the church who seek modern medical treatment are ostracized and shunned.

Let's just face it. There is a dangerous irrationality inherent in fundamentalist religion. Without reason, distorted religion quickly becomes a force for dysfunction, chaos and darkness.

Rule number 1 of understanding inspiration of the Bible: *You simply cannot always take the Bible literally in every passage.* When Jesus is called the lamb of God, it does not mean He was covered with wool. He was being described in figurative, symbolic, language.

When Jesus said, "If you have faith you can move mountains," He did not mean that literally, physically. He meant figuratively that if you have enough faith in God, you can face any difficulty successfully. Many of the Bible's teaching are definitely not made to be taken literally. Those who do appear foolish and may also do great harm to themselves, others, and the image of Christianity.

Some years ago, Pastor Ed Dobson was teaching religion classes at Liberty University. One day he was lecturing on Jesus' Sermon on the Mount, where the Lord says, "If your right eye causes you to sin, gouge it out and throw it away." After class a male student came up to talk. The teacher noticed the young man was missing his right eye. The student said, "That verse you read---I tried it! I have a problem with lust, so I literally gouged out my right eye. And I am here to tell you, I am a left-eye luster."

When Satan tried to tempt Jesus, he did it by trying to get Him to make the mistake that you and I often make. *Satan tried to get Jesus to take the Scriptures literally*. He took Jesus to the highest point of the temple and said, "If you are the Son of God, throw yourself down, for it is written: He will command his angels concerning you and they will lift you up in their hands so that you will not strike your foot against a stone." He was quoting Psalm 91:11. "See, it says so right here," he said temptingly, throwing out his proof-text.

Jesus did not fall for it. He knew that some Scriptures are not to be taken literally. There are no angels assigned the task of going ahead of Christians and kicking sharp stones or any other problems out of their path! Satan loves it when he can trick believers into becoming Biblical literalists because they then become a danger to themselves and to others! (By the way, that is what constitutes grounds for forcibly admitting someone to a mental institution! So you see that proves there is a connection between fundamentalism and insanity! Kidding. Just kidding.) Many fundamentalists become harsh, judgmental, even ruthless. Charles Scriven, writing about the perils of fundamentalism, put it this way: "fundamentalism is a ...conceit that murders curiosity and leads thereby either to listlessness or to destructive passion. Fundamentalism is a dread disease ... a groundwork for madness." 1.

Isn't it scary when you meet someone who is utterly certain of something? Andrew Sullivan in his book *The Conservative Soul* warns of the hazards of holding all of one's religious beliefs with "utter certainty." He cautions about the dangers of preaching absolute adherence to inerrant Scripture. Sullivan calls Christians to a kind of spiritual humility that precludes dogmatic certainty. He suggests that from a humble faith comes tolerance and openness to others, both necessary ingredients for relationships in our own society and with people of other nations and other faiths. Much of the tension in the world today he says, including that between Islam and the West, comes from fundamentalists of different faiths operating from positions of what they believe to be absolute truth. He points out that Jesus taught in stories and parables rather than teaching a rigid creed. Sullivan says,

If God really is God, then God must, by definition, surpass our human understanding…there is…something we will never grasp, something we can never know—because God is beyond human categories. And if God is beyond our categories, then God cannot be captured for certain. We cannot know with the kind of surety that allows us to proclaim truth with a capital T. There will always be something that eludes us. If there weren't, it would not be God. 2.

Sadly, those with the fundamentalist view of Biblical inerrancy often end up believing that if you find one mistake or contradiction in Scripture, you have to throw the whole thing out. Many in this group end up renouncing their faith because they eventually grow up enough to come across some of the discrepancies in the Scriptures. In fact next to the attitude and behavior of some church-goers, there is nothing that causes more people to turn their back on Christianity without accepting it, or to reject it after they have been a part of it, than this very serious problem that so often goes unaddressed in Christian circles. Believers sometimes prefer to keep their heads deeply buried in the inspirational sands.

BIBLE WORSHIPPERS

There is a kind of bibliolatry that goes on with this distorted view of inspiration.

For the record; *the Bible is not God*. It is not ever to be a substitute for God. To make the Bible into God is idolatry. As Bible scholar Alden Thompson says: "it is not enough to know Scripture. One must know God." Scott McKnight, another theology professor has written: "Missing the difference between God and the Bible is a bit like the person who reads the book of Jonah and spends hours and hours figuring out if a human can live inside a whale—and what kind of whale it was—but never encounters God. The book is about Jonah's God, not Jonah's whale. 3.

There is a great deal of "Bible abuse" that goes on in Christian circles. One example is using it as a hammer to beat others into believing or behaving in a certain way. (The way you do!) There is also the hazard of taking one's own interpretation of a passage with utter certainty as to that interpretation being the absolute truth. There is the peril of taking the Bible as the lone foundation of one's faith, while neglecting or ignoring a personal intimate connection to the Person, the living Presence, the Bible is there to point to. In their splendid book *The Sacred Romance*, Brent Curtis and John Eldredge warn:

There comes a place on our spiritual journey where renewed religious activity is of no use whatsoever. It is the place where God holds out his hand and asks us to give up our lovers and come and live with him in a much more personal way. It is the place of relational intimacy that Satan lured Adam and Eve away from so long ago in the Garden of Eden. We are both drawn to it and fear it. Part of us would rather return to Scripture memorization, or Bible study, or service—anything that would save us from the unknowns of walking with God. We are partly convinced our life is elsewhere. We are deceived. 4.

Many believers are fond of unthinkingly stating that the Bible is the foundation of their religion. The Bible may indeed be the foundation of one's system of beliefs and of one's morality. However even the Bible has its limitations It is not to be the foundation of one's personal spirituality. Jesus is. "For no one can lay any foundation other than the one already laid, which is Jesus Christ" (1 Corinthians 3:13).

Your spiritual foundation is not your understanding of a book. Your spiritual foundation is your relationship with a living Person. The right emphasis here is on a person, not on a book. Can you handle it? There is Someone greater than Scripture! The Master put this in proper perspective Himself when He said, "The Scriptures bear witness *to me*"(emphasis supplied). Our intimate connection with Jesus by the miracle of His indwelling Spirit is to be the foundation of our spirituality. Anything else, while it may be good, is not sufficient. How could we forget? Jesus did not say the church is the way. He did not say religion is the way. Jesus did not even say Scripture is the way. He said, "*I am the way.*"

IMPORTANT BUT NOT SUFFICIENT

Some believers imply that it is only through the scriptures that we can know God's will for us. Paul, Christianity's greatest theologian acknowledges that there are alternative ways to spiritual growth besides scripture, when he counsels, "Do not conform any longer to the pattern of this world, but be transformed by the renewing of your mind. Then you will be able to test and approve what God's will is -- his good, pleasing and perfect will" (Romans 12:2).

Certainly, the study of the Scriptures is an important way to come to understand the will of God. But it is not the exclusive way. A mind surrendered to, renewed and transformed by the indwelling Holy Spirit can be an equally valid revelator of the will of God for your personal life in this time and place. Look closely at that verse again "… when he, the Spirit of truth, comes, he will guide you into all truth." Do you realize that the Holy Spirit *has not made Himself dependent solely on the Old and New Testament in order to guide us into all truth?* Do you understand that the Spirit has many, many avenues, some of which may not have occurred to you and of which you might not yet be aware? Of course, the Spirit uses and works through the Bible. It is His prime source. But He has many other means by which to touch human hearts and minds. Please, be open to those.

David Larson, who teaches religion at Loma Linda University, writes;

The primary source of truth for Christians are Scripture, tradition, reason, and experience. Because it creates the Christian community like a constitution invents a nation, Scripture is the most important of the four. The idea that Scripture is the Christian's only source of truth is accurate if it means that none others share its primacy. It is false if it suggests that we can flourish as Christians by studying only it. 5.

Part of the dynamic new paradigm of spirituality Jesus came to introduce shifted the foundation of spirituality from reliance on learning and scripture alone to a whole new world of worship and connection with God based equally on scripture and personal, intimate personal fellowship with the Father by the indwelling of the Holy Spirit. (Think the garden of Eden before the fall!) Thus Jesus could proclaim with vigor, "Yet a time is coming and has now come when the true worshipers will worship the Father in Spirit and in truth, for they are the kind of worshipers the Father seeks. God is spirit, and his worshipers must worship in spirit and in truth" (John 4:23,24). (emphasis supplied)

Some of us have been mighty long on truth and mighty short on Spirit in our worship experience for most of our lives. This book is an attempt to correct that deficiency. The members of my church have long bragged that they are "people of the Book". Well and good. I wish they would declare with equal fervor that they are "people of the Spirit." True worship consists of worshipping in "both Spirit and in truth." One of the most deeply spiritual of Christian leaders, A.W. Tozer wrote:

> Sound Bible exposition is a *must*...But exposition may be carried on in such a way as to leave the hearers devoid of any true spiritual nourishment whatever. For it is not mere words that nourish the soul, but God Himself, and unless and until the hearers find God in personal experience they are not the better for having heard the truth. The Bible is not an end in itself, but a means to bring men to an intimate and satisfying knowledge of God, that they may enter into Him, that they may delight in His Presence, may taste and know the inner sweetness of the very God Himself in the core and center of their hearts. The modern scientist has lost God amid the wonders of His world; we Christians are in real danger of losing God amid the wonders of His word. 6.

There is simply no alternative to reading the Bible "in the Spirit." Indeed, to read it otherwise is dangerous and potentially harmful to your spiritual health. Let's be clear what the Bible is not. It is not a history book. It is not a scientific manual. *It is a salvation manual!* You can read the Bible with a microscope and get caught up in the minutia. You can read the Bible with a telescope and get too narrow of a view. Things will be way out of perspective either way. Best to read the Bible, with a surrendered heart and a humble, prayerful, teachable spirit. Read it through a wide-angle lens, so you can see the big picture. What is the big picture? Simple. 1. God is love; 2. Jesus saves; 3. The Holy Spirit wants to fill you *now*. Everything else in the Bible is commentary. Helpful? Surely. Instructive? Yes. Essential? No.

Even Paul, schooled as he was in the teaching of Moses, as a Pharisee, recognized the limitations and insufficiency of part of the Old Testament. "For what was glorious has no glory now in comparison with the surpassing glory.... Even to this day when Moses is read, a veil covers their (God's people's) hearts (2 Corinthians 3:10, 15).

JESUS AND THE OLD TESTAMENT

Remarkably, Jesus Himself declared, "The Law and the Prophets (the Old Testament) were proclaimed until John. Since that time, the good news of the kingdom of God is being preached..." (Luke 16:16). In other words, the

New Testament's teachings bring us into a whole new incredible spiritual paradigm! John 1:17 bears this out. The law came through Moses, but grace and truth through Jesus Christ." You may not like me saying this, but I must... *It is a kind of blasphemy to put some of the teachings of the Old Testament on an inspirational par with the incredibly spiritual, incredibly enlightened teachings of Jesus Christ in the gospels.*

Here is a quick and shocking contrast between the Old Testament and the New; referring to the babies of the enemies of Israel, "happy is he... who seizes your infants and dashes them against the rocks." (OT) "Let the little children come unto me." (NT) To sum it up, there are many harmful, dysfunctional primitive ideologies portrayed in the Old Testament that are not worthy to be our model of behavior and relationships today. The Psalmist can boast, "Do I not hate those who hate you, O Lord? And do I not loathe those who rise up against you? I hate them with a perfect hatred, I count them my enemies." Psalm 139:21,22 Go ahead, contrast that with what Jesus said in Luke 6:27; "Love your enemies, do good to those who hate you."

The Old Testament was the only scriptures Jesus had. Yes, He studied them and used them, but he carefully *picked and chose* from those Scriptures and *often* took exception to them and taught something 180 degrees from what they taught. He often told His listeners, "Moses said to you...but I say unto you" then revealed a truth that was either directly opposed to or far advanced beyond an Old Testament teaching. Doing that in fact, was one of the things that got Him killed. *Yes, Jesus picked and chose from the Old Testament and under the guidance of the Holy Spirit you are authorized to do the same. You may disregard any teaching in the Old Testament that is not in harmony with the greater revelation of the teachings of Jesus Christ. Under the example of Jesus Christ you have the authority, guided by the Spirit to be a picker and chooser of Scripture!* Can you handle it? To scary? More comfortable and less threatening to just accept every word of the Bible as inerrant and above evaluating and questioning? Here is a sobering thought...a person who bases their spiritual life on the total inerrancy of Scripture is likely not to survive the reality of the discrepancies they will find from a careful reading of the Bible and a careful comparison of the Old and New Testaments.

To take the Old Testament as word-for-word infallibly inspired is a recipe for absolute disaster. There are even parts of the New Testament where one has to use the same discretion, as in the attitude of some New Testament writers toward women and slavery to cite one example. Many New Testament scholars believe that Paul's injunction to women to be "silent" in church and to be obedient and subordinate to their husbands was not written by him at all but was put in later by scribes who wanted to keep women in their place! When we look at how the church has treated women in the last two thousand years and how it still, in many cases, treats them as second-class citizens to the present day, it is certainly not a stretch of the imagination to see how this could have been the case. Let me just put it right out there. It is a disgrace; it is a grievous moral failing for a church to refuse to ordain a woman as a pastor because of her gender. Guys, we have to stop treating women as our spiritual subordinates! Hello, the patriarchy is dead!

Always, always, the Scripture reader's safety net is to compare what is said with the life and teachings of Jesus. That is the ultimate standard of truth against which all other truth (even other Scriptural truth) may be safely judged. Take a look at what the writer or the later supplementer to 1st. Corinthians said about women and then contrast it with how Jesus treated and valued them. Do you realize that He entrusted the best good news the world was ever to hear, the very gospel itself to a woman first of all? Not to Peter, not to John or to some other patriarch, but to Mary Magdalene was first given the incredible truth that the Lord was risen from the dead. Jesus revealed Himself as the resurrected Son of God first to a woman and then He even commissioned here as the first "missionary" the first bearer of this good news! "Go...and tell..." He told her. Now there is a commission for you! There is a Divine ordination! And Mary went in great wonder and joy and proclaimed the truth that was to change history. "I have seen the risen Lord" she said. She was the first to ever be able to speak those words!

When I read parts of the Old Testament, I at times feel like Mark Twain did when he said: "Most people are bothered by those passages of Scripture they do not understand, but the passages that bother me are those I do understand."

Taking the Old Testament literally would lead to condoning the punishment of homosexuals by death. It would allow the killing of adolescents by their parents for being disrespectful. It would allow the societally and religiously approved killing of someone who gathers firewood on the Sabbath or breaks the Sabbath in some other way. It would tell a woman who has been raped that she must marry her rapist! It can be used to justify slavery and the total subjection and objectification of women. It justifies genocide including the extermination of innocent women and children. It advocates a theocracy (think Islam and Sharia law, think Iran's type of government) as the absolute best form of government for a nation.

In the Old Testament God was often pictured as violent and intolerant. Here is a chilling passage about how to deal with those who differ with you over religion.

If your very own brother, or your son or daughter, or the wife you love, or your closest friend secretly entices you, saying, "Let us go and worship other gods"... do not yield to him or listen to him. Show him no pity. Do no spare him or shield him. You must certainly put him to death. Your hand must be the first in putting him to death, and then the hands of all the people. Stone him to death (Deuteronomy 13:6-10).

Christian fundamentalists who take the Bible literally can not dodge these troubling instructions. They are not metaphor, they are not symbolic, and they are not allegorical. They are clear, specific instructions how to treat those who do not believe the way you do. And Christians piously condemn Muslims when their Koran suggests that infidels should be killed??

Centuries later the Psalmist conveyed the same attitude. "Do I not hate those who hate you, O Lord? And do I not loathe those who rise up against you? I hate them with a perfect hatred. I count them my enemies" (Psalm 139:21-22).

One author who says he did an honest, objective, thorough reading of the Old testament came up with this description of the god he found there;

The God of the Old Testament is arguable the most unpleasant character in all fiction: jealous and proud of it; a petty, unjust, unforgiving control freak; a vindictive, bloodthirsty ethnic cleanser; a misogynistic, homophobic, racist, infanticidal, genocidal, filicidal, pestilential, megalomaniacal, sadomasochistic, capriciously malevolent bully. 7.

Yes, I know, you wish I hadn't quoted this writer, especially when I tell you that it is Richard Dawkins. I know, I know, the Old Testament also speaks of a God who is merciful and just and long-suffering. But Dawkins is not making this stuff up. Someone has said that the God presented in parts of the Old Testament would be considered a war criminal today under the terms of the Geneva Convention!

A case can be made that some of the Old Testament writers, at times, did present a picture of God that was distorted. They projected some of their own fears and anxieties and judgmentalness and harshness on their deity. They wrote of a severe God who was rigid, intolerant jealous and condemning and seemed to want conformity and control instead of relationship. A God who ordered and demanded and threatened rather than supporting and encouraging. A God who kept telling people, "turn or burn"!

Can you see how bad theology equals bad behavior? A distorted picture of God leads to dysfunctional, destructive behavior. If God can smite the rebellious then a man can justify hitting his wife. If God can destroy innocent babies and children then a parent can explain abusing a child. Your view of what God is like is so critical because it has everything to do with how you treat other people. If God is not really severe, rigid, judgmental and intolerant then what right do you and I have to be that way?

God was the very first victim of identity theft! Satan's masterful manipulations have succeeded in creating a picture in people's minds of a God who is more like the deceiver himself, than who the Father really is. This false picture of a violent, intolerant God has caused all kinds of grief.

This concept of God has led many fundamentalist Christians through the centuries to oppose any scientific or medical breakthrough that to them seems to contradict their impression of what the Old Testament says God is like. For example, Timothy Dwight, a Presbyterian clergyman and the president of Yale University from 1795 to 1817 went on a crusade against the new practice of vaccination. "If God had decreed from all eternity," he said, "that a certain person should die of smallpox, it would be a frightful sin to avoid and annul that decree by the trick of vaccination."8.

There was a time in distant history when, coming out of paganism and barbarism, a theocratic, religion-centered and controlled government was a step toward order and civilization. That was then. This is now. The Old Testament represents a great advance in religious thought and teaching three and four thousand years ago! But it was a lesser light pointing to a greater light. It was a shadow of the reality to come. To put it in computer terms, it was version 1.0. The best there was for its day and time. *But when will we ever get it? Truth is progressive. It is constantly evolving.* How effective would your computer be if you took out your current version 8.0 and tried to run your programs with the old version 1.0? When the unseen hand of God dramatically and publicly ripped down the thick curtain that screened the Holy of Holies in the Jewish temple immediately upon the death of the Savior, the old system came to an end. The Holy Spirit, the Shekinah glory, was released out into the entire world, carrying the flame of love and grace, now seeking the heart of every person as His tabernacle.

The writer of Hebrews contrasts this dramatic difference between the Old and New clearly. Describing the Old Testament paradigm of law, an experience with God based on fear, he says:

You have not come to a mountain (Sinai when the law was given) that can be touched and that is burning with fire; to darkness, gloom and storm; to a trumpet blast or to such a voice speaking words that those who heard it begged that no further word be spoken to them, because they could not bear what was commanded; "If even an animal touches the mountain, it must be stoned." The sight was so terrifying that Moses said, "I am trembling with fear."

Then he moves to a contrasting picture of what the new spiritual paradigm as proclaimed
by Jesus in the New Testament is like:

But you have come to Mount Zion, to the heavenly Jerusalem, the city of the living God. You have come to thousands upon thousands of angels in joyful assembly, to the church of the firstborn, whose names are written in heaven. You have come to God, the judge of all men, to the spirits of righteous men made perfect, to Jesus the mediator of a new covenant, and to the sprinkled blood that speaks a better word than the blood of Abel (Hebrews 12:18-24).

What a difference! What a contrast! A religion from the past based on fear and law. A whole new spirituality for our time based on joy and grace! Rules vs. relationship. Law vs. grace. Dogma vs. devotion.

The author of Hebrews really shows he gets it when he begins his letter with one of the most profound statements in the entire Bible:

In the past God spoke to our forefathers through the prophets at many time and in various ways, but in these last days he has spoken to us by his Son, whom he appointed heir of all things, and through whom he made the universe. The son is the radiance of God's glory and the exact representation of his being..." (Hebrews 1:1-3).

So there you have it. Jesus Christ is the ultimate revelation of truth and love! His life. His teachings. Not the Old Testament. Jesus. Not even the last book of the New Testament, even if it is called "Revelation." Jesus is the ultimate revelation. All other scripture and spiritual writing and religious teaching (including Paul's) is to be judged by and looked upon through the lens of what Jesus taught and how He treated people and how He lived His life. "Now Christ is the visible expression of the invisible God" (Colossians 1:15, Phillips).

Yes, the Old Testament does point forward to Jesus, quite clearly and beautifully in the Psalms and Isaiah. But that is the point. It is a pointer. It is a signpost. We are all grateful for signposts on our journeys, but how much time and energy on your spiritual journey do you want to spend with a signpost? Are you going to stop and build an altar around the sign post? Are you going to stand there and study and worship and glorify the signpost or get on with the journey, move on toward the ultimate destination, the Ultimate Revelation? You and I have been taught to call the Scriptures the "Holy" Bible. Sorry, but that worries me sometimes. There is only one Holy thing, and that is God Himself. The Bible, written by imperfect men, points us beautifully *toward* the Holy. Toward the Holy One. It is the map, not the journey, not the destination. One spiritual teacher has said that many of us are like the dog, who, when his master is calling to him, "Over there, over there," and is pointing him where he wants him to go, sits and stares fixedly at his master's finger! Or, think of it this way. If you substitute rays of light for the Source of light, you will quickly find yourself in darkness. We can not and must not substitute the Scriptures for God. We can not and dare not substitute truth and doctrine for God. The devil knows the truth better than any of us, but that does not make him a Christian! We can not substitute the purity of our doctrine for the purity of our heart.

WHAT DOES INSPIRATION GOT TO DO WITH IT?

Jesus warned that the diligent study of scripture is not enough to give a complete foundation to a spiritual life. "You diligently study the Scriptures because you think that by them you possess eternal life. These are the Scriptures that testify about me, yet you refuse to come to me to have life" (John 5:39, 40). Ponder for a moment the startling idea that we might still be doing this today. Some Christians I know believe in a trinity that goes; Father, Son and Holy Scriptures! Excuse me! Then they wonder why they don't have any power in their life! I recently heard a pastor say something profound: "It's hard to have the same faith as the early church when you value a book they didn't have above the Holy Spirit they did have".

Why am I taking the risk of addressing a controversial issue like inspiration and one's attitude toward scripture in a book on the Holy Spirit you ask? *Because I am alarmed that many believers are not open to the experience of the baptism of the Holy Spirit because they feel that their belief in and study of the Bible is a sufficient foundation for their personal spiritual life.* I'll say it again. You just can't substitute the study of the Scriptures for the baptism of the Holy Spirit. The Bible is very important but it is not sufficient. Only Jesus is sufficient. I am also addressing this issue in this book because I believe that the topic of inspiration is one of the "growing edges" for the church right now.

Yes, Spirit filled Christians still need the Bible! They will love and appreciate it all the more after they receive the Spirit. It will always be true that the scriptures will serve as a safety test for any experience of the Spirit. Particularly the gospels. Particularly the life and teachings of Jesus. If the Spirit appears to be leading one into an action or a teaching that is at odds with the life and teaching of the Savior, than one can be sure he or she is misguided, *for the life and teachings of Jesus are the gold standard for both belief and behavior.* The scriptures, once again, particularly the gospels, will serve as a standard and a safeguard to keep believers from excesses or from violating the will of God or from assuming that something the Spirit seems to be leading them into is God's will when it really is not. But that being said, please remember the words of Jesus when He said that truth, scriptural understanding, is just one part of a two-part spiritual foundation.

I know it is hard for you to look at what appears to be a challenge to the supremacy of the scriptures. But I am not challenging the scriptures. I am challenging the misuse and the abuse of scripture. I am challenging the idea of investing the scriptures with a perfection that they do not claim for themselves. I am challenging the priority they are given in some believers' lives to the detriment of something just as vital and foundational.

Here is a warning you may not have heard before: Bible doctrine and rules without the presence of the Holy Spirit can actually be hazardous to your spiritual health! They can be deadly. "The letter kills, but the Spirit gives life" (II Corinthians 3:6). I want you to appreciate and study the Scriptures daily. But wait a minute; what good would it do if you just read the recipes in the cookbook but never made a meal? You wouldn't get fed nor would the people you love. More than anything else I want this book to help you understand that you must take the next step beyond studying the Bible and let the very real experience of the filling of the Holy Spirit personalize and internalize the great principles of Scripture and the great Person of Scripture *in you.*

As extraordinary as it sounds, and as scary as it seems, you and I are called to follow Jesus in becoming the living, evolving, dynamic word in our world! I am wondering, are you willing to trust the Master when He says, "When He, the Spirit of truth is come, he will guide you into all truth." He said this in the amazing context with His disciples, where He declared to them, "I have much more to say to you, more than you can now bear." Can you believe that there were deeper truths the Lord had that had not been revealed in Old Testament writings, had not even been revealed while Jesus was instructing His followers for three years, but were to be revealed in the future through the vibrant, progressive leading of the Holy Spirit working through the minds and hearts of people like you and me in the future! The expansion of Spiritual truth did not stop when the Bible writers laid down their pens sometime in the 70's AD. Through the incredible agency of the Holy Spirit, it continues to this day, and you and I can be part of it if we are willing to be open to it!

LOVE LETTERS

I still keep and treasure the love letters my fiancé wrote to me when we were apart years and years ago! (Thank goodness that was in the days before e-mail, or everything we wrote would have vaporized long ago into cyberspace!) I remember pouring over those letters when they came, reading them again and again. They were wonderful. But what if we had just contented ourselves with a relationship based on written communication? What if we had never moved on to personal connection and intimacy? There would have been no marriage. There would have been no children. No family! We would have missed the greatest of blessings.

Here is a bit of advice that ruffles a lot of fundamentalist feathers and if I do it long enough I will surely get the temple police called out on me...Never study the Bible! Please, allow me an explanation before you pick up that... The Bible is a love-letter. You would not "study" a love-letter from your sweetheart! No. A love-letter is something you read with your heart not just your head. You cherish it. You look for the subtle meanings. You meditate on it. Always read your Bible "in Spirit." Surrender yourself to the Spirit before you dare open it up. Come at it with an open heart and in an attitude of reverence and meditation. Then, your time with the Bible will be an exciting adventure. George Muller said, "I have read the Bible through one hundred times, and always with increasing delight. Each time it seems like a new book to me...I look upon it as a lost day when I have not had a good time over the Word of God."

105

Here is an incredible exciting promise for the Spirit-filled person: "Call to me, and I will answer you, and show you great and mighty things, which you do not know" (Jeremiah 33:3). New, fresh insights will leap out at you and feed your soul. As you read, dare to claim this promise from the Master: "But when he, the Spirit of truth come, he will guide you into all truth...He will bring glory to me by taking from what is mine and making it known to you" (John 16:13,14). Yes, that includes fresh new truth and insights that, while founded on and supported by and never in disagreement with Scripture may actually be beyond Scripture! New light! New truth! Truth specifically for this time. Truth specifically for you.

Dietrich Bonhoeffer wrote: "Just as you do not analyze the words of someone you love, but accept them as they are said to you, accept the Word of Scripture and ponder it in your heart as Mary did. That is all. That is meditation." He recommended to students in his seminary that they spend a silent half hour every day on meditation of the Scripture. He advised them to spend a whole week on a single text! There is so much more to reading the Bible than just finding out what it says and what it means. It is to be read much more with the heart than with the head. Meditation is after all more a function of consciousness than it is of intellect. Scriptures are to be much more meditated on than studied. The real value of reading the Scriptures is when you can answer positively the question, "Did you experience God in your reading?" Have you moved from "reading about" to "entering in"? Through the Bible God speaks to our hearts.

Fundamentalists, literalists, fail to understand that the Bible is the love letter, not the marriage. It is the menu, not the meal. It is the map, not the journey. In his book *The Blue Parakeet*, Scott McKnight speaks of the importance of regarding the Bible relationally and not authoritatively. "The relational approach *distinguishes God from the Bible*. God existed before the Bible existed; God exists independently of the Bible now. God is a person; the Bible is paper. God gave us the papered Bible to lead us to love his person." McKnight suggests that *instead of viewing the Bible as an inerrant and as authoritative we should see it as a profound guide to a personal relationship with God.* He says that the psalmist did not say to God, "your words are authoritative, and I am called to submit to them," but rather, "your words are delightful, and I love to do what you ask." The difference between these two approaches is enormous. One of them is a relationship to the Bible; the other is a relationship to God." 9.

We must remember that the writers of the Bible were from a pre-modern, non-scientific world. Thus their perspective was limited as was their vocabulary. The Bible is not a book of science. We abuse if we try to make it so. It was Galileo's colleague, Cardinal Baronio who, attempting to support Galileo during his time of persecution by the church said, "The Bible tells us how to go to heaven, not how the heavens go." The Bible reveals that God is the Father-Creator of the world and of all life. It does not detail for us how He did it or exactly when He did it. The Bible is not even primarily a book of history. *It is to be read for one main purpose: to enhance one's relationship with God.* It was given to bring us to God consciousness and to love and to salvation.

Fundamentalists forget that all of the Bible's writers were imperfect human beings. They forget that these penmen were all (darn it!) male. That is, of course, thanks to the culture of the day that considered women to be sub-standard mentally and which did not allow them an education. Can you imagine how awesome it would be if along with good old Matthew, Mark, Luke and John, we had a gospel of Mary! A gospel according to Martha! The Acts of Dorcas or Phoebe? Imagine the beautiful, insightful, perspective a feminine writer could have brought to the life and teaching of Jesus as she witnessed it! The authors of scripture *wrote primarily for their own people in their own time and in their own language for their own culture.* "Thy word is a lamp unto my feet and a light unto my path," wrote the Psalmist. Note however, that the scriptures while helpful are *not* the path. There is only one Path, the one who said He was "the Way" (Psalm 119:105 KJV).

An eye for an eye was the Old Testament standard of behavior. Sadly, it continues to be the criterion today. The absolutely disastrous results of this choice are well-illustrated in the seeming unsolvable Israeli-Palestinian conflict that has been going on for almost 60 years now. With both sides deeply

107

committed to the policy of returning violence for violence, with both sides unwilling to consider for even a moment the concept of forgiveness, it still threatens to pull the entire world into a holocaust. (His friends admiringly described a former Israeli Prime Minister as a "real warrior" whose motto was "two eyes for an eye"). Jesus, that Holy radical, on the other hand, made the incredible paradigm-shattering statement, "Resist not evil." He said that when a person encounters violent behavior toward them they should "turn the other cheek." The problem .... the Old Testament sanctions violence, war and capital punishment. Jesus did not. Some of the Old Testament writers present an inaccurate and distorted picture of God. He is viewed as harsh, judgmental, eager to punish and the source of calamity, pain, suffering and death. The really good news? God is not the kind of person Satan has made Him out to be! Paul wrote: "God's kindness leads us toward repentance" (Romans 2:4). Jesus said: "God is ... kind to the unthankful and evil" (Luke 6:55). (Note to evangelists, why not give up fear, judgment, hell and damnation as tools of your trade?!)

The Master made a startling announcement to His disciples one day. It is sad and shocking that the ignorance of the religious people at the time was so deep that He needed to state it. It must have come like a thunderclap to their ears. *The Father himself loves you.* (John 16:27). How sad is it that they did not already know and understand this?

When I was growing up my church gave me the impression that God was really a tough customer. He was pretty much out to get me and my only hope was Jesus somehow blocking God's wrath and punishment so I wouldn't be destroyed! One writer describes it better than I:

Jesus and God were presented as partners in a mission to save the world. Jesus was the good cop, gentle and sympathetic, willing to take a bullet for us. God was the bad cop, standing in the background with his arms folded across his chest, glaring at us. As long as we responded to Jesus, God remained in the shadows. But, should we resist, we were reminded that we wouldn't want Jesus to leave us in the room alone with God. At which point God would crack his knuckles and scowl. 10.

Googled your neighbor lately? Googled your boss or your pastor? Ever try Googling yourself? You might be surprised about what you can learn about someone! What if you could Google God? Do you understand that what comes into your mind and heart when you think about God is the most important thing about you? What you believe about God affects absolutely everything about you… what you do, what you say, how you treat other people. If you could Google God, here is what you would find out… *God is Christ-like!* Jesus Christ came to change people's warped image of God. He came to tell the truth about God. He came to set the record straight. That is one of the most important reasons for His incarnation. He came to demonstrate to us the incredible truth that God is Christ-like! When will we ever get it? When will we ever let go of our twisted picture of God and stop behaving so judgmentally and harshly?

Misrepresenting the truth about God is the most damaging of all sins. A. Graham Maxwell has pointed out that Jesus was gentle with the worst of sinners, including the woman taken in adultery and even with Judas who betrayed Him. However, when some of the religious leaders of the day denied Jesus' teaching about the good news of what God was really like, when they echoed Satan's lies about God's character, Jesus gave them the incredibly strong rebuke, "You are of your father the devil" (John 8:44). While there was no disagreement between Jesus and the religious teachers over the Sabbath or Creation or the Ten Commandments, their dispute with Him was all about *the character of God.* Rather than change their distorted view of God, they ended up killing Him because He viewed God a great deal differently than they did. 11. They took the Old Testament literally. Jesus did not. Their interpretation of the Old Testament and what God was like was so different from His that they could accuse Him of heresy and blasphemy.

I guess now is as good a time to tell you as any… Dear readers, with all humility, I must tell you that I have discovered the "Theory of Everything" that the physicists have been searching for so long and so hard. And at no extra charge I am going to give you the most important formula in the universe, right now! Are you ready for this? Can you handle it? *God is Love!*

The second most important formula for your life is a direct result of the first formula: *Jesus + 0 = Eternal Life.* (Chris Blake suggested this prayer of forgiveness many believers need to pray: "Forgive us for ever placing the word "but" after the words, "You are saved through Jesus Christ.")

Q&A:

Q. You make it sound like the Old Testament shouldn't even be in the Bible. Are you saying I shouldn't bother to read it?

A. Every Christian should be Old Testament literate. Yes, you should read it. There are many parts that are informative, beautiful and uplifting. However, as you read it you must understand the limitations of its authors. You must understand that it does not present a totally complete and correct picture of God. You must understand that the words and even some of the ideas it presents are not perfect, not word-for-word infallible. You must understand that every word of it must be measured carefully against the greater light of the life and teaching of Jesus Christ as revealed in the gospels.

FOOTNOTES CHAPTER 6:

1. Scriven, Charles, *Spectrum Magazine,* May 1993, p. 45.

2. Sullivan, Andrew, *The Conservative Soul.* (Harper Collins, San Francisco, 2006)

3. McKnight, Scott, *The Blue Parakeet.* (Zondervan, Grand Rapids, MI, 2008), p.88.

4. Curtis and Eldredge, *The Sacred Romance.* (Thomas Nelson, Nashville TN), p.137.

5. Larson, David, *Spectrum Magazine,* Jesus and Genocide, Another Alternative, Volume   issue 3 Summer 2006, p.66.

6. Tozer, A.W. *The Pursuit of God.* (Christian Publications, Harrisburg, Pa, 1948), pp
9,10,13

7. Dawkins, Richard, *The God Delusion.* (Houghton Mifflin, New York, 2006), p.51.

8. Spong, John Shelby, *Why Christianity Must Change or Die.* (Harper Collins, San Francisco, 1998) p.7.

9. McKnight, Scott, *The Blue Parakeet. (*Zondervan, Grand Rapids, MI, 2008), p.87, 85.

10. Gulley, Phillip, Mulholland, James, *If God is Love*. (Harper San Francisco 2004), p.21

11. Maxwell, A. Graham, *Can God be Trusted?*. *(*Southern Publishing Association, Nashville, TN, 1977), p.36.

CHAPTER 7

THE ELEPHANT IN THE CHURCH

The Christian church has a really big problem. Unfortunately we have to talk about it here because it has blocked the Spirit for decades. It is sort of like the elephant in the church aisle. Everyone walks around it, nobody wants to talk about and they all pretend it is not there and that it is not doing really bad things to the rug! This is going to upset some of you I know, but please, give me a chance, hear me out. The Problem: over-valuing the Old Testament, the Jewish scriptures... taking it literally and as word by word infallible and assigning them equivalent spiritual value with the New Testament, the Christian scriptures. This has contributed to preventing the application of Christ's radical, reformative New Testament teachings to the existing order of the world. The real issue is inspiration of scripture, what it is and how it works. This is a true growing edge for a lot of us.

In the twentieth century alone, over 180 million people were killed in one war or atrocity or another. This is a far larger total than any other century in human history! The 21st century seems to be jealous of that record and is already doing its best to equal or exceed it. The Prince of Peace came over two millennium ago. What happened? Much of this could have been avoided if Christians would have really lived the gospel, including Christ's teaching in the Sermon on the Mount regarding non-violence and not returning evil for evil. If only His revolutionary teachings would have been followed by individuals and by governments over the last two thousand years! When we are confronted with a choice to pray for our enemies or bomb them into oblivion the latter course usually seems most expedient! When will we ever get it? (Note to Israeli and Palestinian leaders and to whoever the occupant is of a big house on Pennsylvania Avenue: In the short term, force always looks like a good solution, but in the long term you cannot out-evil evil. You can not destroy violence with more violence. It didn't work in Vietnam. It didn't work in Iraq or Afghanistan.

Fredrick Beuchner has written poignantly about the fall from grace of the United States.

The nation that once dreamed of being a new hope, a new haven, for the world has become the number one bully of the world, blundering and blustering and bombing its way, convinced that it is right and that everyone who disagrees with it is wrong. (Axis of evil?) Maybe that is the way it inevitably is with nations. They are so huge and complex. By definition they are so exclusively concerned with their own self-interest conceived in the narrowest term that they have no eye for holiness, of all things, no ears to hear the great command to be saints, no heart to break at the thought of what this world could be—the friends we could be as nations if we could learn to listen to each other instead of just shouting at each other, the common problems we could help each other solve, all the human anguish we could join together to heal. 1.

THE SERMON ON THE MOUNT: DO WE TAKE IT SERIOUSLY?

The Sermon on the Mount is a vivid picture of how we would be living our lives if the Holy Spirit was totally getting His way with us. One simply cannot accept the teachings of the Sermon on the Mount and actively support non-defensive warfare. (Some would argue you cannot support any kind of warfare at all.) Nor can one support capital punishment. The United States is the only large democracy in the world that continues to practice what many call this "cruel and unusual punishment." (Sadly, the United States is also the world's largest arms supplier by far). Between 1976 and January 1, 2012, 1295 prisoners were executed in the USA. There are 3,189 who await their fate on death row now. (723 in California alone). As this is written there are 62 women on death row, many of them mothers. Ponder this frightening fact... 140 death row inmates have been totally exonerated, found innocent, (largely due to DNA evidence) since 1973. A recent poll showed that over 61% of US voters would choose a punishment other than the death penalty for murder.

Opponents of the death penalty argue that it cheapens human life. They say it puts the government on the same low moral level as criminals who have taken life. Let's face the nasty truth; capital punishment exists in the U.S. today primarily because fundamentalist Christians who take the Old Testament literally, find their support for it there. The New Testament, the teaching of Jesus, do not support the death penalty.

Here is another discrepancy between the Old Testament and the New. The OT gives the message over and over again, that God shows His blessing on His people who obey Him by prospering them financially and materially. He is always assuring them that if they will obey Him they will be blessed with abundant crops and much cattle and lands. "If they obey and serve him, they will spend the rest of their days in prosperity and their years in contentment" (Job 36:11).

The theology of the Old Testament is clear that worldly prosperity and wealth are an important indicator that the possessor enjoys God's favor. Sometimes it seems Israel was almost a kind of cargo cult that served God only to be able to receive His material blessings. It's there over and over again. Obey, and the milk and honey will flow. Your cattle will breed very successfully and you will become wealthy. Manipulating people with rewards is as wrong as preying on their fears in order to get them to believe something or to do something.

The Old Testament idea that religious obedience is rewarded by material prosperity and wealth is totally at odds with the teachings of Jesus. If we would have been willing to let the prosperity theology of the Old Testament be superseded by the remarkable principles Jesus presented in His astonishing sermon, we would not be living in a situation in the twenty-first century where there are 7 billion people in the world, more than half of whom struggle to survive on less than $2.00 a day! We would not live in a world where the wealthy 20% of the earth's population consume 86% of the world's goods and services while the poorest 20% of the earth's population (1.35 billion) receive just 1.3% of world's goods and services!

Jesus gave some very clear instructions about money in His Sermon on the Mount: "Do not store up for yourselves treasures on earth"… "No man can serve two masters"… "You cannot serve both God and money", (and the advice that just drives the financial planners a little crazy)…"Do not worry about your life, what you will eat or drink, or about your body, what you will wear, do not worry about tomorrow, for tomorrow will worry about itself."

If we only could learn to follow His counsel, the wealth of the world would not be so unfairly distributed. No longer would it be the case that every year 40 million people would die from starvation and diseases that are treatable. That number is equal to the deaths in ten WWII Jewish Holocausts, and it happens every year! And most of the deaths are preventable! It is even more upsetting to realize this number breaks down to 125,000 people who die every day and 40,000 of those are children!

Meanwhile, *Newsweek Magazine* in its October 16, 2006, issue, reported that in the United States the market for "affordable" high-end cars, costing between $150K and $200K has boomed in recent years. *Newsweek* calls them budget! luxury cars and says that 2,890 of them were sold in 2003, whereas in 2005, 16,880 were purchased. (Thank God for the Bill Gates and Warren Buffetts, Oprah Winfreys and Bonos and yes, even Ted Turners of this world who are an exception to the rule. They are inspiring examples of people who are passionately committed to sharing their wealth with the less fortunate). In his book *Giving*, Bill Clinton relates the stories of many people who have exchanged corporate or money-centered lives to devote themselves to service and volunteerism.)

We consistently have written off Jesus' most profound teachings as impractical in the real world. As a result, the most powerful and civilized governments in the world today still feel that violence must best be prevented with more violence. By choosing to take the Old Testament literally and as a model for behavior by today's governments, by considering war and capital punishment as justifiable options for response to evil and violence, society is saying that Christ's teachings are mistaken in so far as they forbid resistance to evil. Those who take this stance are, as Tolstoy points out in his book, *The Kingdom of God is Within You*, really saying that: "the teaching of the Sermon on the Mount is only a string of very pretty, impractical dreams".2.

If you are truly interested in entering into the Spirit-filled life, you must be willing to stand boldly for the radical and revolutionary teachings of your

115

Lord. A life in the Spirit is not for wimps and conformists! Becoming Spirit-filled has the potential to get you into a great deal of trouble. Following closely in the Master's steps will inevitably bring you to your own cross sooner or later. You must be truly willing to renounce materialism and consumerism as the focus of your life. You must become willing to lead a countercultural type of lifestyle that eschews possessions and money as the source of your security. You must be willing to appear as a fool in your society by refusing to buy in to popular dysfunctional culture that is centered on consumerism, celebrity and hedonism. You must refuse to go along with violence as a solution to political problems. You must have the courage to stand and be heard as rejecting capital punishment as a legitimate tool of government. I know, some of you don't like me dragging the capital punishment thing in here. Too loaded, too political, too controversial for a devotional book you say. But think about it. Would Jesus pull the switch on someone in an electric chair? Would Jesus give a lethal injection to someone? Would you? And if He wouldn't and if you wouldn't then how can you ask a public servant who represents you and is working for you and is paid by you, to do such a thing?

In his book, *The Jesus of Suburbia: Have We Tamed the Son of God to Fit Our Lifestyle?*, Mike Err says there is a growing difference between being a follower of Christ and a follower of Christianity. He thinks we Western Christians have forsaken Jesus of Nazareth for Jesus of Suburbia. He says that Jesus of Nazareth was a revolutionary who took a stand against the kingdoms of the world. Jesus of Suburbia, he says, is more interested in the comfort and prosperity of his followers. Err challenges Christians to live the revolution that is Christ-centered Christianity by giving ourselves away and exhibiting the acts of love and compassion that distinguished the early church.

How long will it take us to understand that it is never what we are not getting so much as what we are not giving that is holding back our spiritual growth? Are you willing to lead a radical life, motivated by love? Focused on serving others? Plain and simple, that is what Jesus is calling you to.

Dr. Tony Campolo, recently addressing a group of ministers dared to challenge them with these words:

Here's the problem. Tell me about this Jesus that you propagate. Does he really incarnate Yahweh? Is he really the Jesus of the New Testament? Or do you preach a Jesus that incarnates the values of this democratic capitalist society? Tell me about this Jesus that you preach. As I listen to the radio and to the television I'm scared. For the Jesus that is propagated in the world today has nothing to do with the Jesus of Scripture...One of the real problems that you are going to have is that if you start preaching the Jesus of Scripture you are going to run contrary to the value system of your congregation. My only response to this problem...well, what's the point of spending your life preaching any other Jesus than the One of Scripture? Do you want to spend your life preaching about a Jesus who never existed?" 3.

Tolstoy said that the critics of Christ's pronouncement of resisting violence with violence, evil with evil consider this to be a naïve doctrine. He believed however, that if it were carried into practice in modern times, it would not allow society continue on as it is at present.

The writer Kurt Vonnegut came up with a poignant thought:

"For some reason, the most vocal Christians among us never mention the Beatitudes. But, often with tears in their eyes, they demand that the Ten Commandments be posted in public buildings. And of course, that is Moses, not Jesus. I haven't heard one of them demand that the Sermon on the Mount, The Beatitudes, be posted anywhere. "Blessed are the merciful" in a courtroom? "Blessed are peacemakers" in the Pentagon? Give me a break!" 4.

Vonnegut may not have realized it, but John beat him to the punch two thousand years ago. "The law came through Moses, but grace and truth through Jesus Christ". John 1:17

Of course, the critics are right. Society would not be the same if we stopped ignoring the principles of the Sermon on the Mount. The point they miss is that if it would dare to take the risk, it would be radically better! For example, Jesus' teaching not to resist evil was championed by Tolstoy when he challenged both his government and his church. This got him into a great deal of trouble and got his book on the subject banned in his home country of Russia. But it was he who deeply influenced Mahatma Gandhi who then led a bloodless revolution to free the entire country of India from British control. Gandhi's principles of non-violence in turn inspired Martin Luther King to lead a non-violent civil rights movement in the United States that revolutionized the

117

country and prevented what could have been a blood-bath of rioting and terrorism and even perhaps another civil war or race war.

Dr. Sakae Kubo, a brilliant New Testament theologian and a former seminary professor of mine has written;

"God condescends to use earthen vessels to present Himself to people and sometimes their limitations show in how they present God to us. We should keep in mind that there is a development and understanding in scripture as time goes on....It is clear there is development from the Old to the New Testament when the author of Hebrews writes, 'Long ago God spoke to our ancestors in many and various ways by the prophets, but in these last days he has spoken to us by a Son...' (Hebrews 1:1-2)."

Kubo goes on to say;

"The fact that there is development shows that we cannot consider the Bible in regards to revelation as a flat or level plane—that is to say, we cannot just select any Scripture and consider it to be of the same value as any other passage from any place in the Bible. In the New Testament we have a better and clearer understanding of God's plan."

Believing in the same level of inspiration in the Old Testament as in the New, giving it equal validity because it is all part of one Bible, undermines the revolutionary new teachings of Jesus. Sadly it leads us to discount and neglect, to our great loss, the incredible depth and wisdom of teachings like the Sermon on the Mount. Brennan Manning says that the role of Christians today is to be a counterculture to our nation's lunatic lust for power and possessions. "If we preferred to be faithful rather than successful, the walls of indifference to Jesus Christ would crumble. A handful of us could be ignored by society, but hundreds, thousands, millions of such servants would overwhelm the world. Christians filled with the authenticity, commitment, and generosity of Jesus would be the most spectacular sign in the history of the human race. The call of Jesus is revolutionary. If we implemented it, we would change the world in a few months. 5.

Q&A:

Q. You say that a person evaluating Christianity or seeking truth should not start reading the Bible with Genesis. Where should they begin?

A. The Book of John. John was the disciple closest to Jesus and reveals His deepest truths most powerfully and poignantly. They should start there, then they should read 1st John, then Matthew, Luke, Mark and go on to Romans, Galatians, to get the true flavor of the gospel.

FOOTNOTES CHAPTER 7:

1. Beuchner, Fredrick. *Secrets in the Dark*. (Harper San Francisco, 2006), p. 143.

2. Tolstoy, Leo. *The Kingdom of God is Within You*.(University of Nebraska Press,   Lincoln NB:1984), p.45 .

3. Campoli, A. quoted in *Good News Unlimited*. (December 2006). p. 7.

4. Vonnegut, Kurt. *A Man Without a Country*. (Seven Stories Press, NY: 2005), p. 98

5. Manning, Brennan, *The Signature of Jesus*, Multnomah Books, 1996). p. 46.

CHAPTER 8:

IT'S NOT JUST ABOUT POWER

What the soul is in our body,

the Holy Spirit is in the body of Christ,

which is the church.

Augustine

There has been an unfortunate idea among some believers that the Baptism of the Holy Spirit is given solely to empower people to witness and spread the gospel. This misconception has resulted in many coming to think that this experience is only for pastors, missionaries and evangelists. The implication is that the person in the pew does not qualify for it, need not be concerned about it and "need not apply" for it. There has been a debate for years about whether the Baptism of the Spirit was primarily about holiness or power. Such boxed-in thinking puts unnecessary limitations on the Holy Spirit. This is the very same Spirit that is like the wind. He comes and goes in His own way as He wills. You can not dictate to the wind. You can not put the wind in a box or lock it up in a doctrine or a creed or a building, not even in a church. The Bible says that the Spirit "divides to every man severally as he will." and that He gives spiritual gifts to each one as "just as he determines." (1 Corinthians 12:11). Christians are liberated by the Holy Spirit from sin and for service.

There should not be an either/or when it comes to the Spirit providing power or personal growth and holiness. It is a both/and situation. Writing in *Christianity Today*, in an article entitled "Embrace your Inner Pentecostal", Chris Armstrong, a professor of church history at Bethel Seminary, says that the Baptism of the Spirit is certainly more than about receiving power to witness. He says the testimonies from people who have experienced the Spirit that have touched him the most reveal one main effect:

"A new, joyous sense of communion with a loving God who counted every hair on their heads and watched over them every minute. The central moment of their Pentecostal experience had opened them to a deep well of living water from which everything else flowed; it had opened them to the personal, relational presence of the Living God." (Emphasis supplied.)

Speaking of his own personal experience with the Spirit, Armstrong says:

"Though it may discomfort the religiously buttoned-down, the rationalists, and the nominal, the Pentecostal God deigns to meet with us and care for us in immediate, experiential ways. We speak to him in a language of love, saying "Abba, Father," and He responds in kind.
This encounter has always been the open secret of Pentecostal spirituality. The belief in God's real, experienced care and the passion for union with Christ—often likened to the thirst of the psalmist's deer for the stream—may turn out to be Pentecostalism's chief contributions to Christianity." 1.

"A passion for union with Christ." I like that! *When people ask me, with some trepidation in their voice, where this thing called the baptism of the Spirit will take them if they ask for it, I tell them it will lead them to a passion for union with Christ, for a deep longing for moment-by-moment connection and intimacy, constant union with the Father.* That is the beating heart of true spirituality. It is the center, the foundation the ultimate destination of our journey. Any religion that does not understand this, and displaces what is so central and foundational with anything else, tragically ends up as only guilt-induced legalism and a set of doctrines to be memorized and rules to be obeyed. You get to decide what comes first in your spiritual life. Rules or relationship? Doctrine or devotion?

Some teach that the baptism of the Spirit is given only for the purpose of empowering a believer for ministry. Wrong. That is an important but secondary purpose. Sacred intimacy is the primary purpose of the gift of the filling of the Holy Spirit. Paul said it so simply and so well in Ephesians 1:17; "I keep asking that the God of our Lord Jesus Christ, the glorious Father, may give you the Spirit of wisdom and revelation, *so that you may know him better.*" (Emphasis supplied.) The Spirit's primary role is to facilitate love, intimacy and connection with God. You will never know a truly deep oneness with Jesus until you come to know it through the experience of the filling of the Holy Spirit. It is only by the Spirit that you and I are truly able to glorify and magnify Jesus. Go ahead, I dare you! Somersault into the inconceivable! Take a spiritual leap! Jump into the oneness!

I can verify Armstrong's thesis. More than thirty years after my own encounter with the filling of the Spirit, two results in my life stand out for me: an understanding and appreciation for unconditional love as the center of life and spirituality and an on-going hunger for moment-by- moment personal connection and intimacy with the Father, my Abba. (Abba is a word from the Scriptures best-translated Daddy or Papa.) Peter Van Breemen has written that intimacy with Abba is one of the greatest treasures Jesus has brought us. 2. That kind of remarkable intimacy comes exclusively through the filling of the Spirit. "Because you are sons, God sent the Spirit of his Son into our hearts, the Spirit who calls out, Abba, Father." (Galatians 4:6).

I really find it a turn-off when Christians run around calling God by Old Testament names. Come on, just indulge me for a moment. It really leaves me cold when He is referred to, even in some contemporary gospel songs as "Jehovah" or "El Shaddai." There are even some, and I have found them usually to be fanatics, who insist that He must only be referred to as "Yahweh." These are not exactly user-friendly, intimacy-producing names to the uninitiated ear! They are kind of scary and mysterious titles, and I think a real turn-off to anyone who might be starting to check-out Christianity for the first time. When the disciples asked Jesus to teach them to pray, He shocked and amazed them by referring to God as "our Father." That's what I like to call my God. Abba. Daddy. Good enough for Jesus. Good enough for me. (Think about it. How would the Muslim world respond if a new, progressive prophet came along and said, "You don't need to call God "Allah" any more. You can call Him "daddy"! Wouldn't that generate a flock of *fatwas*!)

The baptism of the Spirit opens up to men and women an unheard of, undreamed of closeness with God. Christ has invited us through the indwelling of the Spirit to share in the very intimacy He had with the Father! We are invited to also become the sons and daughters of God! "…those who are led by the Spirit of God are the sons of God. For you did not receive a spirit that makes you a slave again to fear, but you received the Spirit of son-ship. And by him we cry 'Abba, Father'."

Only the Holy Spirit filling your heart brings you into the unique relationship, into the sacred place where you can confidently call the Almighty creator by the intimate and tender term "Daddy." Get it? The Holy Spirit is given to teach you that your heavenly Father absolutely adores you! You are the apple of His eye! His banner over you is love! In his powerful book, *Forgotten God, Reversing our Tragic Neglect of the Holy Spirit*, Francis Chan writes; "...there's nothing better than being absolutely sure that the most powerful Being in the universe adores you as His own child. This is precisely the confidence the Holy Spirit offers us." 3.

Q&A:

Q. Our church service lacks energy and enthusiasm. Do you think if more of us ask for the Spirit this would change?

A. Yes. But. Contrary to popular opinion, the Holy Spirit is not given primarily to get people to clap their hands in church. Or to get them to loosen up and raise their arms when they pray. Or to say "amen" or "praise the Lord" more. Or to get them to sing more praise music with a good drum set on the platform. Don't get me wrong. I enthusiastically support the freedom of people to engage in all the above mentioned practices and often participate in and enjoy and am blessed by some of them. But here's the real deal ... when you get ready to ask for the baptism of the Spirit, the big question is: are you ready to give yourself to others? Because that is what it is all about. *Being baptized with the Holy Spirit shifts you from self-centered thinking to other-centered thinking.* The gift of the Spirit is given to us, to equip us and empower us for witness and ministry and service to others. The bottom line of Christianity, the true test of whether or not you are baptized with the Spirit, has always been and will always be whether or not your life is about doing acts of unconditionally loving service for other people. You were created to love and serve and you are most alive and fulfilled when you are actively doing love, actively giving of yourself. *To be baptized with the Holy Spirit is to begin a journey into the heart of love.* That, above all else, is why we seek the Spirit. *You can truly worship God only to the degree you give away your life and your love to other people.* The Spirit teaches our hearts that nothing matters more than love and that nothing can defeat love. Love is your very purpose in living. Love is your hope. "And hope does not put us to shame, because God's love has been poured out into our hearts through the Holy Spirit who has been given to us." (Romans 5:5 English Standard Version.)

FOOTNOTES CHAPTER 8:

1. Armstrong, Chris. *Christianity Today.* (September 2006), p.88.

2. Van Breeman, Peter. *Called by Name.* (Dimension Books, Denville, NJ, 1976), p. 43.

3. Chan, Francis. *Forgotten God, Reversing our Tragic Neglect of the Holy Spirit.* (David Cook Publishing, Colorado Springs, 2009), p.103.

CHAPTER 9:

THE SEDUCTIVE POWER OF FALSE FOUNDATIONS

Knowledge puffs up, but love builds up. The man who thinks he knows
something does not yet know as he ought to know. But the man who loves God
is known by God.
1 Corinthians 8:1-3

I started out with my denomination as the foundation of my religious life. It was my chief identity. I might as well have worn a banner across my forehead stating in bold black letters, "I am a..." That is how I primarily thought of myself. It was who I was. I gave away a lot of my power and my ability to think for myself to the leaders of my church. I firmly believed that my church had an exclusive on "the truth" and that those who refused to accept it would be lost forever. (I know now that this is one of the definitions of a cult.) Therefore it was my primary duty in life to convince and convert as many people as possible to my church.

I remember flying into Los Angeles one night when I was in my early twenties, looking out the window at the endless sea of lights, and in a virtual fit of spiritual narcissism, thinking to myself, "What a mission field! I should take on the burden of this whole big city and convert every one to the truth and get them all into my church!"

We can be such spiritual narcissists. So incredibly arrogant! We think everyone should relate to God just the way we do! We think they should believe exactly what we believe or they are in danger of the judgment! And furthermore we have no patience with people's natural pace of spiritual growth. Rather than patiently waiting for them to come into their own unique relationship with the Father in their own time, we demand immediate obedience and conformity to the religious system we happen to subscribe to! We would have them become religious clones, formed in our image, subscribing to our view of how they should behave, how they should worship and what their walk with God should be like!

125

Oh what great food for the ego when we think we have something no one else does that is critical to their survival. How that allows us to "lord" it over them. On what a high and lofty peak that places us! It makes us so unique! So special! (Such egotistical posturing should not be confused with the genuine privilege and delight of being able to humbly share as one beggar telling another beggar where the bread is, the good news of the true gospel.) We spiritual elitists need to learn to practice a radical humility.

From the time of Constantine, the church was given a place and a power it never was intended to have. It was decided that the church was holy, apostolic. It was decided that its leader could speak with infallibility. Some Protestants fell into the same distorted thinking when they decided that the Bible was literally infallible or that their church had the exclusive on spiritual truth and "unbelievers" or "outsiders" could not be saved without their church's truth. I finally had to come to realize that it is not my church that saves me! I had put my church in the place of God. I had to learn to let go of my "churchiolatry."

In his classic book *The Seven Habits of Highly Effective People*, Stephen Covey describes what it is like for the person who centers his or her life around their church:

Your security is based on church activity and on the esteem in which you are held by those in authority or influence in the church. You find identity and security in religious labels and comparisons. You are guided by how others will evaluate your actions in the context of church teachings and expectations. You see the world in terms of "believers" and "nonbelievers", "belongers" and "non-belongers. Perceived power comes from your church position or role. 1.

I have discovered that while the church is an important component of the spiritual life, the chief reason for its existence is to allow believers to work together to accomplish through organized service to the world what could not be accomplished through individual service. When the church goes beyond being a vehicle for witness and practical, unconditionally loving service to others, it loses its vision. It becomes at best a social club or, at its worst, imperious, political, dysfunctional; it becomes a distraction, even a detriment to genuine Christianity. An example of a church acting outside legitimate boundaries would be a bishop instructing his parishioners not to vote for a candidate because of that individual's personal beliefs or previous votes the church did not agree

126

with. Such behavior illustrates the total inappropriateness of the church trying to manipulate events in the political arena.

The worst case scenario of the church, or religion gone beyond its boundaries is a theocracy, a form of government in which church leaders rule a country by religious laws. Fortunately our founding fathers had the wisdom to protect us from this supreme political folly. This sort of government inevitably leads to the worst kind of distortions and repression of freedoms. Think Afghanistan as ruled by the Taliban. Iran as governed largely by the *imams* and *ayatollahs*. Think of what might happen if Iraq, Egypt, or Libya or Syria do not succeed in becoming a democracy but instead becomes theocracies ruled by fundamentalist mullahs! Frighteningly, the goal of Islam is to create not just a theocracy in every Middle East country but to create a global theocracy based on the rules of the Koran. If a Christian church were to propose to rule a country or the world by biblical laws, it would be no less dangerous.

BLOOM WHERE YOU ARE PLANTED

Just a side-note here. Having justifiably cautioned you against giving your own religion, your own denomination, your own local church too much significance and power in your life, I want you to understand there is another side to the coin. I am not encouraging you to condemn or leave the Christian religious tradition that you have inherited from your parents and grown up with. In spite of the flaws and frustrations of my own denomination, I have stayed with it since I was 8 years old, and I have never regretted that. Thankfully there is enough freedom in my church now that I am allowed to be who I am within it and practice the faith in a way that is true to who I am and where I am at in my spiritual journey. I believe it is far better to try to light a candle where you are than to curse the darkness. I have several friends, some of them pastors, who left the church. In most cases, this decision did not improve their spiritual lot like they thought it would. In some cases it led to great disillusionment, disappointment, loneliness and isolation. It may be that for many, they are better off staying in their faith if they have the courage to adapt it to their own needs and increasing level of spiritual maturity. Realize that you have the permission and the freedom in Christ to become your own kind of Methodist or Adventist or Baptist or even Catholic. The grass is not always greener on the other side of the religious fence!

Kathleen Norris tells of a young man she knew who grew disillusioned with the religion he had grown up with. He was stunned when he went to Thailand and tried to join a Buddhist monastery. "Go back home and become a Christian monk first," the monks there told him. "Learn your own tradition first."

A reporter once asked the Dalai Lama what he would say to Americans who want to become Buddhists. "Don't bother," he said. "Learn from Buddhism, if that is good for you. But do it as a Christian." Perhaps there is something to be said for "blooming where you are planted." In his own personal quest for the spiritual, Steve Jobs discovered the same truth. At one point he was considering going to Japan to enter a Buddhist monastery. His friend and spiritual advisor counseled him not to go. "He said there is nothing over there that isn't here, and he was correct," Jobs later wrote. "I learned the truth of the Zen saying that if you are willing to travel around the world to meet a teacher, one will appear next door." 2.

HOLY CITIES?

For others, the center of their religious life is what they regard to be a sacred site or building or object. For the Israelites in Old Testament times, it was the temple at Jerusalem with its Holy of Holies, a special room no one could enter except the priest and then only once a year. Inside that room was kept what they considered a sacred object, the ark of the covenant.

The Muslims consider Mecca to be their holy city. No non-Muslim may enter the city upon the pain of death. Each Muslim according to the Koran is required to make a pilgrimage to the holy city at least once in their lifetime. Inside the mosque in Mecca resides an object called the *kabala*. It is a large black stone, apparently meteoric in origin, venerated as a sacred.

The Mormons aren't required to make a pilgrimage to the temple in Salt Lake City, but most of them I know don't feel good about themselves until they do. Non-Mormons are forbidden to enter that temple. When Mitt and Ann Romney were married in the temple, she was required to convert to Mormonism first and her parents, not Mormons, were not allowed to attend the service.

I am sorry. There are no sacred holy places on this earth. Not for Christians. Not for Jews. Not for Muslims. Neither are there any sacred physical objects. All these things do is give us something to argue and fight over. Furthermore, there are no holy men. No holy women. I am sorry, but Jerusalem or Mecca is no more sacred than Modesto. The Dome of the Rock is no more sacred than Half Dome or Ayers Rock. The only thing sacred on this earth is the surrendered heart of the believer made sacred by the living presence of the Holy Spirit of God dwelling within him or her.

THE INSUFFICIENCY OF DOCTRINE AND THE LIMITS OF REASON

There are other people who consider their doctrines to be the core of their religious experience. Intellectually understanding and conforming to a set of particular unchangeable religious beliefs, or a certain theology, is what they would call their foundation. However, if Christianity were entirely based on intellectual understanding, then the people with the highest IQ's and the most education would have a distinct advantage! I love that statement from the former professional baseball player and old-time evangelist Billy Sunday. "I don't know any more about theology than a jackrabbit does about ping pong, but I am on my way to glory!" Doctrines can instruct us and illuminate our path, but they must never be allowed to define it. Only the Holy Spirit can do that for us.

The limits of the intellect, the limits of reason when accessing the spiritual life need to be acknowledged. When will we intellectuals or quasi-intellectuals or pretend intellectuals ever get it? There are levels of consciousness in each of us that are far deeper than thought, far deeper than our thinking can take us.

Christians have finally come to understand the insufficiency of their own righteousness. Now, we need to just as clearly acknowledge the limits of our own knowledge and intellect. The Bible counsels, "lean not to your own understanding." Knowledge is knowing stuff. Facts. Scientists have the technical *knowledge* to make the atom bomb. That does not mean they have the *wisdom* to know how and when to use it.

To relate in depth to God we can not rely on our religious knowledge. In fact, we must often empty ourselves of our own wisdom and instead rely on the Holy Spirit to provide His Divine truth which can easily appear as foolishness to the non-spiritual person. Jesus said, "I praise you, Father, Lord of heaven and earth, because you have hidden these things from the wise and learned, and revealed them to little children." (Matthew 11:25) Think about it. It was the wise and powerful and deeply religious people of His day who most derided Jesus and eventually had Him killed! Furthermore, Jesus never appealed primarily to His hearer's intellect; He primarily was concerned with capturing their hearts!

The limits of intellectual, doctrinal-based religion are profound. This is born out by the now acknowledged truism that theology divides but mission, service to the world, to others, unites. Believers can quickly get into a host of divisive quarrels over theology, doctrine, biblical interpretation, religious rules and church tradition. Yet, when they come together to evangelize or to serve human needs a wonderful unity and synergy is usually present. That reminds me of the phrase, what I believe is not what I say I believe; what I believe is what I do!

When will we ever get it? There are times when our frantic attempts to intellectually explain or understand our faith only cheapens it! I am sorry, but we can never ever prove the existence of God scientifically. We can never prove the existence of God by reasoning or logic. Thus the validity of the great phrase: "Stop thinking! It is a mystery!"

There is a level of sacredness that simply cannot be accessed through thought. This may make you uncomfortable but here is the deal… our souls are the deepest part of who we are. Our souls are larger than our minds, our intellects. They also transcend our emotions. Our souls allow us to travel to spiritual places to which our minds can not always come. Our souls can penetrate behind the veil where our thoughts can not come, to the deeper places of God. *There is a depth of spirituality far beyond thinking.* Your mind is a powerful tool for monitoring your behavior but it does not possess the power to change your nature!

Every one knows that IQ is a measure of one's "intelligence quotient". Generally it refers to the amount of factual knowledge a person has plus their problem-solving abilities. In the last few years studies have led us to understand there is a measure for another level of wisdom and maturity that has been labeled EQ or "emotional intelligence". It is quite apart from IQ. It has to do with one's ability to relate well to other people and to how a person may handle difficult and challenging circumstances. I would propose to you that beyond IQ and EQ we should consider another even more significant category. SQ. Spiritual intelligence. Unlike IQ which is about the intellect and EQ which is about emotion, spiritual intelligence can not be acquired by learning more facts or assimilating more information. Thought has to subside for men and women to encounter this dimension. It is not mind-based or emotion-based. You do not achieve it by learning or information or effort. It is something that is received only through surrender. It is soul-based. Joel Goldsmith wrote: "The real seat of intelligence is Soul or Spirit, … The whole secret lies in making the transition from a thinking, plotting, planning scheming mind to a mind at rest in a state of awareness, through which divine ideas can flow." 3.

We can not put God or the Holy Spirit in some kind of test tube and demonstrate Him to the skeptics and the new energetic crew of enthusiastic, evangelistic atheists who have risen out of the existential desert in the last few years. (you've got to love it though, when Richard Dawkins wears his t-shirt that says, "Atheists for Jesus"!)

Preston Foster has pointed out that as our knowledge, education, exposure and access to information has exploded, people are demanding more and more empirical proof of everything, including God and the Spirit. Many moderns resist the idea of being connected to and led by an unseen Spirit. For them, it is just asking too much. They do not realize that God is simply beyond proof. At least beyond logical and intellectual proof. God is a holy mystery. Surrendering our incredible drive to have to know and explain and logically understand everything and just to learn to be content with *not knowing* certain things is a kind of gift we can give the Father. Not knowing everything is okay! It was Victor Frankel who advised, "Sell your cleverness and purchase bewilderment."

In seminars I like to draw a line the whole length of the blackboard or whiteboard and tell the group, "Let's assume this line represents God." Then I ask them to mentally extend that line to the far corner of the room. Then, out to the parking lot. Then, to the outskirts of the city. Then, to the state line, to the edge of the continent. Then, all the way around the world. "After all, is not God infinite?" I ask. Then I go back to the board and mark off one inch on that long line. "This is how much you and I know about God." And to think that some of us belong to churches that claim to have "The Truth"! Being blind to our own blindness is a serious fault of every human being. The psychologist Daniel Kahneman has observed that we are generally overconfident in our opinions and our impressions and judgments. We exaggerate how knowable the world is, he says. I am afraid Christians wildly exaggerate how knowable religious truth is. Or even how knowable all the truth about God is. We think that only those who follow our narrow religious viewpoints are authentic followers of the Lord. There is a word for that; exclusivity. Remember, there is no worse arrogance than religious arrogance.

THE WONDER OF IT ALL

Sometimes we have to release ourselves from our desperate need to understand everything about the spiritual world and just bask in the wonder of it

all! The wonder of the Holy Spirit's willingness to incarnate Himself in us!
The astounding mystery of the incarnation! The marvel of God's limitless,
unconditional love! By the way, wonder and awe are great foundations for
worship and praise. Ask yourself, does your religion overflow with passion?
Have you allowed your heart to be ravished by God? Have you given the Holy
Spirit permission to *overshadow* you, as He did Mary? Do you live in a constant
state of spiritual amazement?

Sometimes we struggle so hard to try and understand everything, to
know everything about our religion. We need to realize that we cannot possibly
know it all, and that *not knowing* is okay. Not being able to explain everything
is okay. In fact our "not knowing" can be a kind of gift we give to God, a kind
of surrender to His splendid infinity and omniscience. *Be oh so very careful that
you do not automatically reject the things you cannot explain!*

Let's just finally admit it. The Christian faith is a mystery. It can never
be explained. It can never be logically or scientifically proven. And you know
what? That is totally wonderful! This is a fact we should celebrate! Imagine
that. It cannot be explained and yet it is beautiful and true! So guess what.
That makes every Christian a mystic! That too new-agey for you? You
uncomfortable with that? Just deal with it because it is oh so true! In fact, it is
quite impossible to be a Christian without being a mystic! Whatever you do,
don't automatically reject something just because you can not explain it or prove
it or demonstrate it. You will end up cheating yourself of the best things in life
and in eternity if you do. Remember, "What is essential is invisible to the eye.
It is only with the heart that one can see rightly" wrote St. Exupery. So please,
don't let the world "mystic" scare you. A mystic is simply a disciple of love. A
mystic is an ordinary human being who, under the control of the Holy Spirit,
becomes fully conscious of love and finds the love and reveals the love that is
present in every relationship and in every circumstance. A mystic realizes as
others do not that there is no problem or situation to which love is not the
answer. A mystic know that love endures, that love always wins.

Something else important about a Christian mystic: He or she lives
primarily in the unseen world. The Psalmist got it when he wrote: "He who

dwells in the secret place of the Most High shall abide under the shadow of the Almighty (Psalm 91). Jim Hornberger says: "The secret place is where faith in God becomes a greater reality than our circumstances. To dwell in that secret place means to stay there, to take up permanent residence. 'Come what may, I am not leaving Lord! You are my reality – not my circumstances'." 4. The question for us all then is: Which reality, which state of consciousness do you live in? The seen or the unseen?

Remember the disciple Thomas, the "doubter"? After the resurrection he said he would not believe in the Lord's resurrection unless he could see the Savior's wounds and touch them. Jesus complied with his wishes but He was hurt by the man's lack of faith. He pronounced a wonderful blessing that I like to claim and I invite you to claim. "Blessed are those who believe but have not seen." Blessed are those who believe even though they don't understand everything!

People often talk about "getting their head around" some concept or idea or doctrine that is difficult to understand. A lot of energy goes into that. I think we should all be more concerned about "getting our hearts around" Someone! Beliefs are useful only as stepping stones to a higher order of spirituality that comes through knowing, surrendering, and connecting. The mind is not the final or best place where we relate to God. It is only when we go beyond and behind mind, to heart and soul that we can truly become one with the Father. And soul is indeed a concept that is intellectually indefinable. Soul is beyond logic, beyond definition. But it is the center of us, it is what makes us more than anything else, made in the image of God. It is the place where we are truly "I am", the little I am, that is the reflection of the great I am. "Thus does God make individual beings, Souls, Identical Souls of the sparks of his own essence." wrote John Keats in *Letters*. We must never forget, *"I am, because He is"!*

Soul is precisely the place where we connect intimately with God. It is the new temple of the Holy Spirit, the tabernacle of God on earth. God does not hang out in sanctuaries in the desert or on the temple mount in Jerusalem any more! Since the cross, He has made you and me His dwelling place! *By surrendering, by emptying yourself, you become the space where God dwells!* Stop reading for just a moment. Still yourself. Contemplate the incredible truth that God is living in you! The surrender of the heart, the soul, is the only path to true intimacy with our Abba. It is the only way to God's presence within, to true God-connection, God-consciousness and God awareness. If you have lost touch with your heart, you are unconscious. It is in the heart that God resides. There is a saying: "unconscious people are trapped in their ego". You can not be self-centered, self-focused, ego-centric and be God-conscious. Here's the thing...*the ego cannot survive surrender!* No man can have two masters. There is room for only one on the throne of your life. With the most important choice you will ever make, you get to choose who it shall be.

BEWARE OF RUTHLESS CERTAINTY

Some religions have been embarrassed when their doctrines proved over time to be faulty and unsustainable. Take the case of the Mormon Church which had to turn away from its own doctrine of polygamy and eventually (but not until 1978) its position that black people were not worthy to be a part of the church priesthood because they were "cursed by God." Spencer Kimball, president of the church at the time, the man who had the "vision" authorizing the full acceptance of blacks into the church reported that he had to argue with God and struggle with God to get Him to finally agree to such a shocking concession! (Conveniently, it came just in time to prevent the U.S. Government from lifting the church's tax free status because of its racist teaching.)

Not long ago the Anglican Church changed its belief on hell. It had previously taught that hell went on forever and ever as a place of fiery torment for all lost souls. Now, its position has changed. The church now says that the wicked are totally annihilated. It says that the doctrine of eternal torment it previously held, "makes God into a sadistic monster."

Presently, the Catholic Church is struggling with its teaching on limbo. Limbo is a doctrine that states that any baby who dies before it is baptized can never go to heaven. Instead the church declared that the child would be sent to an in-between place, sort of a spiritual parking lot, where he or she would live forever but be denied most of the benefits of heaven, including not being able to experience the presence of God or of their parents. This non-biblical teaching has caused incredible amounts of heartache, grief and guilt for bereaved Catholic parents.

Struggling to find a way to deal with the anguish the teaching of limbo has caused, spokesman for the church, Archbishop Forte said, one can "set aside certain formulations without compromising the faith of the Church in any way." He noted that the concept of limbo had "never been defined by the Church, although it was a very common teaching." In this case, the archbishop said, the International Theological Commission is reaching the conclusion that the concept of Limbo is "neither essential nor necessary."

Before he became Pope, Joseph Cardinal Ratzinger had called this doctrine "problematic." It is now expected that he will approve a document which discards the doctrine of limbo and allows un-baptized babies full access to heaven! Yes, it can be problematic for someone to base their faith solely on church doctrine. It is also a reminder of the great bit of advice extrapolated from Thoreau: Question authority. Always question all authority. Especially question all religious authority!

THE GIANT LEAP FROM BELEIVNG TO KNOWING

Once the esteemed psychiatrist Carl Jung was asked, "Do you believe in God?" He quickly replied, "No. I don't believe in God, I know there is a God." Moving from belief to knowing, from religion to personal spirituality, from doctrine to connection, from second-hand religion (your parent's, your pastor's or your church's) to first-hand spirituality (your own) is the kind of paradigm shift we are talking about here. We must all ask ourselves the question, "Have I taken the enormous spiritual step of moving from religious beliefs to personal faith, to knowing?" "Have I passed definitely from belief to experience?" It is the filling of the Spirit that we need so critically to make God a living, burning presence in our life instead of a mere intellectual concept. This experience alone makes God a living reality in our personal experience instead of a theological perception.

The well-known pastor Tony Campolo, put it this way, "You can know all about God, but the question is, do you know God. You can have solid theology and be orthodox to the core, but have you experienced God in your own life?" "All of us" he says, "are looking for transcendence in the midst of the mundane." 5.

There has been, in some minds, the sadly mistaken assumption that believing correct doctrines and committing oneself to a certain church were automatically synonymous with spirituality. This is not true. Doctrines, beliefs can be one of the false boundaries which are used to limit oneself spiritually. Kathleen Norris, in her New York Times best-seller, *Amazing Grace*, says that she finally came to mature enough spiritually to understand that her faith was, "Not a list of "things I believe," but the continual process of learning (and re-learning) what it means to love God, my neighbor, and myself" 6.

For many, the soundness and purity of their theology has been the center of their religious experience. They have worn their denominationalism and the infallibility of their doctrines like an unholy badge. When will we ever understand that we do not have all "the truth," we do not have all the answers but we can have Him!

Brennan Manning says that Jesus lanced the infection of religious belief that had lost its soul and did not even know it. He says that if our religion is based on laws, rules and obligations, we are living at a pre-Christian level. He speaks also for an all new spiritual paradigm when he says, "We are called by Jesus Christ into an intimate friendship in which one member is a human being and the other the eternal God." 7.

I am going to repeat them in this book again, because these are so simple and so essential. I call them the "three angel's messages" because they are such good news. There are really only three "doctrines" that matter for the Christian.

1. God is love.

2. Jesus saves.

3. The Holy Spirit wants to live out the love of God in you.

Everything else beyond that is commentary.

As someone has said, "It is almost impossible to overestimate the unimportance of most things." And I would hasten to add, especially most theological things.

Thomas Moore in his best-selling book, *Care of the Soul,* warns of religious people who go "warring against those who disagree, proselytizing for our own personal attachments rather than expressing our own soulfullness or taking narcissistic satisfactions in our beliefs rather than finding meaning and pleasure in spirituality that is available to everyone."8.

It is a very great struggle for some to finally grasp the concept that John Wesley had so succinctly put in words three-hundred years ago: "Orthodoxy...is a very slender part of religion."

Ask yourself; are you a truth keeper or a truth seeker? True spirituality is not about an unbending allegiance to a narrow orthodoxy.

Religious knowledge is no less infallible than any other form of human wisdom. Indeed it is perhaps the most fallible! Most of us Christians are not nearly humble enough about this. One of the best theology professors I know always made this statement to his students at the end of each semester: "Thank you for listening and studying. Remember, half of what I've taught you is wrong. The trouble is, I don't know which half!

Lisa Miller, a *Newsweek* columnist writes, "What's dangerous about the world today is not belief in God—or secularism or unbelief ... but ruthless certainty." 9.

I am not a big Jean Paul Sartre fan, but he wrote something I find striking: "The rational man groans as he gropes for the truth; he knows that his reasoning is no more than tentative, that other considerations may supervene to cast doubt on it. . . . Only a strong emotional bias can give a lightning-like certainty;"

Most non-Christians find the inflexible certainty of some believers to be a real turn off. Sadly, it can be a factor in keeping people away from a relationship with God. When the singer Sting was asked about his belief in God, he said, "I'm essentially agnostic. I don't have a problem with God. I have a problem with religion. I have chosen to live my life without the certainties of religious faith. I think they're dangerous."10.

Our egos thrive on the idea that we may know something or have some truth, especially some religious truth that no one else has. A. W. Tozer said, "There is no pride so insidious and yet so powerful as the pride of orthodoxy."

The most brilliant living theologian is... the devil in hell! After millenniums of service by His side, Lucifer knows more about God than any human being ever has. The Bible says, "Thou believest that there is one God; thou doest well; the devils believe and tremble. (James 2:19, KJV)

It is a very great myth that the more religious knowledge you have, the closer you are to God. You could have all the knowledge in the Library of Congress in your head and still know nothing of God.

Brennan Manning writes:

For too long and too often along my journey, I have sought shelter in liturgies and cerebral Scripture studies. I have received knowledge without appreciation, facts without enthusiasm. Yet, when the scholarly investigations were over, I was struck by the insignificance of it all. It just didn't seem to matter. 11.

It was Manning who in his provocative way also said: "We can only shudder at the pain caused by cavalier Christian crusaders across the centuries in the name of orthodoxy."

The path to God is not through knowledge. The path to true spirituality, the path to God is through surrender of the heart! Only surrender can open the door to spiritual passion. That is as true in a relationship with God as it is in an intimate relationship with a husband or wife.

Once a man came to the Lord and asked him the question, "Teacher, what must I *do* to inherit eternal life?" Notice he did not ask, "What must I *believe?*" By acknowledging the legitimacy of the question and the way it was phrased, Jesus established that doing acts of love holds a place above doctrinal beliefs. As He elaborated on His answer, He made startlingly clear the inadequacy of correct theology and religious belief as qualifications for entrance into the kingdom of heaven. It is in Matthew 25:31-46 where He speaks of what will separate the sheep (those who get to enter the kingdom) from the goats (those who are left without). In the great judgment day, the decision of who is rewarded by God and who is not turns on just one point! The issue is: what have people done or neglected to do for the poor and the suffering? The writer Anne Lamott says that it seems to her when she reads this passage that we all might need a letter of recommendation from the poor in order to get into heaven! No questions on doctrine. No pop theology quiz! Just the simple question, "How have you shown your love to me by ministering to my needy children?"

Thomas Merton showed his grasp of the true place of theology when he said: "theology really happens in relations between people ... Because we love, God is present. When Jesus comes back, He is going to have just one question for you and me ... 'Have you been compassionate?'"

Merton wanted us to understand that every time we encounter another, we encounter Him. We are called to be Jesus to people. My friend Chuck Scriven says, "You are not meant to sit and marvel at the Jesus story. You are meant to *be* the next chapter, to *be* nothing less than the ongoing ministry of Christ on earth, the presence of Christ on earth." Think about it. Jesus didn't just send help! He didn't just send money! He came to this world as God "undercover"! He came in "under the radar" to a stable in Bethlehem. He came to be with us, to minister to us and serve us. He tells us that we are now, "the light of the world!" It is now up to us to show the world the truth about God! We are the instruments, the transparencies, through which God's grace is appearing, through which the Divine can manifest and express itself on earth. We have taken the place of Jesus to reveal the nature of the Father to people! To show them how He acts, how He thinks, how He loves! We now represent Christ to the lost! *We are to be the Christ! We are to be God's love-letter to the world!* Can you imagine it? God has chosen to operate in the world only as our personal consciousness of Him manifests His glory, His love and His light to us and through us! Your life and mine reveal the presence of God! We are, in fact, God bearers! "You are a child of God. Your playing small does not serve the world. ... We are all meant to shine, as children do. We are born to make manifest the glory of God that is within us". 12.

140

Steve Job's parents wanted him to have a religious upbringing so they took him to the Lutheran church most Sundays. When he was thirteen he became conscious of all the suffering of innocent children in the world and could not reconcile that with the image of God he had been taught. When his pastor could not provide answers to some moral questions that troubled him, he never went back to church. His spiritual quest continued on and off throughout his life however. Not long before he died, he said that religion was at its best when it emphasized spiritual experiences rather than dogma or doctrine. "The juice goes out of Christianity when it becomes too based on faith rather than on living like Jesus or seeing the world as Jesus saw it." 13.

Saint Francis of Assisi recognized the importance of love shown by action when he said, unforgettably, "Preach the Gospel at all times and when necessary use words."

Theologians attempt to explain the gospel. Evangelists proclaim the gospel. Nothing wrong with either of those professions, but the ultimate calling is to *live* the gospel in the power of the Spirit, to live God's love. To be Jesus to people. To be love to people. Can you believe it? *God has made Himself dependent on you and me to manifest Himself in the world!* People run around chasing apparitions of the virgin Mary in cloud formations and pieces of burnt toast; they look for proof of God in granite statutes with bleeding hands. They seek for proof that He is real in enthusiastic healing services or tongues speaking, forgetting that Jesus said, "an evil and adulterous generation seeks a sign." All the while, God is waiting for you, for me, to manifest Him in this world in the genuine way… by simply living His love. Who knew! People, His Spirit-filled children, the ultimate manifestation of God in the world today! We simply must remember who we are to be to one another; that we *are* one another.

Christianity in a nutshell; we serve God by serving others. Is your life focused around self-centered ego-driven ambition or loving service? Dr. Albert Schweitzer, a pastor, theologian, philosopher and medical doctor, a man who forsook the comforts and wealth of European culture and sacrificed a large portion of his life serving the medical needs of very needy, primitive people in

141

the jungles of the Congo, said, "The only really happy people are those who have learned how to serve." The Master said, "Whoever wants to be great must become a servant" (Mark 10:34). Thus in the judgment, the Father will not be looking to see how many people you have serving you, but how many people you have served. "If, as my representative, you give even a cup of cold water to a little child, you will surely be rewarded." (Matthew. 10:42 Living Bible). In a wonderfully concise summary of His mission says, the Bible says of Jesus, "he went about doing good." Most people today are engrossed with just "going about."

FOOTNOTES CHAPTER 9

1. Covey, Stephen, *The Seven Habits of Highly Effective People.* (Simon & Schuster, New York: 1989) p.121.

2. Issacson, Walter, *Steve Jobs.* (Simon and Schuster, New York: 2011)

3. Goldsmith, Joel, *The Thunder of Silence.* (Harper San Francisco, 1961) p.71.

4. Hornberger, Jim, *Come Walk with Me.* (Pacific Press, Nampa Id, 2010) p.84.

5. Campolo, Tony, *Newsweek,* August 29, 2005 p.50.

6. Norris, Kathleen, *Amazing Grace.* (Riverhead Books, New York: 1998) p.2.

7. Manning, Brennan, *The Signature of Jesus.* (Multnomah Books, 1996) p.163.

8. Moore, Thomas, *Care of the Soul.* (Harper Collins, New York: 1992).

9. *Newsweek,* December 31, 2007, p. 89.

10. Time November 21, 2011 p. 64.

11. Manning, Brennan, *Abba's Child.* (Navpress, Colorado Springs: 1994), p.58.

12. William, Marianne, *A Course in Weight Loss.* (Hay House, Carlsbad, California: 2010) p.218

13. Issacson, *Ibid.* p. 15

CHAPTER 10:

OH, OH! LOOK WHERE HE IS GOING WITH THIS!

I was being interviewed on a radio show to help promote a new book of mine a few months ago. This particular station was part of a network that covered a great portion of the Southern United States, the "Bible Belt." It was a show where listeners could call in and speak with whomever was on the air. Based on a chapter he had read in *Living in the Light*, the interviewer asked me if it were true that I believed that there would be people who would get to heaven who were not members of my church. I replied, "Jesus said, 'In my Father's house there are many mansions'. I think there will be some Baptist mansions in heaven, some Methodist mansions, and some Catholic mansions, and I think there may very well be some Muslim mansions and some Buddhist mansions and some atheist mansions." Well, that did it. The switchboard lit up like a Christmas tree. The lines were full of irate callers who were appalled at my statement implying that there could possibly be some people allowed to enter heaven who did not understand Christian doctrine.

For those who think that their denomination provides the only passport to heaven I would suggest a little dose of humility that comes from the story of a little girl who says to a little boy, "Are you a Presbyterian?" And he says, "No, we belong to another abomination!"

Since we are considering the problem of denominational exclusivity, the labels "Catholic" and "Protestant" are frequently thrown about judgmentally. Anthony de Mello, a Jesuit, tells the story of a man who went to his priest and said, "Father, I want you to say a Mass for my dog who just passed away." The priest was indignant. "We don't offer masses for dogs here. You will have to try that denomination down the street." Ask them to have a service for you." As the man was leaving, he said to the priest, "Too bad. I really loved that dog. I was planning to offer a million-dollar stipend for the Mass." And the priest said, "Wait a minute, you never told me your dog was a Catholic!"

After all, *church is not where we go, church is who we are*. Doctrine and denomination must never become more important than Jesus. Worship must never become more important than love.

WHO CAN BE SAVED?

Coming to understand that, according to Jesus in Matthew 25, the sole criteria of compassion and loving service to the poor and the unfortunate is the standard for entrance into the kingdom of heaven takes us inevitably toward another neglected and profound truth that fundamentalists absolutely do not want to acknowledge. It opens up access to the kingdom of heaven to those who may not believe the way you and I do or may not believe much at all. Astonishing. And humbling. So much for my old idea that no one could go to heaven unless they joined my church! Jesus said: "Other sheep I have which are not of this fold." In Romans, Paul quotes God as saying: "I will call them 'my people' who are not my people; and I will call her 'my loved one' who is not my loved one, and it will happen that in the very place where it was said to them, 'You are not my people,' they will be called 'sons of the living God'" (Romans 9: 25, 26).

Darren Morton has asked the question, "Is space so tight in heaven that God needs to be exclusive?" 1 It is not correct to assume that all those who have never heard the gospel, and all those who were born before Jesus came to the world will be lost. To take such a position only shows our ignorance and jugdgmentalness. Certainly, no one will be in heaven without benefiting from the incredible sacrifice that Jesus made. He is truly the door to eternal life for all. Yet, there will be those who benefit from His gift without ever having had the opportunity to hear His name or learn of His teachings or be baptized into His church. They will be those who no matter where they are from on the globe or what millennium they have lived in, have responded to the guidance of the Holy Spirit on their heart, leading them toward a life focused on kindness and on loving service to others.

The author of one of my favorite spiritual books, *The Desire of Ages*, wrote that the eternal destiny of all who stand before God:

"...will be determined by what they have done or have neglected to do for Him in the person of the poor and suffering... Those whom Christ commends in the judgment may have known little of theology, but they have cherished His principles. Through the influence of the divine Spirit they have been a blessing to those about them. Even among the heathen are those who have cherished the spirit of kindness... they are those who worship God ignorantly, those to whom the light is never brought by human instrumentality yet they will not perish. Though ignorant of the written law of God, they have heard His voice speaking to them in nature, and have done the things that the law required. Their works are evidence that the Holy Spirit has touched their hearts, and they are recognized as the children of God. 2.

On a more personal note, my mother was killed in the year 1944. She was 21 years old. Her favorite brother had already died while flying for the Royal Canadian Air Force. Her other brother, my uncle Jack, was flying as a tail-gunner in B-17's over Germany at the time. She must have really loved her brothers and her country and wanted desperately to serve in the incredible war effort that was going on. She was killed in an accident while she was in the process of training to fly bombers from Seattle's Boeing Field to Alaska where they would then be taken on to Siberia and the Russian Front. I was 18-months-old at the time, so sadly, I have no conscious memory of her but I was raised by a loving grandmother, her mother, who helped me develop a sense of what my mother was like as I grew up.

When I was six-years-old we joined a church for the first time. In those days, the church's teaching was very clear that you had to become a member of that particular organization if you wanted to get to heaven. We were taught that our goal in life was to "save" as many people as we could by getting them to become members of our church. In this way we would get "stars in our crowns." It was our responsibility to convert people to "the truth" and if we failed, their blood could be upon us eternally. As a young boy, I remember agonizing that my mother was surely going to be lost forever because she had not been a member of our church. I would never get to see her. This idea brought a great deal of anxiety and pain to my young heart.

Just a few months ago, I brought my youngest daughter to visit the grave of my mother for the first time. Vanessa is now as old as my mother was when she died.

145

From some pictures I have of my mother, yellowed now, it seems to me that my daughter looks very much like her grandmother did at her age. As we were standing by the grave together that day a powerful thought suddenly hit me. I may see my mother again one day after all! I realized that over the years, my beliefs have changed a great deal. I no longer accept the cultish concept that a person has to be a member of my particular church to be saved. I have managed to shake off some of my exclusivist righteous judgmentalism. The church has grown and matured too and no longer teaches such appalling cultic distortions either. Furthermore, I now understand that God with great wisdom and compassion will look at the hearts of those He decides to bring into His kingdom, that He is willing to open the doors of heaven to anyone who has responded to the Spirit's promptings toward a life of love and kindness and service, regardless of how much "truth" or doctrine they had a chance to understand.

STANDARDS AND TRADITIONS

Then there are those to whom their standards of behavior are all important. To them, their religion is all about how they behave and how others behave. They may focus obsessively on religious rules, strict standards regarding dress, diet, entertainment, jewelry and cosmetics. They may feel compelled to urge these standards on others. They do not understand that standards in society change over time, though moral principles do not. Their mistake is equating rules with moral principles. This is the same group who build their religious experience around church traditions. Jesus warned about this trap when he told a group of very religious people, "You have a fine way of setting aside the commands of God in order to observe your own traditions!" Mark 7:9 This penetrating remark was prompted when religious leaders, Pharisees and teachers of the law, criticized Jesus and His disciples for not living according to the "tradition of the elders" when it came to the ceremonial washing of hands before eating. Jesus was usually not one to respond to criticism, but this time He was all over the accusation. It must have been very

146

important to Him to set things straight. "He replied, 'Isaiah was right when he prophesied about you hypocrites; as it is written, these people honor me with their lips, but their hearts are far from me. They worship in vain; their teachings are but rules taught by men. You have let go of the commands of God and are holding on to the traditions of men." (Mark 7:6-8)

There is a wonderful old Buddhist saying, "Seek not to follow in the footsteps of the men of old; rather, seek what they sought." Are you letting religious tradition dictate how you live your life? Are you burdened with a load of unexamined, unquestioned authority and tradition? Do you see how this could be effectively blocking your personal connection to the Holy Spirit?

A distorted emphasis on rules sucks the life out of religious experience. It turns living flesh into dry bones. As if the rules of one's denomination aren't enough, some people make up their own list of religious rules that they beat themselves up over if they break them. "Thou shalt not do this, Thou shalt not do that," on and on and on. When they break one of these self-imposed rules many feel that they are cut off from God and suffer despair and discouragement. This is not Christianity, this is legalism. No Christian can lead a full spiritual life by obeying a set of rules outside of themselves. Your life is either going to be about legalism or liberty. The new paradigm is all about surrendering all notion of struggling to obey external laws and rules and allowing the experience of the filling of the Holy Spirit to write God's law of love in the heart. Abiding, not trying. Surrender, not struggle. That is the formula.

When I am giving a seminar in a church the focus is on the great and profound and beautiful truths such as the assurance of salvation, the character of God as shown in the life of Jesus, the cross, the coming of the kingdom into the heart of the believer right now and the assurance of the baptism of the Holy Spirit. Since I believe strongly in audience participation I will always open the floor for the sharing of experiences, ideas or questions. Inevitably there will be one or two persons in the crowd who want to talk about wearing wedding rings or going to movies or wearing makeup or dancing! I know how Jesus must have felt. This just drives me nuts! I want to holler at the person: Grow up! Get out of spiritual kindergarten! Get a life! I can understand why Paul said to some of the Corinthians, "My friends, stop thinking like children. Think like mature people. 1 Corinthians 14:20 *Contemporary English Version.* (Note: I try to be very patient and kind to people who want to focus on the non-essentials because I realize that I was once in the same place they are and God-alone knows how skewed my perspective still is in many areas! As Shakespeare said so famously, "Forebear to judge for we are sinners all.")

It is important for you and me to be clear about our own personal standards as the Holy Spirit leads us at our own pace toward a godly life. It is not our task to concern ourselves with someone else's standards or to hit them over the head with ours. That is just a big distraction that keeps people away from the deep truths of the gospel.

GURUS

Some religious people center their faith around an individual human person. For the world's more than one billion Catholics, it is the Pope. He is still considered the absolute head of the church, God's vicar, God's mouthpiece on earth, with the authority to make pronouncements regarding doctrines and behavior that are considered infallible by the true believers in his flock. Some religious types develop an even more dysfunctional, cultish connection to a pastor, teacher or guru of some sort.

On November 18, 1978, the world was shocked to learn that 918 people died in the largest mass murder/suicide in American history. The victims had followed their charismatic preacher, Jim Jones, to a jungle encampment in Guyana, South America. There the members of The People's Temple died after drinking a fruit punch he provided for them, laced with cyanide and tranquilizers. Jones, a former ordained Protestant pastor with the Disciples of Christ denomination, managed to create an atmosphere of religious persecution and paranoia and fear among his followers that led to the tragedy. He has become the poster-boy for the dangers of cults and cult leaders.

Vernon Howell was raised as a Seventh-day Adventist. He attended an Adventist high school. The Branch Davidians were an apocalyptic offshoot of the Seventh-day Adventist church. Howell joined the Davidians in 1981. He assumed control of the sect in 1986 and changed his name to David Koresh. He settled himself and his followers in a compound called Mount Carmel, ten miles outside of Waco, Texas. Koresh believed he had a unique last-day message from the book of Revelation to give to the world. Something about the seven seals. On April 19,1993, he died, along with 73 of his followers, 21 of them children in the Waco, Texas compound tragedy.

Of course there have been many others. The Heaven's Gate suicide cult in San Diego. There was the Bagwan Rajshneesh in Oregon. His followers tried to take over a whole county government. The more blatant examples that have been picked up by the media are just the tip of the iceberg. There are countless fanatical, cultish religious groups in America whose ideology may be just as radical and destructive as some of those we have mentioned but who have not yet acted it out or who have simply not been noticed by the media and come to public attention. There are many religious para-military groups in Idaho, Montana and in Oklahoma that call themselves Christian and are dedicated to opposing or even overthrowing the United States government. Most of them believe that African-Americans, Jews and Hispanics do not belong in this country. It appears that Timothy McVeigh may have been inspired and influenced by members of a right-wing "Christian" separatist group such as this as he planned the Oklahoma City bombing. The Bible shows great wisdom when it warns, "O put not your trust in princes, nor in any child of man; for there is no help in them." (Psalm 146)

Q&A:

Q. You seem to be trying to take away everything that is important to me... my church, my pastor, my beliefs, my standards, my relying on the Bible... .

A. Only in a state of emptiness can you be filled. I want you free of all religious and intellectual and emotional and social crutches. All the things you have mentioned are important in a person's spiritual life. Only when they are misused do they become dysfunctional or dangerous. None of them however is sufficient as a spiritual foundation. Only Jesus is. Only your personal connection with His living presence through the indwelling of the Holy Spirit is. Do not let the good distract you from the best. In the words of the old hymn: "On Christ the solid rock I stand, all other ground is sinking sand."

Q. The Bible says that no man comes to the Father except by Jesus. How dare you say that there will be people in heaven who have not heard of Jesus?

A. No one will get to heaven except through the sacrifice of our Lord. It was His death on the cross alone that allows anyone to enter the Kingdom. Even those who have never heard of Him, but who have nonetheless responded to the Holy Spirit's promptings in their heart. In spite of doctrinal ignorance, they have become people whose lives are all about unconditional love, compassion and service to others.

Q. You mean there could actually be Muslims and Buddhists in heaven?

A. Yes, quite a handful of them. And maybe a few atheists too! When you get to heaven you are going to be shocked, shocked, at who is there you did not expect to be and shocked at who you thought would be there but is not!

FOOTNOTES CHAPTER 10

1. *Spectrum* Magazine, Vol. 32, Issue 3, Summer 2004, p. 9.
2 White, Ellen G. *The Desire of Ages*. (Pacific Press Publishing Association, Nampa,   Idaho: 1898) p. 638.

CHAPTER 11:

A WHOLE NEW PARADIGM: SPIRITUAL DSL, THE TRUE FOUNDATION

"For no one can lay any foundation other than the one already laid, which is Jesus Christ."
1 Corinthians 3:11

One's personal relationship with Christ towers over every other consideration.
Brennan Manning

Our whole business therefore in this life is to restore to health the eye of the heart whereby God may be seen.
Saint Augustine

They say that now, thanks to computers, we live in the information age. That's fine, but what I am looking forward to is the inspiration age! This will come when more of us are living the inspired life; that is to say when more of us are living in-Spirit. Hold that thought. Back to computers for a moment. They are such a big part of our lives nowadays. Many people spend far more time with their computers than they do with another human being. They say you know that you are too involved with your computer if you are reading a book and you keep looking for the space bar to get to the next page! Or you get on an elevator and you double-click the button for the floor you want!

There are even "bumper stickers" for computers now. Ponder the wisdom of a few that show the complex emotional, behavioral and moral quandaries computers present us with:

Smash face on keyboard to continue.

Backup file not found. Press A to abort, C to continue, P to panic.

Thou shalt not covet thy neighbor's password nor his software nor any other digital thing that belongeth to thy neighbor.

Thou shalt not hack.

It was a great day when DSL came to our house. Some people who try to install it themselves say DSL means "Driven Slowly Looney" but it actually stands for Digital Subscriber Line. It allows a computer to stay continuously connected to the Internet at a very fast speed over an ordinary phone line. It also plugs into a router that sends a wireless signal all over your house so that many computers or other devices can connect to the Internet without wires. (Similar broadband services are available by cable, satellite or wireless phone service.) It really revolutionizes the way your computer works. It's like a whole new platform, a new paradigm of connectivity. It's two-way too. You can upload or download information very quickly. You are always on line, always plugged in!

WHAT IS YOUR FOUNDATION?

DSL got me to thinking about how we need a whole new paradigm spiritually, a revolutionary new foundation for our connection to God. Just to show you how old I am, my first computer could only take in data from an old cassette tape player! What a miracle it was when floppy drives became available! Now they are even so outdated most computers don't even use them anymore. Just what is your spiritual foundation anyway? Does it need an upgrade? Are you trying to work spiritually with version 2.0 when version 10.0 is now available and so much more effective?

A new service, a new kind of connection to God became available some time ago. Sadly, a lot of people have not heard of it. I am wondering if you have signed up for it? I am wondering if you are connected yet? It offers a whole new platform, a whole new foundation for your spiritual life. That's right. Version 10.0. The ultimate in connectivity! It's wireless too! You can use it wherever you go! Available since the cross! With it, you are always plugged in to the Divine… always on line with God! There is no lag time getting on the spiritual Internet. You are always connected! You can receive incoming calls while you are online! You can multitask and still stay in touch! It is the Holy

Spirit's two way information superhighway! I like to call it DSL. Direct Service to the Lord!

All right, all right: so you are not a techie. You may have chosen to lead a computer free life! Or maybe you have gotten the victory over your Blackberry. That's okay, you are still a practicing member of the human race! But maybe you are struggling to identify with my DSL analogy. So this verse from John 15 is for you. "I am the vine; you are the branches. If a man remains in me and I in him, he will bear much fruit; apart from me you can do nothing… as the Father has loved me, so have I loved you. Now remain in my love." (John 15:5,9) The vine and the branch… you can't get much tighter, much more intimate, and more dependent than that relationship! It means that by His Spirit, God wants to absolutely *permeate* every area of our lives and personalities. I live in America's premier grape-growing region. I am literally surrounded by vineyards. I love thinking about these precious words of Jesus every time I walk through or drive by the vineyards that surround my home.

How long can a branch live once it is removed from the vine? If the branch is separated from the vine, the result is lifelessness, corruption, death. If it stays connected the result is fruitfulness! The branch grows gorgeous fruit, not by struggling to do so, but by simply abiding in the vine! The life-force, the nutrients and energy contained in the sap rise up through the vine into the branch. The Holy Spirit is like that sap. It you stay connected to your Source, the Spirit will rise up in you and produce the fruits of love and joy and kindness in your life. "I am the vine, you are the branches." *Connection is everything.* The opposite of connection is separation. And separation is death. The baptism, the in-dwelling of the Holy Spirit, is all about connection. The ultimate spiritual connection. I like the helpful acronym CCC. It is the goal, the high calling of all Christians: Constant Conscious Communion. That is what "praying without ceasing," practicing the presence of God, is all about. Frank Laubach, founder of the Each One Teach One literacy program, committed himself to thinking about God, being consciously aware of God at least one second out of every minute!

The Holy Spirit is drawing you and me constantly toward an inner attentiveness to the Divine. He is teaching us to learn to *delight in the presence of God*: to become continually mindful of the Father so that we do not fail to sense His nearness and love. Once we surrender our ego and respond to the One knocking at the door of our heart we can let go of ourselves at the deepest level and move forward into the loving presence of the Father, right on into the kingdom of heaven! Now. Your life will begin to be taken over by love, by joy and peace and kindness and gentleness and self-control. Thus surrendered, we can not help but be continually drawn ever more and more toward the heavenly. Madame Guyon wrote: "... you will discover that God has a *magnetic* attracting quality. Your God is like a magnet! The Lord naturally draws you more and more toward Himself." 1.

THE NEW SPIRITUAL PARADIGM

The old religious paradigm just does not cut it any more. Where has it gotten us? I mean think about it. We know we are missing something because the Latter Rain has not yet fallen! The Lord has not returned yet! There is not nearly enough love and joy and peace in our lives and in our families and in our churches and in our community and in the world! That alone tells us we need to start doing something differently. God would like to have cleaned up this mess a long time ago! The fact that there is still so much missing in our lives and in the world gives us a kind of permission to search for a new spiritual paradigm.

A lot of us have been like the people Stephen Covey describes as struggling and working diligently to climb the ladder (in our case the religious ladder) but all the while we do not recognize that we have placed the ladder against the wrong wall! We are living with the illusion that what we are doing is pleasing to God, but the results leave a great big gap, a huge hole, a great emptiness in our hearts and lives! "To change the results, we need to change the paradigm." says Covey, in his best-selling book *First Things First*.2.

I want to suggest a whole new radical paradigm for Christianity. A paradigm shift is another name for a revolution or a reformation. This is beginning to happen in the church today. Believers are beginning to move from a doctrine-based theology to a spiritually-based connection. They are moving from information to inspiration. From truth to Spirit. From struggling to surrender. From knowledge to spiritual consciousness. From believing to knowing. I want you to have your ladder up against the right wall, a spiritual wall. Not a religious wall or a material wall or a money wall. Dietrich Bonhoeffor, must have had this perspective. While in his prison cell in Nazi Germany, waiting for his execution, he made a profound call for believers to move toward a "religionless Christianity."

Permission to speak freely? Can I talk to you as adults? The sad truth is that a lot of us have been doctrine-believing, Bible-studying, text-proofing, law-promoting, rule-keeping religionists. The ladder we have been struggling to climb has been against the wrong wall.

While having a structure of religious beliefs and studying the Scriptures and going to church can be helpful, none of these activities is sufficient. We need something radically different as our personal spiritual foundation. Outrageously different even. Folks, we need a whole new religious paradigm.

From religion to relationship

From law to grace

From belief to experience

From doctrine to devotion

From believing to knowing

From platonic religiosity to passionate spirituality

The questions that arise from the old religious paradigm would be like: "What should I believe?" or, "What is truth." In the new spiritual paradigm the questions become: "How can I experience the Holy Spirit?" "How can I become truth?" "How can I become love?"

Instead of basing our spiritual foundation on some outside source, whether it is our church or our beliefs or our standards or on a charismatic leader or even on the Bible itself, I would suggest that we need to do a daring reassessment of what is truly foundational for us on a deeply personal level. *I would like to see another reformation in Christianity which moves men and women from a faith-based not on doctrines or standards or denomination- but on a personal, intimate, moment-by-moment relationship with the living person of Jesus Christ through the in-dwelling presence of the Holy Spirit.* Why? Because nothing else is sufficient. Helpful, informative perhaps, but not sufficient. It fact, all else is a counterfeit if you are trying to use it as a spiritual foundation. Paul put it so simply. "For no one can lay any foundation other than the one already laid, which is Jesus Christ." (1 Corinthians 3:11) Jesus said that we should "love the Lord our God with all our heart and all our mind and all our soul." Here's the thing … the church has overemphasized theology and obedience and underemphasized friendship and relationship. Too often, our worship has been an intellectual exercise. The question really is, are you going to worship the idea of God with your intellect or the person of God with your heart? Are you willing to take the longest journey in the world? The one-foot-drop from your head to your heart? Richard Foster says we may: "…descend with the mind into the heart and live in quiet wonder and adoration and praise."3. But wait! There is another one foot drop! *This one from the heart to the hand!* This is all about the Spirit –filled Christian moving out into the world to become the compassionate hands of Jesus. It is all about the Spirit leading us to represent the Savior by focusing our life on doing acts of loving service to others.

THE TRUE FOUNDATION

"Jesus did not say that religion was the truth … or what people taught about Him was the truth, or that the Bible was the truth, or the church or … theological doctrine. "I" he said, "I am the truth."

Here, profoundly, simply and eloquently put is the very best description of what should be the foundation of your spiritual life and mine. "And this is life eternal, that they might know thee, the only true God, and Jesus Christ whom thou hast sent." (John 17:3 KJV) There you have it. Spirituality 101. But paradoxically, also spirituality version 10.0. The simplest, most basic spiritual truth is also the absolutely most profound!

In the Bible, the word "know" is the same word used for sexual intimacy. By using this kind of language, God is telling us that He does not want some Platonic, intellectual connection with us! He wants something more from us than to merely have us believe in Him like we believe in atoms and gravity. God longs for a *passionate* intimacy with us! He wants to know you and me in a very personal and direct way. There is this tendency for many church people to get uncomfortable when someone becomes spiritually passionate. They immediately want to normalize someone who becomes too radical or sacrificial. Calm them down. Mellow them out. Re-institutionalize them! Good church-goers can attend a football game and stand up and yell and holler and wave their arms for their favorite team, but hey, if someone shows a similar level of passion in church… call in the temple police! Guys, what if we had the kind of passion for God we had for the woman we first fell deeply in love with? Remember how painful it was when you had to be apart from her? How you spent every possible moment with her that you could? How eager you were to spend a fortune on a gift for her? How you thought about her constantly?

For each of us, there must come a time in our spiritual journey when traditional religious belief and practice are no longer adequate or satisfying. We must come to hear the call of a God who is holding out His hand to us, asking us to give up all our other lovers and attachments and come into intimate relationship with Him in a much more personal and passionate way.

The shocking truth is, God wants us to come into such intimacy with Him that through His Spirit we all become pregnant with the Christ child! *He wants His Jesus forming within the heart and soul of you and me, just as the Spirit formed Him physically in Mary!* "And in him you too are being built together to become a dwelling in which God lives by his Spirit" (Ephesians 2:22). "Don't you know that you yourselves are God's temple and that God's Spirit lives in you? (1 Corinthians 3:16). You see, you are invited to experience an incarnational event in yourself! Can you believe it? The incarnation

157

continues! In you! Jesus came to teach the world love. Now you get to do that. Jesus came to teach the world the truth about God. Now you are called to do that! Here's the thing. In the Old Testament, we are told about "Jehovah", "God Almighty" a very external and somewhat distant God. In the New Testament, along came a whole new dimension. "Immanuel" God with us! The very Son of God, incarnate in Jesus Christ, right here in our world. Then, miracle of miracles, there came the day of Pentecost, the fire fell, the Comforter came and now, God the Holy Spirit can be *in us!*

LIVING CHRISTS

One of the most powerful texts in the New Testament says simply and poignantly, "The Word became flesh and dwelt among us." Now, miracle of miracles, the Word wants to become flesh in you! By the power and wonderful presence of the indwelling Holy Spirit, your hands are to do the work of God. Your smile, your face is to come to reflect the benevolent face of Jesus, full of kindness and compassion! We are, as C.S. Lewis so succinctly stated, "to become 'little christs'."

"Be ye partakers of Divinity", the Scripture alluringly invites. When this incredible invitation is accepted, and this experience becomes a living reality for you and me, we can truly say with Paul, "I no longer live, but Christ lives in me" (Galatians 2:20).

"The Spirit is the breath of Christ in us, the divine power of Christ active in us, the mysterious source of new vitality by which we are made aware that it is not we who live, but Christ who lives in us" (Galatians 2:20).

Indeed to live a spiritual life means to become living Christs. It is not enough to try to imitate Christ as much as possible; it is not enough to remind others of Jesus; it is not even enough to be inspired by the words and actions of Jesus Christ. No, the spiritual life presents us with a far more radical demand; to be living Christs here and now, in time and history. 3.

The greatest discovery you will ever make is that God lives in you!
Jesus came to teach us the powerful truth that we have the potential to embody God! Right now. Incredible! Do you get it? The Spirit wants you to be Jesus to people! That means that every time the phone rings, before you answer, you pray that you may be love, that you may be Jesus to the person you are about to speak to. It means that every time you meet someone you will pray for them. Yes, that means the UPS guy and the check-out clerk and even the policeman that stops you for talking on your cell! Doing these things blesses you immeasurably too because they are portals to God's presence that help you stay closely connected with Him throughout the day. Every single contact you have with a person becomes a God connection! You are called to be an agent of the sacred in this world, in this place and time!

Many years ago a missionary to China visited an obscure village in the interior of that vast land and began to tell the people about Jesus --- how He went about doing good, how He suffered because others suffered, how He made the burden of others His own.

As the villagers listened, their faces lighted up. "We know him! We know him!" they cried eagerly. "He has been here. He used to live among us. He is buried in our cemetery."

Amazed, the missionary asked, "Show me where he is buried." So they took him to their cemetery and pointed to a tombstone on which appeared the name of a Christian physician whom the outside world had forgotten. Henry Scougal said it so well, "The throbbing heart of the church is the life of God in the soul of man."

There is simply no substitute for the Spirit's filling as the foundation of our personal spirituality. I wrote this book you are reading about the baptism of the Holy Spirit for only one reason … the baptism of the Spirit is the foundation of the drastic new spiritual paradigm we need because it is the filling of the Holy Spirit that brings us into intimacy with the Father! That is the most valuable gift the Spirit gives us. "I keep asking that the God of our Lord Jesus Christ, the glorious Father, may give you the Spirit of wisdom and revelation, *so that you may know Him better*" (Ephesians 1:17 emphasis supplied). How dare anyone say the baptism of the Spirit is primarily about tongues! It is not about tongues or exorcisms or even healings. It is about intimacy! Intimacy with our Abba. Taking on His nature. Embodying His presence in our flesh and blood!

CONSCIOUSNESS RISING

Can you agree with me that one of the greatest works of the Spirit is to enhance consciousness? God consciousness. The writer of Acts understood the essence of God consciousness. "In Him we live and move and have our being (Acts 17:28). The baptism of the Spirit causes God to become a conscious reality, a living presence in our lives. As a result of this we feel His closeness personally as we never could before. We enter into a sacred, moment-by-moment relationship with Him. The filling of the Spirit is the impartation of the very life of Christ into us. A great Christian man wrote a remarkable book in 1928. It was called *The Coming of the Comforter*. In it, Leroy Froom said beautifully and simply: "There are three outstanding things that the fullness of the Spirit brings: The presence of Christ; the likeness of Christ; and the power of Christ." 5. That really says it all.

When will we ever get it? Christianity is not a religion. It is a relationship. If practicing the living presence of Jesus in us by His Spirit becomes the ground of our being, the great central purpose and theme of our life, then God can empower and transform us. It could then be said of us as it was of a certain man in the past, "The Spirit of the Lord will come upon you in power ... and you will be changed into a different person." (1 Samuel 10:6)

You see, the baptism of the Spirit not only regenerates, it renews! It is one thing for the Lord to redeem us and reform us, thank God for that, but we don't have to stop there! He also, through the second blessing of the indwelling Spirit, is willing to transform us. It is always by love that He does His incredible work in us. One of my favorite texts becomes a living reality for the Spirit-filled Christian. "Think of the love the Father has lavished on us, by letting us be called God's children; and that is what we are." (1 John 3:1) Oh, how I like that word lavished!

Do you think this new paradigm, this experience of intimacy I keep talking about is just some sugar-coated, airy-fairy, blissful, emotion-saturated

New Age, meditative state where you become so heavenly minded you are not earthly good? Think again. Of course you will be blessed at some point with some wonderful feelings when you come closer to God. Enjoy them. Delight in them. But never forget, the Spirit-filled life comes from the set of your will, from the power of your personal choice and it is primarily a call to action! It is a call to service. It was after Jesus was baptized with the Spirit that He went to work! He returned to Galilee "in the power of the Spirit" and began preaching and teaching and healing and casting out demons. "He went about doing good."

Through focusing on the new paradigm of intimate Spirit-filled connection with the Father, our lives can become the simple outworking of His will for us. We come to know our purpose. We come to understand that our life is about mission. We finally get it that we are all priests! Every Christian is a minister! It brings us as nothing else can to the bottom-line of Christianity: doing acts of unconditionally loving service for others. It allows us to make the quantum leap in life from the bondage of self-preoccupation to the true freedom of self-forgetfulness.

Q&A:

Q. You said you live in a grape-growing region. Do you drink wine?

A. Father, forgive them for they know not what they ask!

Full disclosure requires that I must tell you I once used the Clinton technique: I have tasted but I didn't swallow! No, relax, as far as I am concerned wine is just spoiled grape juice that makes you sleepy! I get in enough trouble in the church just talking about the Holy Spirit without being a wine-drinker! I sure love the non-spoiled grape juice though. It is the nectar of the gods. But since you brought up the subject … you have given me an excuse to quote a couple of my favorite wine texts, of which there are many in the Bible. "Do not get drunk on wine… instead be filled with the Spirit." (Ephesians 5:18, NIV)

We have put so much thought and energy into not drinking … when I was 10 years old the temperance secretary of the conference came around and got us kids to sign up our little pledge card not to ever drink alcohol. This was all fine and good, but what is deeply disappointing and frustrating to me, is that while we were so anti-alcohol, we forgot the other half of that verse, an actual command, "Be filled with the Spirit". I wish that when I was 10 years old someone would have put at least as much energy into teaching me about the Holy Spirit as they did teaching about the dangers of alcohol, drugs and tobacco. We had *Listen* magazine, which was great, but why not a magazine on the Holy Spirit for teens? The Holy Spirit is for kids too! "In the last days, God says, I will pour out my Spirit on all people. Your sons and daughters will prophesy, your young men will see visions" (Acts 2:17).

On the day of Pentecost, when the disciples were baptized with the Spirit, they became so exuberant and expressive, that people who were watching "made fun of them and said 'they have had too much wine.'" Peter was quick to correct this misconception. "Fellow Jews, let me explain … these men are not drunk as you suppose." Then he went on to explain that instead, the believers had been filled with the Spirit. (Acts 2:13-15)

The well-known psychiatrist, Carl Jung, astutely understood a connection between a craving for alcohol and a need for the spiritual. He wrote, "Alcohol in Latin is '*spiritus*', and you use the same word for the highest religious experience as well as for the most depraving poison. The helpful formula therefore is: *spiritus contra spiritum*". 6.

Do you understand that the Holy Spirit is offering to make you God intoxicated!? We can scarcely imagine the joy of such. In his amazing little book, *Letter by a Modern Mystic*, Frank Laubach speaks of experiencing "the electric ecstasy of God."

If we let the Spirit fill in the empty places in our lives, we won't need to try to stuff those empty, lonely spots with alcohol or drugs or money or busyness or misuse of food or sex. We will be filled up with something, with Someone, so much more wonderful! So thanks after all for asking about my "drinking habits" because it gave me a chance to expound!

FOOTNOTES CHAPTER 11:

1. Guyon, Madam*Experiencing the Depths*. p. 53

2. Covey, Stephen, Merrill, A. Roger, Merrill, Rebecca R. *First Things First*. Simon and Schuster, New York,1994) p.200.

3. Foster, Richard J. *Prayer, Finding the Heart's True Home*. (Harper, San Francisco, 1992) p.71.

4. Nowen, Henri. *The Selfless Way of Christ*. (Orbis Books, Maryknoll, NY 2007) p.20.

5. Froom, Leroy E. *The Coming of the Comforter*. (Review and Herald Publishing,   Washington DC, 1928) p.181.

6. Jung, C.G., letter to Bill W. *AA Grapevine*, 1968 p. 12.

7.   .

8. CHAPTER 12:

GO AHEAD, PLUG IN AND DOWNLOAD!

Here I am! I stand at the door and knock.

If anyone hears my voice and opens the door,

I will come in and eat with him, and he with me.

Revelation 3:20

The only way we can make the paradigm switch from materialism and narcissism to spirituality and intimacy is by a moment-by-moment dependence on God. Think of it as being constantly online with God! Of course you have to be plugged in first. That is your part and mine. Simply making the decision to plug in! There is an old spiritual saying, "the sunshine can not get in if the shutters are closed!" "Behold I stand at the door and knock. If any man open to me... ." Go ahead. Make your day! Stick your spiritual Ethernet or USB cable into the great socket of heaven! Or if that is too technologically complex a task, reach out and turn that door handle! Think of a sailing ship about to embark on an adventuresome voyage. Before you can get away from the dock you have to do two things... loose the lines that are holding you and *put up the sails!* Only when you put up the sails can the wind empower you! The wind of the Spirit is blowing today. It has the power to move you quickly along on your journey toward the kingdom. But *you* must put up the sails. That is your part.

Open the door to intimacy! That is your part. That is what you can do. A simple choice. A decision. "Taste and see," "Ask... and the Spirit shall be given unto you." Imagine what is possible when you chose to have connection. You are linked with super DSL to the mind of the Almighty! You are connected, so you are able to instant message with the Father! Furthermore, anytime you need it, you can get a download from the Divine! Tempted do indulge yourself again in some ego-building and appealing but unnecessary possession or luxury? Download some wisdom, temperance, and unselfishness! Did you have a nasty argument with your spouse this morning? Download some forgiveness! Your teen's hairstyle driving you a little nuts today? Download some patience and perspective! "Sometimes you have to look very hard at a person and remember he's doing the best he can," said Ethel Thayer, in *On Golden Pond*

Most important of all, if we are linked up intimately with the Father, we may receive the best gift of all flowing down into our life: unconditional love for others. What is unconditional love? It is doing or saying what is for the best good of another person, regardless how you feel about them. It is an unfailing commitment to love other people who think and act in ways we find unacceptable. To just love them. Period. Regardless of their beliefs or behavior.

Oh, and if you have slipped away and let yourself be exposed to something dangerous or destructive that could hurt you or shut you down, your DSL line to God also comes with virus and spy ware protection that can root out and destroy any harmful thing that threatens to contaminate you! (Okay, let's push this a little further just for fun; the Devil is a malicious hacker who wants to take over control of your religious system and search and destroy all that is good and use it for his own evil purposes!)

If we have established our connection with Him, God does not leave us to struggle on our own. He can protect us and guide us. "God has given us his Spirit. That's why we don't think the same way that the people of this world think." 1 Corinthians 2:12 *Contemporary English Version*

TRUE SPIRITUAL FREEDOM

This new paradigm I am inviting you to switch to can be very challenging and very scary. Thinking outside the box, especially the traditional religious box can be threatening. It is very rewarding, but it can make you feel very much alone. "The spiritual man makes judgments about all things, *but himself is not subject to any man's judgment.* For who has known the mind of the Lord that he may instruct him? But we have the mind of Christ." 1 Corinthians 2:14-16 (emphasis supplied)

165

Here is another even scarier text for those who do not have absolute confidence in the ability of the Holy Spirit to lead them personally and directly: "But the anointing which you have received from Him abides in you, *and you do not need that anyone teach you*: but as the same anointing teach you concerning all things, and is true, and is not a lie, and just as it has taught you, you will abide in Him." (1 John 2:27) (emphasis supplied) Traditionally Christians have felt they should not dare to explore truth on their own. They think they need their priest or their pastor or theologians to do this for them and then to instruct them. The Bible on the other hand dares to inform you that if you are a person who abides in the Lord, the Spirit can instruct you personally and directly in the way of truth and in the things of God.

Are you really willing to be daring enough to trust the words of the Master when He promises you that when His Holy Spirit fills you, He is capable of leading you into progressive, startling, dynamic new truths *that may even be beyond those revealed in Scripture*? "When he, the Spirit of truth, comes he will guide you into all truth." (John 16:13) "Call to me and I will answer you, and show you great and mighty things, which you do not know." (Jeremiah 33:3)

Paul understood the profound implications of the Spirit revealing to us that which is far beyond what has been revealed by the prophets of the past. "No eye has seen, nor ear heard, no mind has conceived what God has prepared for those who love him but God has revealed it to us by his Spirit." (1 Corinthians 2:9) It has been the tendency of some expositors to equate this exciting passage with what we can expect to encounter in heaven. Not so. Please notice the words "*has revealed.*" These new wonders are here, available to us now!

Can you do it? Can you handle that kind of freedom? No question about it, it can be scary! There is an incredible freedom in Jesus Christ that we scarcely have begun to understand. It makes some people very edgy and uncomfortable. Legalists and fundamentalists especially. There may be those within your own church who would try to put you back under the law, under judgment, under fear, under religious slavery. Paul spoke of those within the church who were "false brothers" who "infiltrated our ranks to spy on the freedom we have in Christ Jesus and to make us slaves" Galatians 2:4.

Are you ready to let go of your spiritual timidity and take bold, decisive even dramatic steps in your personal spiritual growth? Are you willing to let go of the need to conform and fit in? Are you willing to resist the pressures of those who would have you deny the freedom you have in Jesus? Are you willing to think outside your, comfortable religious box? Can you dare to rely on the Holy Spirit to release you from the need to be free of other's judgments? It has been said that the greatest freedom of all is to be free of seeking the good opinion of others. Can you really let yourself go to such a unique and sometimes lonely place? Can you let go of your constant need for the validation of others? From concern about what they think of you? From your need to rely on others for your spiritual guidance and for the interpretation of what is truth? St. Augustine once said, "Love God and live as you please." This is a terrifying thought to the fundamentalist but a glorious passport to freedom in the Lord to the enlightened Christian.

You do not need your husband or your wife to validate you spiritually. You do not need your parents or your pastor or your friends or your church to validate you. Jesus validates you! Jesus is the validator-in-chief!

FEAR OF FREEDOM

Consider the story of the children of Israel as slaves in Egypt. They were held in what became the most demeaning and oppressive kind of slavery for over four-hundred years. Bondage became a way of life to them. Ruthless slave-masters extracted the maximum amount of toil they could get from them. Grandparents, parents, children, generation after generation knew nothing but a life of slavery. They continued to multiply so rapidly even in this atmosphere however that Pharaoh was threatened by their increasing numbers. He decreed that all their baby male children should be killed in order to keep the population in control. Then, everything changed incredibly quickly. Moses came on the scene, then the plagues. Pharaoh was convinced to release them. Talk about a dramatic paradigm shift! The whole population free at last! They began their journey to freedom and into the adventure of the great unknown. But it wasn't long before fear came in to haunt them. They were not very far into their liberating exodus before some actually began to think about returning to Egypt!

Can you believe it? They had been set free by God to go to the Promised Land, a land flowing with milk and honey, and land of freedom and prosperity. And yet, the doubts began to arise. The anxiety, the fear began to grow in their hearts. You see, for many of these people, slavery was their paradigm. Slavery had defined them. Their identity was that of slaves. They could not seem to let go of it and move toward a new awareness and understanding of themselves as liberated and free. Not long into their journey they rebelled against their liberator. The whole community of Israel spoke bitterly against Moses and Aaron. "Oh that we were back in Egypt. It would have been better if the Lord has killed us there! At least we had plenty to eat. But now you have brought us into this desert to starve us to death!" (Exodus 16:2-3)

"Why did you bring us out here to die in the wilderness? Weren't there enough graves for us in Egypt? Why did you make us leave? .Our Egyptian slavery was far better than dying out here in the wilderness!" (Exodus 14:11-12)

These people could not shake off their slave mentality. They could not be open to the whole new paradigm of freedom that lay before them. The uncertainty, the individual responsibility was just overwhelming to them. The security of the old ways had more power over them then this new incredible option that God was offering them. Sadly, because they lacked the courage to change and move ahead into greater light and opportunity, because they were caught up in conformity to the old way of thinking and of seeing themselves, many of them did die in the wilderness. The pressure to conform, especially to conform religiously can be extreme. Maurice Maeterlinck wrote, "Each progressive spirit is opposed by a thousand mediocre minds appointed to guard the past." The poet e.e. cummings understood the incredible pressure to step out beyond the bounds of the mediocre and the ordinary, to be true to one's own soul and one's own personal spiritual quest. He wrote, "To be nobody-but-yourself in a world which is doing its best, night and day, to make you everybody else means to fight the hardest battle which any human being can fight; and never stop fighting".

No one had to fight this battle harder than Jesus Christ. He was truly a stranger to the world. In a sense He was the ultimate loner, the ultimate individual. He was pressed so very hard to conform to the religious expectations of His day. Yet, with great courage, He stood fast and followed the unique new direction the Holy Spirit led Him in. As you learn to walk in the Spirit, I caution you to be aware that it may be those closest to you in your own family or in your own church who will put the greatest pressure on you to conform to the old accepted, comfortable ways.

Like the Israelites who were so afraid of change, there are many people who are not only made uncomfortable but are terribly threatened by the new life of freedom and promise, spiritual opportunity and adventure that comes from being baptized by the Spirit.

The hand of God ripped down the curtain secluding the ark of the covenant in the Holy of Holy chamber of the Jewish temple. Above the ark rested the burning fiery presence of the Shekinah glory, the earthly symbol of the Holy Spirit. The moment Christ died, the curtain was torn. The Holy Spirit was unleashed into the world. He was no longer confined but could begin His work of inspiring and liberating men and women everywhere. This incredible event and the day of Pentecost that followed shortly thereafter resulted in a spiritual paradigm shift. There was a whole new foundation available for a person's spiritual life: a personal, intimate, moment-by- moment connection with God through the indwelling of the Spirit.

Like the Israelites who were called out of Egypt however, there are many believers who resist the opportunity to make a quantum leap forward spiritually. The prospect of the new life guided by the Spirit within rather than an outer set of religious rules and doctrines is just too threatening to them. There are those comfortable, conforming Christians who insist on ignoring the stupendous fact of Pentecost and who insist on trying to mend the curtain God ripped and hang it back in place in order to keep the Holy Spirit confined and cocooned in a safe place where the freedom and adventure He offers is not a threat to their status quo! They choose to live in slavery to their fear-based, rule-based religion.

YOUR CELL DOOR IS UNLOCKED!

Today, the Spirit of God is moving in the land and in individual human hearts. He is calling people out of slavery. Slavery to fear. Slavery to materialism. Slavery to addiction. Slavery to selfishness. Slavery to egoism and narcissism. Slavery to religiosity. The gates of the prison have been opened but there are some who insist on staying in their cells because it is so familiar there and besides their husband or wife or parents or friends don't see any reason to leave! It is so comfortable there! They have decorated their cells so carefully, and besides, they have cable! But the Spirit keeps calling out, offering freedom, a whole new identity as cherished sons and daughters of God. He urges all to begin at once a journey toward the Promised Land. A land overflowing with love and joy and peace and connection and intimacy with the Father.

It is a journey, a great spiritual adventure. For some, it might mean moving beyond the Bible's literal precepts and words and stories to the greater principles God wants you to grasp for your relationship to Him and to others in today's world. You may be called to learn to separate religious fundamentalism and extremism from true personal spirituality. *For some, it may mean moving from a theology or belief-based religion into a relationship or intimacy-based spirituality.* It may mean moving from the Bible as your spiritual foundation to the filling of the Spirit as your spiritual foundation. R. A. Torrey puts it almost bluntly in his book, T*he Person & Work of the Holy Spirit.*

No amount of mere reading the written Word (in the Bible) and no amount of listening to man's testimony will ever bring us to a living knowledge of Christ. It is only when the Holy Spirit Himself takes the written Word and interprets it directly to our hearts that we really come to see and know Jesus as He is.1.

True Christianity is progressive. Revelation is progressive. David Larsen, a professor of religion at Loma Linda University, says that we should:

trace the direction in which the whole of Scripture is moving so that in our day we can travel even further down the same road. It is right to move beyond Scripture in the same direction but wrong to go against it. To be a Christian today is not the task of simply believing and doing what the ancients did. It is the adventure of plotting the trajectories of Scripture and doing all we can to advance them in our time. 2.

Dare to consider what Jesus meant when speaking of what would be possible through the Holy Spirit being able to indwell every believer after He returned to heaven. He said in a very exciting statement, "I tell you the truth, anyone who had faith in me will do what I have been doing. He will do even greater things than these, because I am going to the Father." (John 14:12) Many don't understand how this could possibly be so. How can you possibly top healing the blind, calming the storm, raising the dead? But you know what? You *can* do one truly remarkable thing Jesus could not. You can stand before your family, your neighbors, your church and the watching world and say, "I am a sinner saved by the grace of God! I once was lost, but now I am found! I once was bound but now I am free! The Spirit of the living God lives within me though I am less than perfect!" You see, Jesus could never give that kind of testimony that so resonates with and encourages other fallible human beings. But you can, and it is very powerful.

There is another way that you can be a part of "greater things" than Jesus was able to do. That is because, before the cross and the day of Pentecost, the Holy Spirit could not fully indwell men and women. Jesus' teachings, even accompanied by His physical presence in the world could only go so deep. There was a limitation on the hearts of His hearers. Now, thanks to His sending the gift of the Spirit of truth that "leads us into all truth," thanks to the Spirit, when invited, being able to enter deep down into the soul of the surrendered person, there is a new level of connection with God available that was not available before Pentecost. The previous limitation was not due to what Jesus could do or teach. It was because of the limitation of His hearers. Now that limitation has been removed by the work of Christ on our behalf and "greater things" can happen in the spiritual realm than when He was physically here. Note that He said these "greater things" could happen because He was "going to the Father." He told us that He was so eager to leave earth and go to the Father so that He could send the Spirit in all its fullness to us. That has made all the difference and allowed for us to be part of "greater things" that could not occur while He was here in the flesh.

If you accept the baptism of the Spirit, you will discover something very energizing and exciting. The Holy Spirit is always revealing something original and unique. If we don't block Him, if we do not get distracted, He will do this in each of our lives and in the church. In fact the Holy Spirit is absolutely ecstatic about making dynamic new things open up to us! He wants to show us things that will transcend our own thinking! "No eye has seen, no ear has heard, no mind has conceived, what God has prepared for those who love him but God has revealed it to us by his Spirit." (1 Corinthians 2:9,10) Note especially the word *has*. Most people think the above verse is talking about what it will be like in heaven in the future. Wrong. This incredible promise is for Spirit-filled Christians right now also! We have received "the Spirit who is from God, that we may understand what God has freely given us. This is what we speak, not in words taught us by human wisdom but in words taught by the Spirit, expressing spiritual truth in spiritual words. (1 Corinthians 2:12,13)

A religion accompanied by the Holy Spirit will never be dull or monotonous! Never trite or boring! The light and truth of God are always expanding. It did not stop with Moses. It did not stop with Elijah. It did not stop with David. It did not stop with Matthew or Luke or Paul. The Spirit of prophecy is not a dead gift! It is alive and well and available right now! With spiritual truth advancing like this, do you *really* want to be content with the religion of your grandparents? Is the religion of 1705 or 1844 or 1920 or 1999 what you want your religion today to be like? Do you realize that your spiritual life is to be formed far more by the Holy Spirit living within you than by your church or your parents or your culture? God wants to do "a new thing" in you! Pushing back spiritual frontiers can be challenging and scary. It is not always comfortable. It can get you in trouble, usually with the religious authorities. (See Matthew, Mark, Luke, and John.)

RELIGIOUS STAGNATION OR SPIRITUAL GROWTH?

Bottom line, do you want to be a part of the exciting progression of spiritual insight and truth or not? Or like some fundamentalists, do you want to lock yourself in a safe, rigid archaic structure. Do you want to practice the 3500 year-old religion of Deuteronomy and Exodus? Do you want your beliefs to be limited to some of Paul's 2100 year-old concepts of Christianity which as progressive and profound as most of them were, also included his acceptance of slavery, the de-valuing of marriage and the family and the inequality of women, as normal? Do you want to practice the 300-year-old fundamentalist religion of the Pilgrims many of whom insisted that God had called them to kill the pagan savages that inhabited the new world and take the land for Christianity. There is the famous lament we hear from Native Americans, that seems to ring all too true. "When the Europeans came, we had the land and they had the Bible. Now, we have the Bible and they have the land." Ah yes, the Pilgrims, who tried to establish their own brand of a theocracy in America. The Pilgrims whose religious convictions led them to try to root out the Devil from their midst by hanging or drowning "witches" most of whom were mentally ill young women or people who opposed the religious doctrines of the majority. The Nobel-Prize-winning American physicist Steven Weinberg said, "With or without it (religion), you'd have good people doing good things and evil people doing evil things. But for good people to do evil things, it takes religion." He was echoing a quote from the great thinker Blaise Pascal who wrote: "Men never do evil so completely and cheerfully as when they do it from religious conviction." Self-righteousness and judgmentalism are diseases of religion for example.

The Muslim faith is perhaps the most recent and frightening example of what can happen when a religion refuses to acknowledge the progression of spiritual truth. Since its founding in early 600 AD, with very few exceptions, it has rigidly locked itself into a fundamentalist stance, insisting on taking every word of the Koran literally. Instead of being open to the progression of truth and encouraging the individual's personal exploration of a connection with God and an exploration of truth for themselves, it has taught its adherents to rely on the interpretation of Scripture by (all male) *imams* and *ayatollahs*. This has resulted in a religion that has become stuck in a rigid, medieval mindset and has created the atmosphere where extremism and fanaticism have bred the terrorism that threatens the entire world today.

The Muslim faith needs nothing more than a reformation, the equivalent of the Protestant Reformation, to break it out of its chains of medieval rigidity. But we must not cast all our stones toward Mecca! Indeed, Islam's shortcomings should serve as a reminder to Christianity that it has been 500 years since its Reformation and that we are past due for another one of our own! Luther led us into a informational/doctrinal reformation of truth. We are now in need of an inspirational reformation of Spirit.

THE BEST GIFT AFTER THE CROSS

Jesus was so excited to be going to the Father because that meant He could send us the Holy Spirit. "I will ask the Father, and he will give you another counselor to be with you forever, the Spirit of truth. The world cannot accept him, because it neither sees him nor knows him. But you know him for he lives with you and will be in you." (John 16-18) *From with you to in you!* Now there is a paradigm shift of the first magnitude!

You may have to be willing to take up the dangerous and uncomfortable task of truly "working out your own salvation with fear and trembling" as you let go of some of the old religious crutches you have leaned on through the years. *Here is one of the key points of this book, one which will give some of you readers fits: to put it bluntly, as important as it is, the Bible can never be your spiritual foundation. It can never be allowed to become a substitute for the intimate connection with Jesus through the Spirit being in you which can lead you to your own unique relationship with God and to the larger principles that come from a personal connection with the Lord.*

DECLARING SPIRITUAL INDEPENDENCE

Do you understand that much of your religious thinking and belief comes from parental and religious programming? Most of your religion was planted in you at a very early age by the beliefs, words and behaviors of your parents. For better or worse. In some ways you may have much to be grateful for what was given you. In some cases you may have been harmed or handicapped spiritually by what was given to you. Your parents may have been doing the best they knew how, yet you may need to let go of some things they taught you or lived out before you that were distorted, dysfunctional or inadequate. The whole point is, you are now free! The Spirit-filled life sets you free and gives you permission to release yourself from any of the old beliefs and behaviors that no longer serve you well. *Now the time has come for you to be a spiritual grown-up.* You are ready for a whole new spiritual paradigm. Your paradigm. A whole new spiritual operating system. It is time to restart and reboot your spiritual life!

In a sense, and I know you will think this is dangerous, but you have been freed to make up your own kind of religion, or to say it better, your own kind of personal spirituality. In fact, it may be your greatest challenge and responsibility to do this now at this point in your life. How exciting! For some of you, this may mean having the courage to look beyond the religion that has been part of your life for years. *Time* magazine recently reported a new trend. Not a few have found that their traditional church does not meet their deeper needs and they are:

turning away from organized religion and yet seeking rich if unorthodox ways to build spiritual lives. The fastest growing religions group in the U.S. is the category of people who say they have no religious affiliation. Sometime called "the nones" by social scientists, their number have more than doubled since 1990; major surveys put them at 16% of the population. 3.

The article goes on to make clear that many of those who have given up on "organized religion" have not given up on faith. The hunger for spiritual connection and community is still very real for them. An example is a group who meet every Sunday and calls itself "Not Church". They are people who have given up on traditional religious institutions. Yet, when they meet they still look somewhat like a congregation. They pray, they talk about spiritual things, they deliver food when someone is sick and serve the poor.

Most of those who have decided to let go of religion do not feel they are rejecting God, but instead are rejecting their traditional churches for being rigid and dogmatic. They are looking for something more; something more personal and fulfilling. They could be called "post-denominational", but not "post-spiritual." Many of them are part of the emerging church movement to "take religion away from musty pews and fierce theological fights by creating small worship communities that often meet in member's homes according to the article.

No, don't worry, I am not recommending that you bail out of your church. Better I think that you stay and light a candle. Bloom where you are planted. After all, a church is definitely *not* a building. Church is not a denomination. Church is not where we go. Church is who we are. In its finest sense, church is a family, a group of people loving and helping each other in this difficult world, helping each other toward the Kingdom. That being said, sometimes in therapy we find that a client is in a job or a church or a relationship that is just so extremely dysfunctional that the only way for them to continue to survive and flourish and grow is to leave.

The real issue for most of us however is this; *are you willing to let go of some of that comfortable religious co-dependence you have had for so many years with your parent's beliefs or your church, or your doctrines, or your religious traditions and standards that may be taking up a lot of your thought and energy and begin to center your spiritual life and energy on practicing the Presence of Jesus in your life through the Spirit's filling you? Are you willing to focus on having the mind of Christ in you?* Are you as willing to put as much energy into that as you are attending church or reading the Scriptures? Are you willing to give up your reliance on the purity of your doctrines to become a Christian mystic? Can you handle a spirituality based as much on relationship as revelation? As much on devotion as doctrine? As much on connection as catechism? Are you willing to take the responsibility of self-managing your

176

spiritual life? Do you understand just how totally responsible you are for your own spiritual growth and development? Can you handle breaking from the crowd, even your religious crowd, from the familiar, the comfortable? Can you dare to trust yourself, surrender yourself to just your moment-by-moment connection to God? Can you come to realize that a life lived in the Spirit gives you this kind of astounding truth and insight and daring freedom? Are you really ready to take the risks that come with this kind of amazing spiritual freedom? Can you trust yourself enough to the Spirit to accept this incredible spiritual independence?

Shockingly, living in Spirit brings freedom from rules and traditions. However, it does not destroy the law, it transcends it! If a person does not have the Spirit, they will tend to cling to law, religious rules and traditions. They will be carrying a huge burden around on their back everywhere they go. "Yes, Jesus said to take up our cross and follow Him," they declare mournfully. Guess what. When Jesus said that, He wasn't talking about carrying the thing around for the rest of your life! He didn't! Pastor Kris Vallotton says: "We are meant to take up our cross and follow Jesus to the baptismal tank, where we identify with Him in His death. We are supposed to enter the death chamber of baptism with a cross and exit with a crown. 4.

Once they receive the Spirit, believers will move into a new freedom, lightness and joy. The burden will be lifted. The struggle will be over. Law will no longer be central in their life. Grace and love will be central and with these great gifts in their hearts, they will be able to keep the purpose and intent of the law much more fully than before. In that sense, to the Spirit-filled person, external laws, rules and traditions become irrelevant. "The law came through Moses, but grace and truth through Jesus Christ," proclaim the scriptures.

HOLY SPIRIT, SOURCE OF LOVE

When a person adjusts from rule-based thinking to a heart-based attitude, centered around oneness with the Father through the indwelling presence of the Spirit, his or her life will be transformed. Look at it this way:

177

Jesus did not need any external rules to constantly act in the most loving and compassionate way. He was love. You and I can become love too. "The love of God is shed abroad in our hearts, by the Holy Spirit, which is given unto us." (Romans 5:5) We simply must become the love that we want to see in the world. But we can only do it through the gift of the indwelling Spirit. This is so essential because unconditional love is the very power and Presence of God alive on earth. "God is love" is the most important and foundational truth in the universe. Without it, nothing else is relevant, nothing else matters. Little wonder that Paul Tillich could say that this kind of God is the "infinite and inexhaustible ground of all being." Aren't you and I so blessed to have at the center of our religion, the center of our spiritual lives, the incredible concept, the incredible truth, the incredible experience that God is love! Oh, the wonder of it! The sheer beauty of it! The sheer joy of it! How exciting it is that we can best worship a God who is love by daring to love others extravagantly, wastefully abundantly and unconditionally! Our religion is love! We are quite simply called to be God's love in this world. This is how we live out the meaning of God. This is how we reveal His character to those who often misunderstand Him. The beloved disciple said it clearest and best of all: "God is love, and whoever abides in love, abides in God (1 John 4:16).

But wait, here is the thing … you and I can't even love our own wives or husbands and children well enough, let alone our neighbor who irritates us or our boss who makes us a little crazy every day! We can never muster enough love out of ourselves in spite of our best efforts and our best intentions. But thank God, He has given us an abundant supply in His Spirit. *To put it simply, we seek the filling of the Holy Spirit so that we may become more loving. So that, in fact we may become love.* Along with Romans 5:5 there is another text in the Scriptures that reveals so splendidly that the Holy Spirit is the source of love, that I am simply compelled to share it with you right now. It is so eloquent that I am not even going to comment on it. Please read it slowly and prayerfully with an open heart and let the Spirit touch you as you do.

I pray that out of his glorious riches he may strengthen you with power through his Spirit in your inner being, so that Christ may dwell in our hearts through faith. And I pray that you, being rooted and established in love, may have power, together with all the saints, to grasp how wide and long and high and deep is the love of Christ, and to know this love that surpasses knowledge— that you may be filled to the measure of all the fullness of God. (Ephesians 3:16-19)

That is one absolutely incredible text! Stop! Go back. Read it again, slowly, with your heart. It is telling us that you and I have access to a virtual spiritual gold mine! We have an incredible source of love that lays far beyond every human boundary. A source of love that is inexhaustible!

Are you willing to relinquish the rites and traditions that may have been part of your family or your denomination for generations if they are holding you back from your personal spiritual growth? These rules often produce separation and enmity from other Christians. Are you willing to acknowledge that the religion of your grandparents does not have to limit your spiritual growth and heritage? Do you realize how progressive spiritual truth is? Think about it. In the second decade of the 21st century, do you really want to be content with the level of spirituality and the religion your church practiced in 1844 or 1915 or 1975?

THE END OF NARCISSISM

There is an old saying that goes, "When man discovered the mirror, he began to lose his soul." Sin in its greater meaning is another word for selfishness, self-centeredness, ego-centeredness. Let's face the truth folks, *selfishness is our default position!* The average person goes through all day, every day, all caught up in themselves. We are, all of us, addicted to ourselves.

Some people think the opposite of love is hate. Not so. The true opposite of love is selfishness. The best definition of sin I know is when the Bible says, "we have each turned to his own way." Sin is not usually some atrocious evil as often as it is the far more subtle practice of putting one's self and one's own interest ahead of a relationship with God, ahead of service to others. *Evil is always a failure to love.* There is no greater and more deadly addiction than self-addiction. No drug has more power than the drug of self!

In the movie *Nine*, the devastated wife poignantly says to the selfish, thoughtless, philandering husband, "You are just an appetite." The Scriptures speak of people "whose god is their belly." Check this out: Jesus promised that out of the belly (read heart) of the Spirit-filled Christian will flow "rivers of living water" to nourish and sustain others. What a contrast! In his way-cool book *Blue like Jazz*, author Donald Miller talks about coming finally to realize the extent of his intense selfishness. "I was addicted to myself. All I thought about was my self. The only thing I really cared about was my self. I had very little concept of love, altruism, or sacrifice. I discovered that my mind (read ego) is like a radio that picks up only one station, the one that plays me: KDON, *all Don, all the time."* 5.

The untamed, un-surrendered human ego is an incredibly destructive force that lurks in every person's heart. I am sorry to break the news to you, but your ego is a needy, greedy beast of a thing! It is absolutely enraged by the idea of surrender. It will fight and kick and scream and justify and manipulate in an incredible struggle to maintain its absolute power over your life. Remember, E G O stands for edging God out! *The ultimate challenging goal for the Christian is to grow toward ego unawareness!* By the leading of the Holy Spirit we may move from a paradigm of "it's all about me" to "it's all about Jesus." Paul really got this. He could report, "I no longer live, but Christ lives in me." (Galatians 2:20) "That in all things He may have the preeminence (Colossian 1:18).

Do you have any idea how terrifying it is to your ego to learn that you are thinking about surrendering your heart and soul fully to God? "No! Anything but that!" the tyrant screams. The ego, that sneaky wolverine-like beast that insists it has full possession and control over you and all you do resents anything that challenges its number-one position! Marianne Williamson says, "What is actually the birth of our spiritual identity feels to the ego like death. The ego, our small and separate sense of self, is an imposter personality. It is a false self. It resists our genuinely remembering God, because in the recognition of our oneness with Him lies the death of the ego..." 6.

God is able to create from nothing. Is it any wonder that He asks us to totally surrender, to become "nothing" so He can make us something? Chrysostom said, "To be another than I am I must abandon that I am." Our surrender must be complete. If we try to hang on to just one little bit of self or selfishness in some little remote corner of our lives that we think no one can see, then that little worm will spoil the entire fruit. I know, it is hard, terribly hard to die to self. But be of good cheer! The Holy Spirit will hand you over a big old spray can of ego-be-gone anytime you need it!

QUIT BLAMING THE DEVIL!

It really bothers me that a lot of Christians are always talking about the devil. When I go to church or a group fellowship meeting I hear a lot about the devil!   The devil did this and the devil did that, the devil is keeping the church form doing this and the devil is keeping the church from doing that. The devil tempted me to do this and the devil tempted me to do that. Just cut it out will you! "The devil made me do this or that" is about as credible an excuse as "the dog ate my homework" (or nowadays, "my computer crashed and I lost my homework"). The Scriptures say: "Each one is tempted when by his own evil desire (read ego) he is dragged away and enticed." Satan's power doesn't hold a candle to the raging power of your own egotiscial mind. It is "the enemy within" that always does the most hurtful damage.

When I look back over the sad record of the sins I have committed, over the trouble I have gotten into, over the many mistakes I have made, there is not one that I do not deserve the blame for. I cannot conscientiously blame the devil for them. Many of us give way too much press, way too much credibility to the devil. I hate to take away our best excuse for screwing up, but here's the deal with the devil. He was whipped at the cross! He is a defeated foe! Oh sure, he is still around for awhile until things get cleaned up, but *the devil has no power over you unless you give it to him!* He is not the main source of your temptations! You are! Your ego is!

By over-focusing on the devil, by making a super big deal out of spiritual warfare, by being afraid of the devil and giving him far more credit for

181

tempting you or influencing you than he deserves, *you are only empowering him!* What we think about, what we talk about, what we express our anxiety and fears about, we empower. "Well" some of you say, "what is wrong with you, don't you know your Bible? It says, 'the devil goes about as a raging lion, seeking whom he may devour'." Hello! Did you ever hear of Daniel in the lion's den? That worked out pretty well, now didn't it? The angels came and shut the lions' mouths! The lions were powerless! Let me tell you something. If you are filled with the Holy Spirit, the devil cannot touch you. He is absolutely powerless in the presence of the living Lord Jesus. He can do absolutely no harm to the one who makes the choice to surrender and abide in the Savior. I can't believe how much time and thought and energy and power some Christians give to "the devil" while they ignore and are totally unconscious of the incredible presence and ministry of the angels. Let's focus on the angels more and the devil a lot less. "Submit yourselves therefore to God. Resist the devil, and he will flee from you." (James 4:7) Jesus Himself said, "Now is the time for judgment on this world; now the prince of this world will be driven out (John 12:31).

SURRENDER, THE KEY TO THE SPIRITUAL

Surrender is the path to spiritual life. "Surrender" is the word the ego wants least of all to hear. Surrender means allowing the Holy Spirit to dwell in the temple of your heart, to fill up the throne room of your life. The ego absolutely hates being kicked off the throne! It does *not* want Jesus on the throne. It will sometimes allow Jesus to be co-pilot, but never "pilot in command." *Jesus as Lord of your life is anathema to the ego.* (After forty years of commercial and private flying, some of it flown as a co-pilot, I can attest to how truly powerless the co-pilot of an aircraft is. It is the captain who is the "pilot in command" and is responsible for absolutely everything about the flight. You people who proclaim "God is my co-pilot" better think again!)

You know what the fruits of the Spirit are... love, joy, peace, patience, goodness, self-control. Well, check out the fruits of the ego by way of

182

contrast: selfishness, gluttony, envy, laziness, pride, lust, fear, rage, greed, judgment, jealousy, neediness, compulsions, addictions, dissension, bitterness, envy, cynicism (life sucks, and then you die!). These fruits of the ego are all *psychological and spiritual toxins!* God is waiting to take them as trade-ins on the fruits of the Spirit! What a deal!

It has been said that EGO stands for; E–edging G –God O-out. The ego feeds voraciously on fear and pain. *The ego says, "it's all about me!" The Spirit says:"it's all about love!"* Egotists are narcissists. A narcissist has been defined as "someone who believes God plans His day around them"! The ego is completely preoccupied with itself. Thus it shuts itself off from the spiritual world and from love. The Spirit-filled person becomes completely preoccupied with Jesus and so opens her heart to love and to service. Don't ever be afraid of being baptized by the Spirit. It is all about bringing you to living in a transformed state of blissful clarity, consciousness, awareness, mindfulness, presence and love. The Spirit-filled person lives in an atmosphere of love. The song of his or her life is sung in the key of love!

Spirit-filled Christians do not have egos. Oh they have healthy self-esteem, and plenty of it, because they know how cherished they are by their Abba. They have humility but they realize the deep truth that humility is not thinking less of your self, it is thinking of your self less. But ego? No. Their ego has been transformed from a wicked wolverine of a beast into a tool for accessing the spiritual. *The spiritual journey is all about moving from egoism to unconditional love*. When the ego is dead, there is left only love. When surrendered to, the wings of the Gentle Dove are quietly capable of lifting us out of our egoism and narcissism as nothing else can. The greatest freedom is the freedom not to have to satisfy the harping demands of the ego.

Here is how it works; the ego, the mind, the emotions all get transformed when we surrender our whole selves to the filling of the Holy Spirit. Then, instead of living from a place of ego, we live from a place of unconditional love. When you transcend egoism, through surrender, when you become love, then you become the person that God created you to be. Then you find the very meaning and purpose of your life. The ultimate example of the power of surrender and sacrifice is what happened on the cross. The greatest act of love the universe has ever seen, that which transformed all of history and the destiny of every soul for all time was the result of the most powerful Being in the universe surrendering Himself to death. For you. For me. Now, we are called to do the same. The goal? Simple. "I no longer live. Christ lives within me."

The Spirit-filled have learned that they have to "die daily" in order to really live. They understand that He is on the throne of all their thoughts, emotions and actions. All great spiritual truth is paradox and Jesus gave us the ultimate paradox when He said so simply, "You must die in order to live." It is your job and mine to die before we die! Then we can really live. Right now and eternally. There are so many unhappy and dissatisfied and anxious and frustrated people in the world because they have not died yet! It was Muhammad who said, "Life is only a dream…you do not wake up until you die." We need to wake up every morning and immediately die to ourselves. Die to self, to ego, and put Jesus at the center of our lives. Surrender! Surrender, the portal to the spiritual. Truth is, without dying, the soul can not come fully to life! If dying to yourself sounds a little scary to you…think of it this way. The process is like sugar casting itself into a glass of water to be dissolved. It is not really gone, but it is absorbed! Oh to be absorbed into the bosom of the Father! To be absorbed into the presence and personality of God! The spiritual teacher, Kabir Edmund Helminski poses the question, "Are you a rock or a fragrance?" Two stones cannot occupy the same space, but two fragrances can. In the world of solid material existence, a stone has a weight and mass that limits what it can do. Fragrance, on the other hand, being matter in molecular form, has powers of diffusion and penetration that allow it to spread at phenomenal speeds over great distances in all directions at once. 7.

Oh that we all would have constantly arising from our hearts the fragrance of the Rose of Sharon, the Lilly of the Valley and that it might be wafted by the winds of the Spirit out into the world!

If we are surrendered and committed to God in the deep personal way we have been talking about, it is the antidote to selfishness, narcissism and egotism. These destructive forces can be swept away along with the fear and anxiety in our lives. They can be replaced by His wonderful assurance, peace and Presence. Closeness to God through the indwelling of the Spirit starts us on a remarkable journey of transformation, transformation "into the likeness of Christ," into more compassionate men and women. John Spong writes beautifully about the transforming effect of the Master:

Jesus … called the egotistical Peter into wholeness; a corrupt tax collector, Levi Matthew, into generosity; the short Zaccheus into an expanded life; the mysterious Mary Magdalene into the apostleship of sharing in the resurrection; the doubting Thomas into a life of faith; the angry John … into being the apostle of love. It was as if the being of Jesus was limitless. 8.

We are talking about nothing less than you getting a heart transplant! A new heart entirely, a transformation brought about by a deep, personal centering in God as you practice His presence each moment. This is the experience He meant when Jesus said, "You shall love the Lord your God with all your heart and soul and mind." (Mark 12:29,30)

This incredible life in the Spirit is the life Jesus Himself knew, and you and I have been invited, commanded even, to live it! We scarcely can begin to comprehend what a life centered in the Spirit and presence of God can mean.

Is this risky? You bet. Because it does not depend on your parents or your spouse or your church, or your doctrines or your knowledge of your scriptures, or how well you follow traditional religious rules. It is entirely dependent on relationship, on connection, on your daily commitment, your moment-by-moment surrender and dedication to your Lord. You and you alone can make it happen and continue to make it happen. Or not.

Q&A:

Q. We have always been told that the Bible is to be the foundation of our religious life.
What could be more important?

A. The Bible is very important, but it is not sufficient. The Bible is the map, it is not the territory. It is the guidebook, it is not the journey. It is the love-letter, it is not the marriage. I have a drawer full of love-letters from many years ago that I still cherish. If I would have been content with them however, I never would have moved on into the relationship that has given me a family, a wife and children. It is the personal, intimate relationship that is foundational. The Bible points the way. Jesus said He is the Way. Your spiritual foundation is not on a book or a belief or a church. It is on an intimate relationship with a living, loving being who wishes through His Spirit to bring His very presence into your heart and soul. He wants you to surrender to Him like Mary did, so that He may overshadow you too with the Holy Spirit. Then He can be re-created in you. He can be spiritually formed in you so He can manifest Himself in the unique person and character and personality that is you.

Q. You say we need this new paradigm, this new reformation in our spirituality. I thought the Reformation already happened in Christianity.

A. The Protestant Reformation was a reformation of information, of beliefs, of truth. The reformation we are talking about here is a reformation of inspiration, a reformation of Spirit. We have been told to worship God in Spirit and in truth. The first Reformation was about the truth part, this reformation is about the Spirit part.

The Protestant Reformation was desperately needed because the Church had drifted toward focusing on political power. It had been infiltrated with pagan philosophy and many non-biblical teachings. The Reformation brought the focus back to the simple vital truths of salvation by faith and the priesthood of all believers. It in fact prepared the way so the new reformation we are talking about could happen.

Q. You make these new ideas about religion sound too easy. Like some sort of shortcut. Like some kind of cheap grace.

A. It is not easy. Paradoxically, surrender is both the hardest work in the world and yet it is the easiest. It is the most important spiritual thing you can do every day. Surrender is what gets ego out of the center of your life and *only in the death of the ego is there true freedom, joy, peace and serenity.* Always remember the spiritual truism that the thing we surrender to becomes our power. Maintaining a quality intimate relationship is never easy, not even with someone we can see and touch. It requires a great investment of time and energy. Even the perfect Jesus had to retreat to the mountains and sometimes pray through the night to stay intimately and consciously connected with the Father. Staying filled with the Spirit requires a continual emptying of the self, a continual crucifying of the ego. It must happen every day, moment by moment. Dwight L. Moody said he had to be filled with the Spirit every day because he leaked!

There are so many distractions that can break our connection to the Divine that we must be continually practicing the presence of God, continually making ourselves consciously aware of Him, continually praying, continually surrendering. The Scriptures tell us to "pray without ceasing." This does not mean all we do is pray, but it does mean that we don't do or say anything without prayer! No, it is not easy. Yes, it requires discipline and strong intent and focus. But does the artist not focus intensely on his canvas in order to create a masterpiece? The composer on his music? Is it a burden? Only the kind of burden sails are to a ship. Wings are to a bird. It is the way to great joy. Great peace. And great love.

FOOTNOTES CHAPTER 12:

1. Torrey, R.A., *The Person & Work of the Holy Spirit*. (Whitaker House, New Kensington Pa: 1996) p.103.

2. *Spectrum Magazine*, Jesus and Genocide: Another Alternative, Volume 34, Issue 3, Summer 2006, pp. 66, 67.

3. *Time Magazine, The Rise of the None*, March 12, 2012 p. 68.

4. Vallotton, Kris, Johnson, Bill, *The Supernatural Ways of Royalty*. (Destiny Image Publishers Inc.,Shippensburg, Pa: 2006) p.108

5. Miller, Donald, *Blue Like Jazz*. (Thomas Nelson, Publishers, Nashville, 2003) p.181.

6. Williamson, Marianne, *Everyday Grace*. (Riverhead Books, New York, 2002) p.51.

7. Helminski, Kabir Edmund, *Living Presence*. (Jeremy P. Tarcher/Putnam, NY, 1992)

   p. 131.

8. Spong, John Shelby, *Why Christianity Must Change or Die*. (Harper Collins, San Francisco, 1998) p. 223.

CHAPTER 13:

FROM CARPENTER TO CHRIST: UNDER THE DESCENDING DOVE

"And the Holy Spirit descended on him in bodily form like a dove"—Luke 3:22

A pioneer missionary to China once gave a refined and educated Chinese gentleman who was not a Christian, a copy of the New Testament. He asked him to read it all the way through. When the missionary met the man again some time later he asked him, "What was the deepest impression made upon your mind when you read that book I gave you?" To his surprise the man said, "The wonderful truth that the body is the temple of the Holy Spirit."

Do you see? Do you get it as clearly as this non-believer did? The Holy Spirit is the One who completely sets Christians apart from every other, philosophy, dogma, creed, cult and religion on this planet! No one, no one, has anything in their teaching or theology that even comes close to it!

How sad that what this non-Christian saw as one of the most profound and remarkable truths of Christianity is so often misunderstood, overlooked and ignored by believers. To understand best its incredible importance, there is no better place to start than to look at the life of Jesus Himself, our ultimate example.

For 20 years the Man from Nazareth made baby cribs and shepherd's crooks and dining table chairs. At first He worked alongside his step-father in the carpenter's shop, observing, learning, perfecting His craft. A carpenter was a very important profession in those days for almost everything made or built or manufactured had to be made out of wood. When Joseph passed away, Jesus took on the additional responsibilities of managing the business. Now He had to be responsible for ordering the finest cedar from the forests of Lebanon, or the black oak imported all the way across the Mediterranean from Spain. Perhaps, from time to time, He even got His hands on some mahogany out of Africa. He had to take on the role of supervising the apprentices and do all the bookkeeping and make sure there were enough *shekels* to make the payroll each Friday afternoon. He had to make sure the accounts receivables were collected. And there were the taxes to be paid. No small business owner can avoid those! The Jerusalem temple tax, Caesar's tax, the Galilean borough tax! All those records to keep and paperwork to file! Endless. Just endless.

He got sawdust in His sandals and woodchips in His beard as He toiled day after day and year after year with the crude and labor-intensive tools of that *T* to support Himself and His mother. But always His work was exceptional. His reputation for quality craftsmanship was unexcelled in the whole region. People came from miles around to place their orders for His products. Can you imagine owning a beautiful wooden fruit bowl made by this Jesus? During this time, the great portion of His entire life, He preached no sermons. He healed no lepers. He attracted no disciples. Customers yes, plenty. Disciples, no.

THE TRANSFORMATION

Just what do you think it was that turned this shy carpenter who was too busy practicing His trade to leave His little village into the powerhouse of a Messiah who would "draw all men unto Him" and who would turn the world upside down? What was it that transformed Him from the carpenter into the Christ?

Well, here it is. "When all the people were being baptized, Jesus was baptized too. And as He was praying, heaven opened and the Holy Spirit descended on him in bodily form like a dove" (Luke 3:21, 22).

The first time the Holy Spirit descended and hovered over the waters was in the beginning of earth's history at creation (Genesis 1:1-3). Once again, the Spirit descended and this time hovered over Jesus. This is a reminder to us that just as God created the world, He is now beginning a whole new creation, a spiritual creation, through His beloved Son.

And look what happened next! "Jesus, *full of the Holy Spirit,*(emphasis supplied) returned from the Jordan and was led by the Spirit in the desert.". "Full of the Holy Spirit! The Bible never said anything about Him like that before! Something exceptional happened to this man when the dove descended!

Now, even the devil took an interest in Him! He came to Him out there in the desert and tempted Him for 40 days. The devil did not like what was happening one little bit. Why, as the years had gone by, 10, 20, then 30, he had begun to hope nothing was going to come of Jesus being on earth. He certainly did not want anything to change from the carpenter-shop status quo. He especially did not want this man to be filled with the Spirit. It was his worst nightmare! Anything but that! Satan had little interest in Him when Jesus was building tables and chairs but now, this carpenter had suddenly become a threat to the whole kingdom of darkness! Trust me, the Devil wants nothing more than to keep you away from the baptism of the Holy Spirit also.

If this Jesus, with all the advantages He had spiritually, His mother chosen for Him, born of a virgin, leading a sinless life, going to church, keeping the law perfectly, still needed the baptism of the Holy Spirit before His life could be transformed from carpenter to Christ, how much more do you and I need this experience!

I want you to think about the fact that for 30 years Jesus led a sinless life. He was fully obedient. He never broke a single commandment. But perfect obedience was not enough! Jesus' own life was oddly enough a testimony for the insufficiency of obedience to the law. Even a perfect life was not enough by itself to empower Him for ministry, not enough to transform Him into the miracle-working Messiah. I just want you to really get that being a Christian is about so much more than believing right and refraining from sinning. After your conversion you still need something more! Was Jesus born again before that day at the Jordan when John baptized Him? Of course. He was born again from the minute He was physically born. Why, He was even conceived by the Holy Spirit as the Spirit overshadowed the virgin Mary. But when will we ever get it? Being converted, being born again, is not the same thing as being baptized with the Spirit. They are not synonymous. They do not necessarily occur simultaneously. In fact, they usually do not occur simultaneously. Even the perfect Jesus needed something more to equip Him for His life of service, for His ministry.

Look what the Scriptures say about Him next, after He finished His time in the desert. "Jesus returned to Galilee *in the power of the Spirit* (emphasis supplied). That was never said about Him before. Soon, news about Him spread through the whole countryside. He taught in their synagogues and everyone praised him" (Luke 4:14,15).

Here is the picture of a man transformed overnight. From carpenter to Christ! From craftsman to Savior! He moved from the simple village life onto the stage of the world. Why? Only one reason. He was baptized with the Holy Spirit! Let's face the truth: without the Holy Spirit, Jesus was powerless. And so are we!

It was the Spirit who led Him to start preaching. He had never done that before. He even came to speak in His home church at Nazareth. And what was His text? He took it from Isaiah 61: "The Spirit of the Lord is upon me." (He had never said that about Himself before.) "He has anointed me to preach good news to the poor, freedom to the prisoners, recovery of sight to the blind, to release the oppressed." Then, He uttered those bold words that announced to the whole world that His Messiaship had begun: "Today this scripture is fulfilled in your hearing" (Luke 4:21).

Soon after this, He went to the town of Capernaum and began to teach the people there. The people "were amazed at his teaching, because his message had authority" (Luke 4:32). In the church, as He was preaching, there appeared a man possessed by a demon who interrupted and challenged Him. Jesus ordered the demon to be quiet and to come out of the man. The devil, who had called Jesus "the Holy One of God", obeyed Him at once. "All the people were amazed and said to each other, 'What is this teaching? With authority and power he gives orders to evil spirits and they come out!'. And the news about him spread throughout the surrounding area" (Luke 4:35-37).

The same day, He left the church and went to the home of Simon, whose mother-in-law was suffering from a seriously high fever. He healed the woman in an instant. When the word of this spread, later that evening, people with all kinds of illnesses began to congregate at the house where He was. "...and laying his hands on each one, he healed them" (Luke 4:40).

All these incredible events are recorded in just one chapter in the book of Luke! It is no coincidence that it is the chapter that follows the account of His receiving the Holy Spirit! The chapter shows Him being transformed from a man who had been a shy carpenter for thirty years, into a teacher, a preacher, a prophecy-fulfilling, demon-defeating, miracle-working Messiah over the period of just a few days!

Do you still wonder how this could happen? Look at the record again. "Jesus, full of the Holy Spirit" (Luke 4:1). "Jesus returned to Galilee in the power of the Spirit" (Luke 4:14). The Master had laid aside His own power when He left heaven. It was by the filling of the Holy Spirit that Jesus received His power to become what He was to be, what He was to do for God and for you and me. "God anointed Jesus of Nazareth with the Holy Spirit and power, and he went around doing good and healing all who were under the power of the devil, because God was with Him" (Acts 10:38).

By the way, notice that it was shortly after Jesus was filled with the Spirit that He was emboldened to cleanse the temple. When the Spirit is lacking, when politics or money or manipulative power have come to be used in the church to try to fill the gap, the temple still needs to be cleansed. Sometimes I wish we could go down to the supermarket and buy a bottle of temple-cleanser for our churches! Maybe someone should give Proctor and Gamble a call! Part of the reason the baptism of the Spirit is called by John the baptism of fire, is because it cleanses.

The anointing that Jesus received, He now makes available to you and me! "...the anointing which you have received from Him abides in you" (1 John 2:27). We too may be anointed to "preach the gospel to the poor, to heal the brokenhearted, to offer deliverance to the captives and recovery of sight to the blind." The Holy Spirit's filling is designed to turn ordinary people into extraordinary people. Not extraordinarily wealthy or powerful but, extraordinarily compassionate, extraordinarily anointed to the service of others. Extraordinarily like this magnificent, bold, compassionate Jesus. Like Him, able to love extravagantly!

May we all come under the descending dove.

Q&A:

Q. Since Jesus was God, didn't He have the ability to work miracles any time He wanted? How dare you say He was powerless without the Holy Spirit?

A. Jesus chose to make the sacrifice of laying aside His Divinity when He came to earth. He chose to make Himself dependent on the Holy Spirit's power to accomplish every phase of His mission. In this, as in all things He was our model and example. We can tap the same power source He did.

Q. You talked about Jesus being changed practically overnight from a carpenter to the Christ, by the power of the Holy Spirit. Should we expect the same dramatic change if we are baptized with the Spirit?

A. The Spirit is truly like the wind. It blows as it wills. How the Spirit will chose to work and manifest itself with any given person is not predictable. That is part of the excitement, the sacred adventure of the Spirit-filled life. I love a quote by poet Mary Oliver and keep it posted above my desk. It says, "Tell me, what is it you plan to do with your one wild and precious life?" I believe the most dramatic and important thing I can do to get the most out of my precious life is to surrender it to the filling of the Holy Spirit every day!

Then, let the adventure begin! The important part for you and me is to ask for the baptism of the Spirit and to surrender to it. I can never, ever emphasize surrender enough. Surrender is the key to everything spiritual. According to Meister Eckhart, surrender "enkindles the heart, awakens the spirit, stimulates our longings, and shows us where God is".

Only when we surrender can, the process of transformation begin for each of us individually, manifesting itself through our own unique identity and personality. It will be a different expression and experience for everyone! You can't even begin to imagine what God might have in mind for you! Jesus whetted our appetite for great spiritual expectations when He said, "I tell you the truth, anyone who has faith in me will do what I have been doing. He will do even greater things than these, because I am going to the Father" (John 14:12). He could make the extraordinary promise because of the gift of the Holy Spirit He was sending. "I will ask the Father, and he will give you another Counselor to be with you forever—the Spirit of truth" (John 14:16). Jesus was so anxious to get back to heaven that He limited His ministry here to only three-and-one-half years! This was because He knew that when He left, the Holy Spirit could be sent in fullness into the world and could in-dwell every believer so that Christ's presence would not just be in one place at one time, but could be manifest everywhere there was a Spirit-filled Christian!

CHAPTER 14:

THE BAPTISM OF FIRE

"I baptize you with water for repentance.
But after me will come one who is more powerful than I...
He will baptize you with the Holy Spirit and with fire."
Matthew 3:11

In the mid-nineteenth century, a party of French explorers established a camp in the heart of central Africa. They had picked a spot in the middle of a forest clearing in the jungle. Each morning they left early for a day of exploration and mapping. When they came back in the evening they would hurriedly gather twigs and branches to light a fire before darkness fell. One late afternoon upon their return to camp they discovered a most unusual sight. In the clearing all around the tents there had been erected little teepee-like piles of limbs and branches. There were more than a dozen of them and they had been very carefully and painstakingly constructed. Dry leaves on the bottom, then smaller twigs and on top of those, larger pieces of wood. Examining their discovery, the men were puzzled by what they had found until they heard a noise behind them. Turning quickly they glanced up into the canopy of trees surrounding them. Above them was the explanation for the mystery. A group of chimpanzees were chattering and swinging among the vines. The animals had watched the explorers build their campfires for several days. When the men left that morning, they had come down out of the trees to try it for themselves. They had done very well indeed. The little teepees looked perfect. They were remarkably similar to the ones the men had made. They had been put together with much care and effort. But there was no fire!

Some of us have spent a great deal of time and energy in our lives erecting our ecclesiastical teepees. After much religious effort, we may be very comfortable with our theology which is arranged "just so." Our doctrinal houses are in order. Our beliefs well-grounded. Our institutions standing proudly. We have an adequate representation of a "form of godliness." But the question is: Where is the fire?

Can you imagine what would have happened on Mt. Carmel if there had been no fire? The forces of good and evil had reached a standoff there that day. Tension filled the air after 450 of Baal prophets had tried unsuccessfully to attract the attention of their god.

Now it was Elijah's turn. The altar was in place. The sacrifice had been divided into its parts. Everyone was waiting with hushed expectancy. "How long will you waver between two opinions." the prophet thundered. "If the Lord is God, follow him, but if Baal is God, follow him" (1 Kings 18:21).

Then as now, there were religious counterfeits, cunning voices proclaimed a deceptive and distorted version of reality. A nation was caught between truth and error. Elijah came to call the devil's hand: "...you call on the name of your god, and I will call on the name of the Lord. The god who answers by fire—he is God" (1 Kings 18:24).

THE GOD WHO SPEAKS BY FIRE

Ah, will the real God please stand up? The God who answers by fire! It was Jehovah versus Baal. Truth versus error. The genuine versus counterfeit. Faith versus works. Genuine Divine spiritual power versus men's own feeble efforts at religiosity.

A huge crowd from all over the country was at the mountain that day as was the king himself. Baal's prophets were intent on his vindication. From morning until noon they pleaded with their god to answer them. "Can you hear me now Baal, can you hear me now?" Baal did not seem to have his cell turned on. Elijah just could not resist it. Try harder guys. "Shout louder! he said.

197

…Perhaps your god is deep in thought, or busy traveling. Maybe he is sleeping and must be awakened" (1 Kings 18:27).

The Baal group were growing more and more frenzied. "So they shouted louder and slashed themselves with swords and spears until their blood flowed. Midday passed, and they continued their frantic prophesying until the time for the evening sacrifice. But there was no response, no one answered, no one paid attention" (1 Kings 18: 28, 29).

Elijah called the people to all come in close to the altar. Three times he had men pour gallons and gallons of water all over the offering and the altar until the trenches surrounding it were filled to the brim. Then he prayed a quiet, simple prayer. "Oh Lord, let it be known today that you are God in Israel." (1 Kings 18:36).

The people waited. The king waited. The 450 false prophets waited. No one moved. Complete silence hung over that vast crowd.

And then the fire fell! It "burned up the sacrifice, the wood, the stones and the soil, and licked up the water in the trench" (1 Kings :18:38). The crowd could not constrain itself. "The Lord—He is God. The Lord—He is God" they roared 1 Kings 18:.39).

History has repeated itself. Today there is again much religious confusion in the land. Who is God? What is God? Is there a God? What is truth? What is love? Meanwhile the church has been busy cutting up its sacrifices and tending its altars.

Current evangelicalism has laid the altar and divided the sacrifice into parts, but now it seems satisfied to count the stones and rearrange the pieces with never a care that there is not a sign of fire upon the top of lofty Carmel. But God be thanked that there are a few who care. They are those who, while they love the altar and delight in the sacrifice, are yet unable to reconcile themselves to the continued absence of fire. 1

Good question. Is there any fire on the mountain top today? Have we called on the God who answers by fire? Have we accepted the gift from the one who wants to "baptize us with fire"? Is there any one today to stand before the doubting crowd and have the courage to say, "let it be known today that you are God in Israel and that I am your servant" (1 Kings 18:36),

This time it is not one small nation that is waiting and watching. It is the whole world. Perhaps the whole universe is holding its breath, waiting for God's champions to stand up. With so much at stake, we must not be content with the religious status quo. There are those of us who are grateful for an altar, we appreciate the sacrifices and are pleased to have a hill on which to worship, but we can not seem to reconcile ourselves to the absence of the fire!

THE UNIQUE CHRISTIAN DOCTRINE

Today God is waiting to reveal Himself to the world through the fire of the Holy Spirit in the lives of His people! Remember, it is Christianity alone that offers this ultimate and exquisite experience to every believer who would chose to have it. Among all the religions of the world, there is no doctrine, no teaching that even comes close to it. Like the Baal worship of old, the emphasis of other religions is on men struggling to appease their god, to somehow find favor with him through their own efforts or sacrifices. Only Jesus Christ came offering to men and women the unique opportunity to have the very Presence of their loving God live right within them now! To inhabit them! To incarnate Himself in them! Without this incredible gift, Christianity would be no different than other religions, merely pointing its adherents toward some distant future reward to be earned by their beliefs, obedience and good behavior. It was only Jesus who proclaimed to the world, "The kingdom of God is here right now. The kingdom of God is within you!" This was because only Jesus could offer the incredible gift of the Holy Spirit.

So you see, God is now filling people with the Holy Spirit. Not tabernacles. In this dark night of the world, "the God who answers by fire" wants to light up your life with the fire of His supernatural love. I love that text that says, "The spirit of man is the candle of the Lord" (Proverbs 20:27). Jesus had made Himself dependent on us to reflect His glory and presence and love in this world! Don't ever diminish your role in bringing light into the world. It has been said, "There is not enough darkness in all the world to put out the light of one small candle."

The question is, when people look at your life and mine, do they see the fire? When they look at our church, do they see the fire? Is your life and mine actually a testimony to the fact that the last Christian did not die on the cross?

A skeptical and hardened lawyer once came to meet a man named John Vianney. The lawyer said of this encounter, "An extraordinary thing happened to me today: I saw Christ in a man". If your religion does not make you a better father, mother, husband, wife, child, parent, friend, employer, or business partner, it is wasting your time. Christianity must demonstrate that it can produce better people here and now. It is a proof of its genuineness. God is calling you to be an extraordinary person, extraordinarily aflame with His love. Extraordinarily filled with His presence.

THE TWO BAPTISMS

John said, "I baptize you with water for repentance. But after me will come one who is more powerful than I. He will baptize you with the Holy Spirit and with fire" (Matthew 3:11). Jesus is the baptizer with fire! Jesus is the baptizer with the Holy Spirit! No church. No priest. No pastor. Jesus. The whole point of this book is to bring you to the question: "Have I chosen to allow Jesus to baptize me with the Holy Spirit? Do I have the assurance of this marvelous gift that can transform my life from one of selfishness to one of service?"

I remember so clearly and so fondly the occasion of my baptism with water. It was in the middle of the Alaska winter. The little church in our small village did not have a baptistery. All the lakes and streams were frozen solid. So solid that the missionary-bush-pilot pastor who flew in to perform the service

200

landed his ski-equipped plane on the lake near the church. A special plywood tank had been built in a nearby school utility room for the occasion. A sweet, rotund, white-haired Eskimo grandmother and myself, a skinny, red-haired twelve-year old were the only candidates. I watched in awe as the lady was immersed. Then it was my turn. Let's just say that day was a peak spiritual experience for me. God reached down and touched my young heart. I will never forget the incredible feelings of warmth and joy and love and peace that I experienced as never before as I walked home on the ice of the lake after the service that day. It was and remains a peak experience for me.

I can look back and say with confidence, on a certain day of a certain month, in a certain little Alaska village I chose to publicly surrender my life to Jesus Christ and I was baptized by Pastor Smith. It was a real, historic event that happened for me.

I want you to see that your baptism by the Holy Spirit can be just as real an event in your life as your water baptism or your graduation from college or your marriage might be. It too can be no less of an historic, real-time reality. It is possible for you to be able to say, on a certain day in a certain year, at a certain place, I first chose to receive the baptism of the Holy Spirit. This event will then become an incredibly significant part of your spiritual history. A peak experience. No, you won't ever be able to say, "Pastor so and so baptized me with the Holy Spirit" because it is Jesus Himself who is the baptizer! But this sacred event can take place for you and become a part of you just as surely as your water baptism. It can be something you can fall back on for reassurance, strength, courage and power again and again as you move through the ups and downs of your spiritual life.

By the way, there is a reason there are two baptisms in Christianity. Water baptism is very important but it is not sufficient (did you know that both Hitler and Stalin were baptized?). Otherwise, why would we need Jesus to baptize us with fire? In a sense, water baptism is a symbol of the cleansing of the sins of the past. It is about getting rid of sin and it is often seen as a motivator to keep one from sinning any more. But notice that when water baptism is seen in this way, it can be made to become all about avoiding sin. If you stop with water baptism, your life and your religious experience can easily become focused on "staying pure," on avoiding sin, yes, even on struggling for perfection! You can become obsessed with maintaining that "sinlessness," that "perfection" that was yours the moment you came up out of the waters of baptism. And that is a very great trap. Sadly, this fear of becoming contaminated by sin, this great centering of the energy on struggling to avoid sin, this obsession about behavior, was in the past and still is at the center of many people's religion. It is always a lose/lose situation, a cause of much frustration, discouragement and fear, since no one is perfect this side of heaven. To center your life on this is to definitely put your ladder against the wrong religious wall! It could be said that water baptism is about not doing bad. Spirit baptism is about doing good.

There was a terrible joke a few years back in the days before righteousness by faith became better understood. The idea behind it was that a person better hope and pray that the Lord would come at the moment they were underwater in the baptismal tank because that would be the only time they would be free of sin and could be guaranteed of being taken to heaven!

As a side note here, there is an interesting warning given by Jesus in Matthew 12:43-45.
"When an evil spirit comes out of a man, it goes through arid places seeking rest and does not find it. Then it says, 'I will return to the house I left.' When it arrives, it finds the house unoccupied, swept clean and put in order. Then it goes and takes with it seven other spirits more wicked than itself, and they go in and live there. And the final condition of that man is worse than the first."

The "cleansing" here being referred to would seem to be the result of the forgiveness of sin that comes with water baptism. When this act rids a person of the evil of sin from their life, rids them of any spirits of evil that were influencing them, then there needs to be something to replace the vacuum, the emptiness. The Holy Spirit needs to come right on in to fill the gap. If that does not happen, then the newly converted person is at risk for backsliding into a place that is worse than before his or her conversion.

So you see, it is a dangerous thing to bring someone only half way into the Christian life. It is not enough to lead them to water baptism and membership in the church. If we stop with this we may be setting them up for failure and spiritual disaster. We are cheating and endangering our converts if we do not give them the full gospel. No wonder that half of them end up leaving the church! We may have helped them receive forgiveness but unless we lead them on to the second baptism, the filling of the Holy Spirit, we are cheating them of the very power they need to be transformed and to lead lives of abundance and victory. We dare not ignore the doctrine of the Holy Spirit any longer. We dare not conduct another evangelistic campaign where we make certain to convince the audience of specific doctrines important to our particular denomination and then neglect the second greatest doctrine in Christendom after the cross, the doctrine, the experience of the baptism by fire, the empowering baptism Jesus brings, the baptism of the Holy Spirit.

The risk then, is that a focus on water baptism alone, sets people up to lead a life of effort, of worrying about their sinfulness and struggling to stay "pure," something they can never achieve on their own. That is why the second baptism is needed so badly. The baptism of the Spirit brings the positive elements of the Christian life into play. Its emphasis is all positive. It is all about the believer receiving the great gifts of love, joy, and peace and patience. It is about becoming an instrument of God's compassion and God's kindness in the world. It is about receiving power to overcome sin and selfishness and fear and negativity. The Bible says the baptism of the Spirit is the down-payment on salvation. It gives us the confidence and the assurance, the peace that alone comes from the certainty that we are saved, the sure knowledge that we will have eternal life.

"And you also were included in Christ when you heard the word of truth, the gospel of your salvation. Having believed, you were marked in him with a seal, the promised Holy Spirit, who is a deposit guaranteeing our inheritance until the redemption of those who are God's possession—the praise of his glory" (Ephesians 1:13, 14).

As you consider the importance of the baptism of the Spirit, think about it in terms of a marriage. Everyone who is married can remember the place and specific date of their wedding ceremony. It is a significant historical event they never forget. Something happens there that changes their lives. Before the vows and the pronouncement of marriage the bride and groom are two separate individuals. Afterward they are united as one. A new level of intimacy is now available to them. Even their legal status before the law changes. Before they could not say they were married. Afterward they can clearly state that they are. They have made their choice to enter into this kind of special relationship and taken their vows before God and man. They have witnesses to prove it. They know they are married. There is no question in their minds. They either are or are not married. If you go up to one of them after the service and ask, "Are you married?" they will answer "Yes." There is no ambivalence. They do not say, "Well, I don't know if I am married or not." They do not say, "Well, I hope I will be married someday."

I am trying to say that you can be as clear about whether or not you have been baptized with the Holy Spirit as you are about whether you have chosen to be married or not. You can have the assurance that you have received this gift, entered into this special intimate relationship where you have certain rights and privileges you did not have without it. In this way, the baptism of the Holy Spirit is like marriage. You either have or you have not chosen to be Spirit-filled. There needn't be any ambivalence. If you have chosen to be Spirit-filled there may be a specific time and place you can look back to that is very real to you. You may even have had some praying brothers and sisters who can serve as your witnesses to this event.

At the risk of trying too hard, I want to come at this experience in another way. I have a friend who became a State Trooper. Let's call him Dan Jones. I knew Dan when he was a carpenter. We took some long floatplane trips and did some fun outdoor things together. We always considered each other equals. But the time came when Dan stood in a ceremony and before witnesses, he took a vow to become a peace officer and enforce the law. He was given a badge and a gun. On that occasion, my friend Dan came to represent a far greater authority than himself. He was invested with a power far beyond his own. He received something he did not have before he chose to present himself for that ceremony. He became a symbol, a representative of something bigger than himself. Dan came to have a power and authority I did not have. Did he have this before the ceremony? No. Did he have it after he chose to participate in the ceremony? Yes. Something had changed because of the choice Dan had made and the vow he took that day.

So it is with you and the Spirit. Your decision to receive the baptism of the Spirit will change your life. It will give you a power and authority that is beyond your own. Not a power to use over others, but a power to love and to serve. It will give you the ability to speak and to teach truth with an authority and a wisdom that is beyond yourself. It will equip you and empower you to minister. Here are the last words Jesus spoke on earth. "You will receive power when the Holy Spirit comes on you; and you will be my witnesses to the ends of the earth." (Acts:1:8). A few days later the precious promise was delivered to the world which has never been the same. When the day of Pentecost had come, they were all together in one place. And suddenly a sound came from heaven like the rush of a mighty wind, and it filled all the house where they were sitting … And there appeared to them tongues as of fire, distributed and resting on each of them. And they were all filled with the Holy Spirit" (Acts 2:1-4, RSV). God's wind. Imagine it! This mighty, rushing force came upon His lifeless and fearful disciples and they were transformed! They came to life. The Spirit was Jesus' final gift to the world.

Can you believe that Mary was there! Jesus' mom! I am like soooo jealous of her. First she had that incredible experience where the Holy Spirit "overshadowed" her, and she became pregnant with the Son of God. And then this! She got to be there on the day the fire fell too! On the day of Pentecost! But wait. I have to put my jealousy aside when I think about it, because, truth is, the same two experiences are available to me. The Holy Spirit wants to "overshadow" me so that the Son of God can be formed in me spiritually! And my Lord wants to baptize me with fire so that I can have my own personal Pentecost! Without this power, we are like a light bulb that is just dull and dead when it is not plugged in. But when we get connected to the Spirit we become transmitters of light and energy with a power that is in us but not of us.

In the middle of one of his books, Brennan Manning quotes the psychiatrist and philosopher William James when he said, "In some people religion exists as a dull habit, in others as an acute fever." Then Manning writes to his readers the same message I want the readers of this book to hear clearly: "Jesus did not endure the shame of the cross to hand on a dull habit. (If you don't have the fever, dear reader, a passion for God and his Christ, drop this book, fall on your knees, and beg for it; turn to the God you half-believe in and cry out for his baptism of fire.)" 2.

Q&A:

Q. Why is this experience called the "baptism with fire"? That sounds scary.

A. Throughout the Bible, fire is a symbol of both the presence of God and the love of God. In the Holy of Holies in the temple at Jerusalem, the fiery Shekinah glory resided above the Ark of the Covenant. That fire was a symbol of God's presence. Now, that same fiery presence seeks to live within you, within your heart and mine, not in some stone temple. "And in Him (Jesus) you too are being built together to become a dwelling in which God lives by his Spirit" (Ephesians 2:22).

One of my favorite quotes comes from French philosopher and priest, Teilhard de Chardin: "Someday, after we have mastered the winds, the waves, the tides and gravity, we will harness for God the energies of love: and then, for the second time in the history of the world, man will have discovered fire."

John said that Jesus was come to baptize us with fire and the Holy Spirit! There is no need to be afraid of the baptism of the Holy Spirit because it is to be baptized into the personal presence and the unconditional love of God. Most simply put, to be baptized with the Spirit is to be baptized with love! Love is just simply the bottom-line of Christianity, of the Spirit-filled life. God is the essence of radical, unconditional, non-exploitive love. The world does not know what this is, and no one can live it out in their life without the Spirit. This is a love well-beyond the human. A love that is simply always there to serve. It never asks anything, not anything, in return. The poet Hafiz in the 14th century described it so beautifully;

Even

After

All this time

The sun never says to the earth,

"You owe

Me"

Look

What happens

With a love like that,

It lights the

Whole

Sky.

Q. You say that being baptized with the Spirit can be a specific event in time. Does that mean that if you are filled with the Spirit once, you will always be filled from then on?

A. No. It is not "once filled always filled" any more than it is "once saved always saved". God does not force you to remain either saved or Spirit-filled. You always have a choice. The great evangelist, Dwight L. Moody, said he had to be filled with the Spirit every day because he leaked! To maintain the Spirit-filled life requires a daily emptying of self, a daily surrender and a daily filling. Paul said, "I die daily." The evangelist R.A. Torrey was preaching the truth about the baptism of the Spirit all around the world in the late 1800's and early 1900's when scarcely a word on the subject was ever heard from any pulpit. He said that he was sometimes asked, "Have you received the second blessing, (the filling of the Spirit)? Instead of simply telling the person that he had, he would say, "Yes, and I have received the third and the fourth and the fifth, and hundreds beside, and I am looking for a new blessing today!" Torrey knew that he needed to be filled again and again. He knew that receiving the Spirit is a continuous process.

Q. I thought that when I was baptized with water I was "born again" of the Spirit already, that I automatically received the baptism of the Spirit at that time. Are you telling me now that I need something more?

A. Yes. There is a great difference between being "born again" of the Spirit (conversion, the new birth) and receiving the baptism of the Holy Spirit (becoming the dwelling place of God on earth and being empowered for your own life of ministry and service). They are two separate experiences. Billy Graham in his book *"The Holy Spirit"* wrote: "…if we wish to be men and women who can live victoriously, we need this two-sided gift God has offered us: first, the work of the Son of God for us; second, the work of the Spirit of God in us". 3.

I have a lot of fun with a little "science" experiment when I am demonstrating the fact that there are two separate baptisms (water and fire, salvation and Spirit-filling) to a group. I bring in an extension cord with two outlets on it. I plug it in in front of the folks. I have a lamp plugged in to one outlet and turned on so people can see there is power in the cord. Then I show another electric cord with one end cut off and the two shiny bare copper wires exposed and separated. Keeping the bare wires widely apart, I plug this cord into power. Everyone sort of cringes and gasps. I hold the two separated wires of the cord by the insulated portions and ask, "what will happen if I touch these wires together? "Sparks"! "Shocks"! "Fire"! the audience cries out! Then I carefully take one of the separated bare wires in my hand. The group cringes again… but I point out that this is perfectly safe if I am only touching one wire, because no circuit is being made. No power is available. Then I ask them, "what will happen if I grab both bare wires?" "You will get shocked," they holler, "you will get power!" Then I proceed to grab both bare wires with my bare hands. People gasp. After a little dramatic shaking and shuddering, I say "just kidding!". Then I reassure them that there is *no power* in the line. In fact, that is the whole point of the demonstration. I show them why. I have broken off one of the prongs from the plug-in end of the cord. That has made it a one-legged circuit. They can see that with only one leg, the circuit is not complete and there is no energy, no power. The point is made that a one-pronged, one-legged gospel is not sufficient. We need both the baptisms of *water and fire, spirit and truth* to be fully completed and empowered as Christians. (Kids, please, don't try this at home)

Anytime I flew my twin-engine plane, I never said, "well I think I will save some fuel and just take off on one engine today." I never would have gotten off the ground. If you want your spiritual life to lift off and soar, to really get somewhere, you need both the engine of conversion and the engine of the Spirit's filling to fly!

FOOTNOTES CHAPTER 14

1. Tozer, A.W.. *The Pursuit of God*, (Christian Publications, Harrisburg, PA, 1948) p.8.
2. Manning, Brennan. *The Signature of Jesus*, (Multnomah Books, 1996,) p. 95.
3. Graham, Billy. *The Holy Spirit*, (Word Books, Waco, Texas, 1978) p. 11.

CHAPTER 15:

SOMETHING MORE

"I tell you the truth: It is for your good that I am going away.
Unless I go away, the Counselor will not come to you;
but if I go, I will send him to you."
—John 16:7

I graduated from a Christian high school. Then I went four years to a Christian college and earned a Bachelors Degree in Theology. Then I went for three more years to a Christian Theological Seminary and earned a Master of Divinity Degree. During this time I spent countless hours, days, months, studying the Bible. I learned Greek to be able to translate the New Testament myself. I (tried to) learn Hebrew to be able to translate the Old Testament from the original language. I took dozens and dozens and dozens of Bible classes on various subjects. Then I became a pastor. And I was a most assiduous and earnest young pastor! I was sure that I absolutely had "the truth." I was sure that all my vast theological training had prepared me well to preach that truth and equipped me to convert skeptics and unbelievers to "the truth." I was sure I had all the right religious answers. Why, I could answer any theological question to my own complete satisfaction! Martin Luther said once that if ever a monk could have gotten to heaven by his monkery, it would have been he! Well, if ever a pastor could have earned his way to heaven by the diligence of his pastoring and the absolute certainty of the conviction of the accuracy of his beliefs, I am sure it would have been me. By the way, a very wise person once said, "the direct opposite of faith is not doubt, it is certainty." To that I would add, beware of certainty. Especially religious certainty!

Then reality hit. Very quickly. Just two days before I arrived at my first church assignment one of the members inconveniently had the audacity to up and die! I got a phone call letting me know that my first ministerial act would be to have a funeral service for this person I had never met. This was unsettling. I looked back through all my notes and textbooks for help and realized that while I had classes in esoteric subjects like Christology and Johannine Literature, the doctrine of the Sanctuary and Eschatology, there had been no classes on how to conduct a funeral. Oh, I had a clear theology and could preach a convincing sermon on the doctrine of the state of the dead, but I was ill-prepared to offer comfort, to minister on a personal, emotional level to the dying or the bereaved. This was just one of the reminders that kept coming at me that I needed "something more" if I was to have a ministry that counted for something in people's lives.

As time went by, I became even more conscious of my limitations-- not only professionally but personally. About this time my wife and I had our first child. Living up to my image of myself as a kind, loving supportive mate, I volunteered from time to time to take a turn getting up with the crying baby in the middle of the night. After an hour or two of futile attempts to calm the infant's penetrating wails, I would find myself much to my chagrin, becoming increasingly angry at this noisy but innocent little human being who was part of my own flesh! I had to ask myself, what kind of person was I, if I became hostile and angry at my own blameless son! How limited must be my love if I could not always love my own child well.

Carrying on my work as a pastor, I tried diligently to preach, evangelize, give Bible studies, visit and counsel, but I became aware rather quickly of my own limitations.
I kept having the feeling that I needed something more to make a difference for the people I was ministering to.

RIVERS OF LIVING WATER

One day I ran across a text that really grabbed my heart. John 7:38. "Whoever believes in me, as the Scripture has said, streams of living water will flow from within him." Now that sounded really promising. It seemed to be the very thing I was needing in my ministry and in my personal life. Imagine that! It was telling me that there could be an ever-flowing artesian well, an endless geyser of goodness gushing out of my life to be a source of blessing and inspiration to others! Is there a pastor or a father or a husband anywhere that would not covet that? Then the next verse really jumped out at me because it told me where I could get this marvelous gift. "By this he meant the Spirit, whom those who believed in him were later to receive. Up to that time the Spirit had not been given, since Jesus had not yet been glorified." v39 italics supplied

Here was a promise that offered me much hope. Yet I knew very little about the Holy Spirit or the baptism of the Spirit. In all those religion classes I had taken there had not been a single one on the topic of the Holy Spirit. That is especially tragic as I look back on it now, realizing that the most important topic in the entire Bible, after the cross and salvation by faith is the doctrine of the Holy Spirit. I also realized that when I was hired to be a minister, the qualifications I needed included being baptized by water, being a graduate of the Theological Seminary, being married (preferably to a wife who could play the piano!), and espousing faithfully without any hint of heresy my denomination's doctrines. While these expectations were made clear, no one ever thought to ask me the most important question of all for someone who wanted to serve as a pastor: "Are you baptized with the Holy Spirit?" Yet I found it interesting as I studied on the topic of the Holy Spirit, that in the New Testament church, even the deacons who served the congregation by running a program to feed the poor and widows and whose efforts freed up the apostles "for prayer and the ministry of the word," even these men had to be qualified for their humble position in the church by being "known to be full of the Spirit." (Acts 6:2-4).

THE QUESTION THAT DOESN'T GET ASKED

To everyone who wants to serve the church in any capacity the question needs to be asked: "Have you been baptized with the Holy Spirit?" It mystifies me why we are so reticent to do this. Actually every Christian needs to answer this question, because every Christian is a minister! Every Christian is called to serve and thus needs the Divine power of the in-dwelling Spirit. The priesthood of all believers was one of the foundational teachings of the Reformation. We must never let go of it. It would be a tragedy to leave the work of ministry to only trained pastors and evangelists! Does it scare you that you are called to have your own ministry? It needn't because all of God's biddings are His enablings. It will also help if you remember that it *is not your ability but your availability* that is important.

With the Holy Spirit filling you, you can simply make yourself available to God for service and He will use you and your unique personality and talents to touch and heal and serve others. When it comes to a ministry of your own, it is not so much what you know as Who you know! "When they saw the boldness of Peter and John, and perceived that they were uneducated and untrained men, they marveled. And they realized that they had been with Jesus"(Acts 4:13).

After seven years of professional theological training in college and seminary, instructed by well-educated and learned religious professors, my own moment of the assurance of personal salvation came from hearing the heart-felt testimony of a housewife!

If a person can not answer the question "have you been filled with the Holy Spirit?" with assurance and certainty, it means only one thing… his or her church failed them by not teaching about the baptism of the Spirit. Such church members have received an incomplete gospel. They should not be looked down upon or judged, because, have we not all been in their place? Instead, we have the blessed opportunity and the sacred responsibility of introducing them to the Spirit-filled life. We must teach them not to rush off into life, into service without the second great blessing.

"Tarry ye," "Stay in the city until you have been clothed with power from on high", were among some of the last and most significant words Jesus ever uttered to His followers (Luke 24:49). He knew that no one should set out on a ministry without the empowering Spirit. He knew that His followers could accomplish more in service in one day with the Spirit filling them then they could in years of labor in their own strength.

I CAN'T WAIT ANY LONGER!

Teaching people about the filling of the Spirit has been one of the great joys of my life. In the early years of doing it I pretty much had to fly under the radar. I recall that when I first started holding seminars on the topic back in the 1970's, it was usually a lay person, a doctor or lawyer or businessman who might have read one of my books and was willing to take the risk of arranging for me to come to their church. Often the pastor of the church would find it expedient to be away over the weekend I was there! Over the years, the climate began to change. Pastors or conference leaders began inviting me to come and talk about the Holy Spirit. I will never forget one occasion when a pastor met me at the airport with much kindness and enthusiasm. As we were driving to the church he suddenly pulled the car over, looked at me and was silent for a moment. Because of what had happened with some pastors in the past, I immediately assumed he must have some quarrel with the topic I was going to present. But then a big smile broke out on his face. He said: "since you were invited to come here a few months ago I have been devoting myself to studying the baptism of the Holy Spirit. I have never before learned so much that is so important and I have never been so blessed. You know what, I can't wait any longer. I can't wait for the meetings this weekend. Can we ask for the filling of the Holy Spirit for me right here, right now!"

At the time I was hired as a pastor I was much like the Christian believers in Ephesus, who though they had been converted and baptized by water, when Paul asked them, "Did you receive the Holy Spirit when you believed?" They replied, "No, we have not even heard that there is a Holy Spirit" (Acts 19:1,2). Please note that this text is one of many that shows the new birth is not synonymous with the baptism of the Spirit.

214

A JOURNEY OF DISCOVERY

My quest for "something more" led me on what was to become a fascinating journey of discovery. As I began to look for the source of those "springs of living water that could flow forth from within me," I found the Bible to be a book overflowing with the truth and the presence of the Holy Spirit. The Holy Spirit appears in the second verse of the first book of the Bible and in the last chapter of the last book of the Bible! There are over 250 references in the Scriptures to the Spirit. The Book of Acts is so full of the workings of the Spirit that it should be called the Acts of the Holy Spirit instead of the Acts of the Apostles! I read through the scriptures, carefully noting every reference to the Spirit and coloring that in. There was scarcely a page of Bible that did not show a great deal of yellow marker!

Other books were a great inspiration to me, such as Catherine Marshall's *Something More*, and *The Helper;* Leroy Froom's *The Coming of the Comforter*. (Nowadays a must-read book on the Spirit is, *Forgotten God, Reversing our Tragic Neglect of the Holy Spirit*, by Francis Chan.)

I came across the inspiring story of Dwight L. Moody, the great evangelist. In my mind his name calls up images of vast crowds gathered to listen earnestly to the great Christ-centered preaching of this mighty man of God. But he had not always had such power.

A preacher for years, Moody began to come to see that he needed something more in his ministry. He began to experience a yearning for the filling of the Holy Spirit. He actually began to feel that unless he could receive this gift, he did not want to preach any more. Moody had his headquarters in Chicago. The city had its devastating fire in 1871. It was the worst disaster in U.S. history until that time. It was on par with the Katrina tragedy with over 90,000 people left homeless. Moody went to New York to help raise money for the rebuilding of the city. But there was something else that weighed more heavily on his mind. "My heart," he confided later to his son, …

… was not in the work of begging… I was crying all the time that God would fill me with His Spirit. Well, one day, in the city of New York – oh, what a day!—I cannot describe it, I seldom refer to it: it is almost too sacred an experience to name. Paul had an experience of which he never spoke for fourteen years. I can only say that God revealed Himself to me, and I had such an experience of His love that I had to ask Him to stay His hand. I went to preaching again. The sermons were not different; I did not present any new truths, and yet hundreds were converted. I would not now be placed back where I was before that blessed experience if you could give me all the world—it would be as the small dust of the balance." 1.

I came to understand that I needed an encounter of my own with the Holy Spirit too if I was to carry on with my ministry and my life in a more significant and powerful way.

HAVE YOU OPENED YOUR PRESENT?

It seemed to me that I and many of those in my denomination were much like my daughter. When she was one year old, she received her first Christmas present. She was so caught up in looking at the colorful wrapping on the package that she refused to open it! Jesus has offered the wonderful gift of the baptism of the Holy Spirit to every believer. Along with salvation, it is part of the hard-earned spoil He won for us at the battle of the cross. Understand that it was not available to all believers before the cross.

Speaking to a group who were already converted believers, the Lord said, "He is WITH YOU (before the cross) and SHALL BE (after the cross) IN YOU." It took Jesus' sacrificial death to make it available to all. To some considerable extent, to ignore this gift is to disparage the sacred blood that made it possible. It is also to ignore the direct, command of the Master Himself when He said, after His resurrection, "Receive the Holy Spirit"(John 20:22). The master spiritual teacher himself gave this commandment and it is just as clear, just as much an imperative as keeping the two great commandments or the ten commandments, so it always puzzles me, when I ask church-goers if they are filled with the Spirit and they can not tell me! So often the responses range from, "No, I don't want anything to do with Pentecostalism" to, "Well, I hope to be filled someday," to "I think I will be filled with the Holy Spirit when the latter rain falls," to, "I am working on getting my character perfected so I can make it through the investigative judgment, so then I can be filled with the Holy Spirit."

THE BABY WITH THE BATHWATER

When I am presenting a seminar on the Holy Spirit, sometimes I like to walk up to someone in the audience and say something like, "Be honest with me now, have you shop-lifted or stolen anything in the last month?" The answer is always an indignant, "Why of course I haven't." I then like to point out how clear and conscientious most believers are about the importance of obeying the ten commandments. When asked if they are keeping any one of them there is no uncertainty in their minds if they are or not.

So it is puzzling to me when it comes to the imperative command of Jesus Himself, to "be filled with the Spirit," that so many church members ignore it or are unclear about whether or not they are obeying it. I have found there is even a strange "backlash" or resistance against the concept of the baptism of the Spirit I have found. For example, when I got excited about exploring the subject I shared my enthusiasm with some fellow pastors at a "workers" meeting. The response was either polite disinterest or cautionary warnings about not getting caught up in fanaticism! I have come to call this "the baby with the bathwater" phenomenon. Apparently, many more conservative Christians have heard about exuberant excesses in music or praise or worship styles or of tongues-speaking among some Pentecostals. Not wanting to be associated with this sort of thing, they have decided to avoid the issue of the Holy Spirit altogether. The truth is, the experience of the baptism of the Spirit is much more about quiet surrender and transformation than it is about rapture and ecstasy.

THE PRECIOUS GIFT

This is truly sad because the treasure of the gift of the Holy Spirit to His people was of such vital interest and importance to Jesus. He was so excited to be able to offer this gift to His children that He could hardly wait to get back to heaven so that it could be delivered. In His wisdom the Master could discern that the world would be better off with Him gone! "I tell you the truth: It is for your good that I am going away. Unless I go away, the Counselor will not come to you; but if I go, I will send him to you" (John 16:7). When Christ was here physically, He was severely limited. The restrictions of physical time and space were on Him. He could only be in one place at one time. He could only be with people, He could not be in them. His desire was to have Himself re-created in His people by the Spirit, so that through them, through you and me, He could be present to minister and serve everywhere on earth! He also knew that without the Holy Spirit we would be powerless.

Something is available since the cross and the ascension that was not available before. Something that was *with* believers before the cross is now able to be *in* them. I will say it again and keep repeating it because it is a vital point that has been missed: *The baptism of the Holy Spirit is a separate experience beyond conversion*. It does not *automatically* come to someone who is converted, born again or baptized by water.

Jesus was incredibly unique in the history of the world. He was conceived by the Holy Spirit. He was "born again" when He was in His mother's womb and He arrived in the world in a "born again" state. He was perfect from birth and He remained that way. But even the perfect, "born again" Jesus did not receive the baptism of the Holy Spirit to empower His ministry until He was 30 years old!

The very moment Jesus came up from the Jordan River water at His baptism, *the Holy Spirit descended on Him and filled Him in a new and powerful and dynamic way He had not experienced in His life on earth before*. He received water baptism and Spirit baptism simultaneously! *It is what moved Him from being the carpenter to being the Christ!* For some of us who are not so perfect, there may be days, weeks, months or years (in my own case 12 years) between the two experiences. The disciples did not receive this gift even when they walked and talked and traveled with Jesus Himself while He was on earth. Of course it was not generally available until after the cross, after the Lord's ascension. When Jesus spoke of His followers coming to have "streams of living water flowing from within them," the Bible explains that, "By this he meant the Spirit, whom those who believed in him were later to receive. Up to that time the Spirit had not been given since Jesus had not been glorified" (John 7:39).

It is important to note that Luke says that *"as he was praying,"* heaven was opened and the Holy Spirit descended on him." (Luke 3:21,22) This is a poignant reminder that as the old Southern preacher said, "The Holy Spirit falls, only when God's people are a-prayin.'" Even the Son had to be in connection and communion with the Father, and in a receptive mood before this priceless heavenly gift could be given to Him. It also instructs us that God values this sacred experience so much, He will not randomly hand it out based on church attendance or membership or correct doctrinal belief. It comes only to those who draw close to His presence in heart-felt supplication and prayer.

In the Old Testament times a handful of specially selected people received some extra measure of the Spirit to empower their work as prophets or leaders. But such a gift was not available to all believers. It was given to only a few, just as an escape from physical death was given to Enoch and Moses and Elijah without being made available to all believers. Both the blessing of the Spirit on a few and the entrance into heaven for a very few were a foretaste of what was to eventually be offered to all after the cross. Those who received these gifts received them contingent upon the sacrifice of Jesus that was yet to come.

Both eternal life and the gift of the baptism of God's Spirit have become available to all because of Jesus' death on the cross. These are the two great engines that propel the gospel! To ignore either one is to totally invalidate Christianity. We dare not minimize the post-cross, post-Pentecost, post-ascension gift of the baptism of the Holy Spirit by implying that it was generally available before the cross or by implying that it is the same as the "born again" experience of conversion, or that it comes to someone by default because they are converted or happen to belong to the right church.

That something is now available to all believers that was not available before the cross is also evidenced by Jesus' remarkable statement in John 14:12: "I tell you the truth, anyone who has faith in me will do what I have been doing. He will do even greater things than these." This text has had Biblical scholars scratching their heads for centuries. How could Jesus' followers possibly do more than heal the sick, raise the dead, walk on water, feed the 5,000 and give sight to the blind! How do you top that! How could His followers possibly do greater things?

Just before His death, Jesus told His disciples that He had to go so that the Holy Spirit might come in a new and powerful way. He had to leave so that the Spirit which was in Him could come to fill not just one Man, but everyone of His followers who chose to be indwelt. He was eager for the Holy Spirit to be sent so that the entire Christian community could have the potential to live and witness for Him in a dynamic new way. So that Christians could take His place in the world! So that we could start being love to people! Truth to people! *Jesus to people!* By the presence of the Holy Spirit living in His people, the work and role of Christ could be multiplied in the world thousands and thousands of times over.

Darrel Bock, a professor of New Testament Studies at Dallas Theological Seminary, says that the works of Jesus's followers today:

"are of a greater quality, since they belong to the era of God's promises fulfilled. These works reflect God's power in a special way, since every good work is made possible by what Jesus did. In Luke 7:28, Jesus says of John the Baptist, 'There is none born of women greater than he,' John is the greatest person of the old era… But all believers in the new era are greater than he was, because their works are empowered by the Spirit…The greater things of which Jesus spoke are greater because of the era our works belong to, not because of what they are in and of themselves. They point to the fact that God, in his grace, has forgiven us and given us his Spirit." 2.

For the disciples, even being physically with Jesus was not enough to give them everything they needed spiritually. They too needed something more internally. Something that was not available to them even when He was with them, before the cross. Something that could be sent down to earth only after He returned to Heaven.

There are those who covet the experience of the 12 disciples who were physically with Jesus. They, say, "Oh, if only I could have traveled with Him and worked with Him and ate with Him and listened to Him speak! How marvelous that would have been!"

In 2006, over 3 million Muslims made the Haj (pilgrimage) to Mecca during one week to visit the Grand Mosque which houses the Kaaba, the "sacred" black stone in whose direction Muslims face to pray five times a day. It was not uncommon for Pope John Paul II to draw a crowd of over one million people at special events in his travels. In l995 at the World Youth Day in Manila in the Philippines, a record of over four million people attended to see the Pope in person as he conducted the Mass.

Let's just say that Jesus decided to come down and hold a week-long revival meeting in Kansas City, Missouri, next June. Can you imagine all the effort and energy and time and money Christians from all over the world would put out to come and see Him physically in person? Imagine for a moment how many airline reservations would be made and hotel rooms booked. All the extra airliners in the world would be chartered! All those passenger jets sitting in storage in the Mojave desert would be put back in service! Every old rail car sitting on a siding somewhere put back on the rails! Every RV in America rented out! Every room within 500 miles of Kansas City would be booked! What do you think, 50 million? 75 million? 100 million would come for the chance to listen to and to see Him physically in person?

But Jesus says, "Don't bother. You needn't go to Kansas. You don't need to go to Mecca or Jerusalem. The kingdom of God is here! Now! It is within you! I have something more, something better for you. I sent you the Counselor, the Comforter. *I am the God who wants to live inside of you by my Spirit! Wherever you are. Right now.* I am the vine. You are the branches. Lo I am with you always. Wherever you are, God is."

A SEPARATE EXPERIENCE

Now, back to understanding that the baptism of the Spirit is a separate experience from the new birth. Paul was converted and became a Christian during his spectacular encounter with Jesus as he traveled on the road to Damascus with the intent to do great harm to the Christians there. Yet three days went by before he was baptized with the Holy Spirit and was empowered to begin a ministry working for Christ instead of against him. "Then Annanias …Placing his hands on Saul, he said, "Brother Saul, the Lord—Jesus who appeared to you on the road… has sent me so that you may see again and be filled with the Holy Spirit" (Acts 9:17).

 After spending a few days with the disciples in Damascus whom he had originally intended to persecute and imprison, "At once he began to preach in the synagogues that Jesus is the Son of God. All those who heard him were astonished" (v 20). Talk about a man transformed and empowered by the Holy Spirit! This nasty, narrow-minded, hostile little Pharisee became a great man of God. It is quite clear that without Paul's Spirit-filled ministry, evangelizing, writing, and his development of a solid theology there would have been no Christian church.

Here's one more example from the New Testament that the baptism of the Holy Spirit is not synonymous with conversion and water baptism. It is another warning that you and I can not just take it for granted and assume that we have it because we are born again or are members of a certain church. Philip was a great gospel preacher. His ministry in Samaria led to the conversion of many: "They believed Phillip as he preached the good news of the kingdom of God and the name of Jesus Christ, they were baptized, both men and women" (Acts 8:12).

Eventually the news of what had happened in Samaria reached the leaders of the church in Jerusalem. "When the apostles in Jerusalem heard that Samaria had accepted the word of God, they sent Peter and John to them. When they arrived, they prayed for them that they might receive the Holy Spirit, because the Holy Spirit had not yet come upon any of them; they had simply been baptized into the name of the Lord Jesus. Then Peter and John placed their hands on them, and they received the Holy Spirit (vss 14-17).

Here is a wonderful way to think about this. Water baptism is for eternal life in the future. Spirit baptism is for internal life now!

TWO KINDS OF CHRISTIANS

In the church today, there are two groups of Christians. There are those who through their conversion experience have the presence of Christ with them or beside them. To some extent this is like the experience the disciples had when Jesus walked on earth with them. But the Master said that He was going away because He had something better than that for His disciples! Now there are those, who through choosing to accept the baptism of the Holy Spirit have Christ in them. "For we are made partakers of Christ" (Hebrews 3:14, KJV). Stop. Read that verse again. Slowly. Contemplatively. Isn't that just about the most amazing, incredible, hopeful thing you have ever read!

This is the greater experience, the truly mysterious and amazing blessing, the one that Jesus said was much to our advantage over the former relationship. *Through the surrender of our hearts and egos, we create the space where God can actually dwell in us!*

Stop again. Take a deep breath and say to your self, "God lives in me." Just sit with that thought for a long while. Ponder the miracle. Embrace the mystery and the majesty of it!

This is the spiritual equivalent of the incredible experience Mary had when the Holy Spirit "overshadowed" her physically and the "Holy One" was formed inside her. Only now as the Spirit is invited to baptize you and me, miracle of miracles, the "Holy One" comes to dwell within us spiritually! This is the experience of the new spiritual paradigm that has been the focus of this book, a paradigm centered not on belief but on connection, a paradigm that is centered on the sweetness of the new intimacy with the Father that is now available to us through the indwelling Spirit. This is the very experience that Jesus had with His Father (Ephesians 1:17) says, "I keep asking that the God of our Lord Jesus Christ, the glorious Father, may give you the Spirit. ... *so that you may know him better*" (emphasis supplied). You see, the baptism of the

Holy Spirit is primarily about opening up to us a new, profound, previously unimaginable intimacy with our God. In a very real sense, Eden has been restored. The oneness with the Father is once again open to you and me! We can have what Jesus had!

The filling of the Spirit is *all about practicing the presence of God*. It is all about connection and continual conscious awareness of the Father, surrendering our own egos, abiding in Him. Oneness with Divinity! "Through these he has given us his very great and precious promises, so that through them *you may participate in the divine nature*" (2 Peter 1:4) (emphasis supplied). Isn't that just an incredible promise! Through this amazing gift of the baptism of the Spirit, the believer can become a partaker of the Divine nature. *We can become hosts to God!* It is the fulfillment of 1 John 4:13: "We know that we live in him and he in us, because he has given us of his Spirit." This is the fulfillment of the amazing experience Paul had. "I no longer live, but Christ lives in me" (Galatians 2:20). Hung up on the complexity of your church's theology? Wonder what Christianity is all about? You just read it in nine words.

This is such a treasure and it is so sad when it is ignored and neglected or avoided. To Jesus, the most precious of all possible gifts that can be enjoyed by His people today is the gift of the Holy Spirit. When it is disregarded it must break the heart of the One who won this precious experience for us through the battle of the cross.

I want to emphasize again the dramatic importance of understanding that this priceless gift is available to us now. In fact, any spiritual experience happens only in the now. There is an intimate connection between receiving the Holy Spirit and really understanding "now" and the "nowness" of the experience. The Spirit leads you to understand that the now is all that you have. In fact, to ignore and not be fully present in the now is to actually deny spirituality and even life itself because life and relationship only exist in the now. There is no past. It is gone. There is no future. It has not yet arrived. The now is sacred space because it is the point where everything is ending and everything is beginning. God in fact, lives only in the now. He is not the "I was" or the "I shall be." He is the "I am" and you can be too if you learn to be fully present in the moment. And what freedom this gives! It means that you are bound by nothing that has happened to you before this very moment! You do not have to be anxious about what you did or who you were before right now. Absolutely nothing from your past has any power to bind you. It has no power whatsoever over God's will for you this very moment.

You have heard God referred to as a "Presence". There is a reason for that. It is because God is always here. Now. In the present moment and nowhere else. (Because there is nowhere else!) *A great peace fills you up from the inside as you learn to rest in the arms of God in the present moment through the indwelling of the Spirit.* This is the place where you come into your true "I amness". Not the capitol "I" of the ego but the "I am" that is a piece of the Creator, the great "I am" who has shared His "I amness" with you when He made you in His image. This is your authentic self. Your true "I am" is not envious or resentful or selfish or proud. When the Holy Spirit is allowed to heal you and enlighten you and bring you to your "I am" state, you will discover there the presence of God, a place of unconditional love.

Many people struggle to connect with the Spirit because they have a tendency to never be where they are. They are never fully present, conscious and aware in the now so they wonder why they have difficulty encountering the Spirit, who is only present in the now. When people are occupied by thoughts of the past or thinking anxiously about the future, they can not present themselves as available to the Spirit.

THE INHERITANCE

To help you remember the difference between the baptism by water and the baptism by the Spirit, think of it this way … water baptism is for sinners. Spirit baptism is for sons and daughters! The Bible says that we are all heirs, sons and daughters of Christ. Here's the real deal … do you see yourself as a hard-working slave, struggling and trying to impress your master by your hard work and obedience? Or do you see yourself as a child of your Abba, held in the embrace of His loving arms? Abiding intimately in His Presence? Are you

225

trying or abiding? Struggling or snuggling? Old covenant or new covenant?
Law or grace? Rules or relationship. You decide.

Upon Jesus' death, we have been given this marvelous inheritance, the
gift of the indwelling Holy Spirit. God holds the spiritual riches of heaven in His
hand and He delights in showering them on you and me. Our inheritance has
made us all spiritual billionaires! We are rich, filthy rich in spiritual assets! "I
pray that the eyes of your heart may be enlightened in order that you may know
the hope to which he has called you, the riches of his glorious inheritance… and
his incomparable great power for us who believe" (Ephesians 1:18,19).

The marvelous fruits of the Spirit have all been provided in super-
abundance for us; the unconditional love, the joy, the peace, the compassion, the
kindness, the tenderness, the patience, the self-control … (Galatians 5) and
thrown in for good measure wisdom! And boldness! And power! "But you will
receive power when the Holy Spirit comes on you"(Acts1:8). Yes! An ordinary
little person like you and me can become a force that will shake heaven and hell
as we receive power to love and to serve and to minister! We can become bold
and strong while at the same time our spirit becomes sensitive to the things of
God. The Spirit also makes us more conscious of the invisible world around
you. This remarkable power transforms ordinary people into extraordinary
servants, giving us a life that has purpose and meaning, a life that makes a
contribution. That incredible power gives us a life that draws us away from our
egotism and our selfishness and our narcissism and our materialism and lets us
fulfill our true purpose as surrogates for Jesus, hosts for God on this earth right
now! No wonder that Jesus came excitedly proclaiming that the kingdom of God
is here now and is within you and me. In his best-selling book *Love Wins*, Rob
Bell says:

Heaven for Jesus wasn't just 'someday'; it was a present reality. Jesus blurs the
lines …inviting us, into the merging of heaven and earth, the future and the
present, *here and now*. To say it again, eternal life is less about a kind of time
that starts when we die, and more about a quality and vitality of life lived now in
connection with God. 3.

What a treasure, all deposited into our spiritual bank-accounts the day
Jesus returned to heaven. What an inheritance we have received! But alas!

There are so many who do not know that they can write checks on this account right now!

Q&A:

Q. Do you need to receive the baptism of the Holy Spirit to be saved?

A. No. The baptism of the Spirit is not about salvation. It is a post-conversion experience available to people who are already saved and have the assurance of their salvation. It opens believers to an even greater love and appreciation for Jesus and for others, it creates a profound intimacy and oneness with God and empowers them for a ministry of service to others. (The thief on the cross, and others who lived before the cross and Pentecost did not have access to the baptism of the Spirit, yet many of these will be saved)

Q. Is the person who is baptized with the Spirit superior to other Christians who are not?

A. No. Being filled with the Spirit does not make you a super-Christian. You will still make mistakes. You will still need grace and forgiveness. You are not better than or holier than anyone else. (Witness the disciples and Paul.)

Q. You say we should all have the assurance of receiving the baptism of the Spirit and be able to say that we are. If I tell people I am baptized with the Spirit, isn't that like bragging?

A. No. It is just the opposite. It is saying, "I need help. I recognize my own insufficiency." I need something more from outside myself to be able to love and to serve."

Q. I think I was filled with the Spirit at the time I was converted or at least shortly thereafter. Are you telling me this is not so?

A. No. I wouldn't dare. Everyone's experience with the Holy Spirit is different. That is part of the uniqueness and joy and excitement of it. That is why the Spirit is associated with the wind, because there is no restriction on how the Holy Spirit chooses to work, He "comes and goes as He pleases." (John 3:8). It is not up to me or anyone to judge or try to measure your experience with the

Holy Spirit. You can not bottle the Spirit up with some kind of religious formula. Thank goodness the church organization does not have a "Department of the Holy Spirit" that pushes pastors to get a certain number of people baptized by the Spirit every year in their churches!

FOOTNOTES CHAPTER 15:

1. Moody, Dwight. *The Life of Dwight L. Moody*, (Fleming H. Revell Co., New York, 1900) p.149.

2. Bock, Darrell. *Christianity Today*, June 2006, p. 56.

3. Bell, Rob, *Love Wins*,(Harper Collins, New York, 2010) p.59

.

CHAPTER 16:

HOW TO BE FILLED WITH THE SPIRIT

"If you then, though you are evil, know how to give good gifts to your children, how much more will your Father in heaven give the Holy Spirit to those who ask him!"

— Luke 11:13

Anything of value that I have ever received in my life came because I first asked for it. I asked to be admitted to a college of my choice and I was. Four years later I had a career. While I was in college, I met a young woman and eventually asked her to marry me. She agreed and I had a wife. When I finished college I asked an organization if they would hire me. They said yes, and I had a job. Some years later I wrote a manuscript then I asked a publisher to print it. They said yes, and I had a book.

As a counselor, one of the most powerful and empowering phrases I have found you can use with a client in therapy is: "How can you make that happen?" Therapy is after all about becoming more conscious and more aware of who you really are and what you really want in your life and in your relationships and then taking the initiative to make change and growth happen for yourself. Part of that process often begins with a person mustering the courage to ask for something that they want or need.

It is up to you to make your spiritual life happen. Don't ever let anyone else tell you how to "do" your religion. No one has the right to tell you how you should be spiritual. That is between you and Jesus as you take Him as your model and let His principles and character be reflected through your own unique personality.

YOU CAN MAKE IT HAPPEN

The most exciting, rewarding thing you will ever do in your life is to co-create your own personal spirituality under the guidance of the Holy Spirit.

No one has the right to tell you how to "do" your marriage. It is a unique, intimate relationship between you and your spouse. Many Christians have no idea how truly free they are. They underestimate the incredible extent of their freedom in Christ. They keep wanting to repair the torn curtain and hang it back up in the sanctuary! They keep wanting to crawl back under the burden of the law or of the authority of the church, or to the pressure to conform to the expectations of their religious peers, or the religious rules and expectations of their parents or grandparents. Remember, one of the greatest freedoms is the freedom from the good opinion of others. Especially the others in your family or your church! I know, I know, now you are getting uncomfortable, but it was the Lord Himself who said, "For I have come to turn a man against his father, a daughter against her mother. Any one who loves their father or mother more than me is not worthy of me. If anyone comes to me and does not hate father and mother…such a person cannot be my disciple." Hard words and I will not attempt to interpret them for you right now, but here's the thing… *Sometimes the Spirit may call you to move on beyond the religious traditions and positions and theology of your family members or friends or fellow church members.* No one, no person, no institution has the right to tell you how to "do" your personal spiritual life. You have been awarded a holy freedom, a kind of holy wildness that gives you sacred permission to develop your own intimate, personal relationship with the God. This God, at your invitation, has entered you and now lives within you as your bridegroom. You get the joy of learning how to live with Him and be intimate with Him in your own distinct way. Just the two of you! Learning to delight in each other! Imagine it! For example, it is up to you to make the baptism of the Holy Spirit happen for you. No one else can do it for you. Not your parents or your spouse or your pastor. You can't sit and wait for your church to have some kind of revival. You can't wait for the "latter rain" to fall. "Work out your own salvation," the Bible says. *You are in charge of your spiritual life.* One more time … *You are in charge of your spiritual life!* The most important first step you can take after conversion is to begin by simply asking for the gift of the Holy Spirit. The Bible says, "You have not because you ask not." You and no one else may start the process.

God does not stand on a street corner and pass out His richest treasures to everyone who passes by. He reserves them for people who care enough to ask. For people who are willing to take the initiative to knock. Not just rap timidly, but perhaps even pound on the door with passionate persistence! "Knock and it shall be opened unto you," is the promise.

It all begins, as it did for me, with recognizing and acknowledging your need. Your need to be more loving. Your need to have more joy and peace and patience and kindness. Your need to have more wisdom and power to serve and minister. *Recognizing your need for Him is the only qualification required for receiving the Holy Spirit!* The only qualification you need to join Alcoholics Anonymous is to be a drunk, to acknowledge your powerlessness over your addiction. The only qualification you need to be saved is to acknowledge that you are a sinner who needs a Savior. The only qualification you need to be filled with the Holy Spirit is to become aware of your own need for the indwelling Divine Presence and power.

When Jesus promised those springs of living water that would flow out of our hearts to others, He said they would be given to those who thirst. Earlier He had said in His great sermon that it is those who hunger and thirst after righteousness who would be filled! One of my all-time favorite texts is Jeremiah 29:13-14. "You will seek me and find me when you seek me with all our heart. I will be found by you,' declares the Lord."

HE IS HERE, NOW

Jesus Himself promised, "Remain in me, and I will remain in you" (John 15:4). The foundation of the new spiritual paradigm that has been presented in this book and the key to entering fully into the Spirit-filled life is developing an awareness of the presence of God in your life. We must come to realize that incredibly, He is already continually present and available to all of us. Paul seemed surprised at believers ignorance of a great spiritual essential when he wrote, "Don't you know that you yourselves are God's temple and that God's Spirit lives in you?" (1 Corinthians 3:16).

In the flyleaf of my 50 year-old Bible I long ago printed a beautiful anonymous saying I found. "The light of God surround me, the love of God enfolds me, the power of God protects me. The presence of God watches over me. Wherever I am, God is." Friends, God-consciousness is everything. I don't understand why some preachers insist on inviting God or the Holy Spirit "to come and be with us" when they start a service. Excuse me. He is already here! Unlike Elvis, the Holy Spirit never leaves the building! Our prayer needs to be, "Father, open our hearts that we may now become fully conscious of your splendid Presence"! Instead of always asking for some object or some outcome, let us more often ask Him simply for Himself. The highest form of prayer is to bring ourselves to God as a surrendered, empty vessel and simply allow God to fill us up!

What an astonishing fact, that since the cross, God through His Spirit has been fully present for us and with us. Our challenge is to simply become aware of Him! Our challenge is to become spiritually conscious! The mystic Thomas Merton was once asked, "How can we best help people attain union with God?" His answer: "We must tell them that they are already united with God."

William H. Shannon wrote: "…I don't have to worry about 'getting anywhere' in prayer, because I am already there. I simply have to become aware of this." 1.

PRAYER … THE KEY

I know that to some of you the triteness of it will send shudders down your spine, but I have to say it anyway. The doorway to the deep spiritual life we are reflecting on here is prayer. Prayer. Plain and simple. Prayer, the key to the Spirit-filled life. Remember Jesus' experience at His baptism? "*As He was praying*, the Spirit descended on Him" (emphasis supplied).

Sometimes I detest the word prayer. I wish we could invent a new and better and more dynamic word that has not been so abused and misused. I generally love and seek prayer and praying people whenever I can now, but in the past, I have had a love/hate relationship with prayer. How many times have I heard someone say, "Let us bow our heads in prayer"? Only to have those words followed by a sinking feeling in the pit of my stomach. Oh, not that again! I don't feel like praying right now! Anything but prayer! I don't want to hear any fancy language. The echoes of the "thees" and the "thous" still haunt me. Not to mention the tongue twister of "wouldest" and "couldest" and "shouldest". Can you believe that until I was in my thirties, it was actually considered indecent and blasphemous to pray up front in church and not use the Old English of the King James Version! If you got up there and addressed The Holy One with the pronouns "you" and "yours," you would get some severe frowns afterward and would not be invited again to, "lead out in prayer."

Some of my adverse reaction to the word prayer comes because I have been a victim of prayer in my lifetime. Boring prayers. Showman prayers. Trite prayers. Knee-aching, back-breaking distended prayers stretched out longer than the Bay Bridge. Sometimes I could just scream when I hear the word prayer. Worse, I have been abused by prayer. I have had prayer pushed down my throat by supposedly well-meaning people when I didn't want it. I have been lectured and preached at in prayer. I have been hit over the head by prayers.

All right, all right, as you see, I have some issues with prayer. My bad. But I am working on it! I have already talked about throwing the baby out with the bathwater when it comes to the Holy Spirit. I sure don't want to do that with prayer. Though humans (including myself) have misused it and twisted it and distorted it, it is truly an essential and wondrous thing. No one had defined it more splendidly and reassuringly for me than Brennan Manning, one of God's itinerant prophets of today, albeit a recovering alcoholic prophet.

Have you ever noticed how remarkably and persistently God insists on using flawed people to be His spokesman? There was Scott Peck. What a guy! An atheist psychiatrist who became a unique and devoted Christian. A man full of insight and precious wisdom who spoke his truth to society in the 1980's so incredibly well that his marvelous book *The Road Less Traveled* was on the *New York Times* bestseller list for years! Sadly, this very wise physician could not break his tobacco habit. The truth is, being human we are of course all flawed "prophets," all wounded healers.

In his deeply spiritual book, *The Signature of Jesus*, Manning writes, "Whatever else it may be, *prayer is first and foremost an act of love*. Beyond any pragmatic considerations, prayer is personal response to the love of God." 2.

Manning sees what he calls "contemplative prayer" as a little child choosing to be with his father, settling down in the Father's arms. (Another writer has spoken of how Jesus constantly "abode in the bosom of the Father." I try to tuck myself in there every night when I go to sleep... and in the morning when I wake up! Yes! It's true. God longs to hold you in His "everlasting arms." to coddle and cuddle you!) Manning proposes taking at least two 20 minute periods of contemplative prayer each day. To help seekers enter into a rich prayer experience, he recommends first taking a few minutes to relax the body and quiet the spirit. He suggests choosing a single sacred word or phrase that captures the essence of your relationship with God. A word like Jesus, Abba, or a phrase like "Help me to live in your presence." Then he says to repeat your personal, sacred word inwardly, slowly and often. He likes to conclude his prayer time with the Lord 's Prayer or some spontaneous words of praise and thanks.

Best of all, we have the example of our Savior. "Jesus often withdrew to lonely places and prayed." (Luke 5:16).

To pray is to descend from the mind into the heart. Prayer is the essential breath of your spiritual life. When, in our own personal way, we learn to open our hearts and spend intimate time with our Father, the Spirit will bring us into such an awareness of Him that we will be staggered with His glory and His loving presence.

AS SIMPLE AS ABC

I love to compare receiving the baptism of the Spirit with receiving the gift of eternal life. Most Christians have at last come to understand the utter simplicity of how to receive the gift of eternal life. We finally have come to realize that God does not grade on the curve, He grades on the Cross! When you grasp the simple process of receiving righteousness by faith, when you come to have the assurance of your salvation, it is much easier to understand how to receive the gift of the Spirit. The process is exactly the same. It is, as they say, as simple as A B C. A, you ask clearly for what you want. B, you believe you have received it because Someone who does not lie has promised it to you. C, you joyfully claim the gift and have the assurance that it is yours. The B, believe part is really important. Here's why: *you can never have anything that you do not believe you can have*. That is spiritual rule number one. But think about it. It is true in everyday life too. You want a job? You have to believe you can get one. You want to get married? You have to believe that can happen for you. You can not have eternal life, you can not have the Holy Spirit unless you first *believe* you can have them. That is your part. God takes care of the rest. Henry Ford once famously said, "You can believe you can or you can believe you can't. Either way you are right."

Here is an important point …believers have no difficulty understanding that though Jesus died on the cross to provide an abiding gift of salvation for all sinners, this precious gift is not randomly handed out. It is clear that each person must individually appropriate salvation to himself or herself personally before it becomes a reality for them. It is strange that so many have a confused picture about the gift of the Holy Spirit. There are those who think that since the Spirit was sent into the world by Christ at Pentecost you don't need to ask for, or appropriate the filling of the Spirit for yourself. It is just sort of "there" and you don't need to ask for it because it is already given. They think it somehow automatically comes to them because they receive salvation and the new birth. Not so. As each person must appropriate his or her own salvation, so they must also ask for, pray for and appropriate the second blessing, the baptism of the Holy Spirit. "You have not because you ask not," the scripture says.

By the way, since we are talking about the assurance of salvation by faith, just a warning: a lot of people (especially those of us who have had to struggle for years to get to this point) seem to feel that once they have come to have the assurance of their salvation and they know that they are saved, that is it.

They have arrived. They are at the end of their spiritual journey. Now, they can sit back and wait for the Lord to come! But guess what? God does not save you in order to put you in a holding pattern.

When will we ever get it? The Christian religion is not primarily about earning heaven or escaping hell! So many Christians seem to think that you get saved and then you skip right on to the second coming or you just sort of hang on or hang out until the second coming! So much is missed if once you are saved, you move your focus off into the second coming in the future. Here's the thing, God does not save you in order to put you on ice until the second coming! He saves you, and then . . . part two, *He wants to light you on fire with the Holy Spirit!* Right now! Salvation is not just about something you get when you are converted. It is not just about what happens when the Lord comes or what happens after you die. Salvation is the beginning of something wonderful. It is not only about you accepting God. It is more about your finally understanding that God has accepted you! Into the beloved! It is a process, a relationship, that begins to open up its splendors for the Spirit-filled Christian the minute they begin to realize how much God loves them and how close He wants to be to them! Heaven begins now for those who understand this.

BEYOND SALVATION

Here's something that may shock you. *The whole point of salvation is not primarily to give the believer eternal life.* It is not all about earning heaven or escaping hell! The primary purpose of the redemption that Jesus Christ died to make possible for you and me is that we might be baptized with the Spirit: "He redeemed us in order that the blessing given to Abraham might come to the Gentiles through Christ Jesus, *so that by faith we might receive the promise of the Spirit* (Galatians 3:14, emphasis supplied).

There it is. *You and I are redeemed so that we can be filled with the Spirit.* And oh, by the way, an added bonus, did I mention you get to live forever?

There is an amazing and overlooked text in Hebrews 6. Speaking to converted Christians, Paul says, bluntly, "Therefore let us leave the elementary teachings about Christ (He (Paul) is talking about the new birth and salvation by faith here!) and go on to maturity, not laying again the foundation of repentance ... and of faith in God ..." (v. 1). He goes on to call the doctrine of baptism and the doctrine of the judgment elementary, and instructs mature Christians to move on! Getting believers to move on to the next dimension of the spiritual life, the baptism of the Holy Spirit is clearly his goal.

Can you believe it? Paul actually saying; "cut it out!" Paul is telling Christians to stop preaching salvation by faith! He of course meant to stop preaching it to the choir who already had got it! John Wesley raised some eyebrows once when he accused those who preached only justification by faith with leaving their converts "stranded at the cross." There comes a time when the maturity level is great enough in our churches that we should stop preaching and re-preaching and repeating the doctrine of salvation by faith and other basic doctrines and focus on something more! We must come to focus on the engine for spiritual growth, on the second dimension of spirituality, the baptism of the Holy Spirit.

BY FAITH ALONE

So, we receive all spiritual blessings by the ABC method. We have covered step A, the asking part. Now let's go to step B, the believing part. The New Testament has some very helpful guidance here. Let's start with a rather profound rhetorical question that Paul asked in Galatians 3:2: "Did you receive the Spirit by observing the law, or by believing what you heard?" Paul has already answered his own question because in a preceding verse, in one of the most striking statements in the Bible he says, "I live by faith in the Son of God who loved me and gave himself for me. I do not set aside the grace of God, for if righteousness could be gained through the law, Christ died for nothing! (Galatians 2:20, 21).

Paul really wants to rub it in. He really wants believers to get it, because again in Galatians 3, he asks another obvious question: "Does God give you his Spirit and work miracles among you because you observe the law, or because you believed what you heard?" (v 5). Then, once again he clearly and precisely answers his own question: "He redeemed us so that by faith we might receive the promise of the Spirit" (v. 14 (emphasis supplied). Excuse me. Why did He redeem us? So that we could sit around and wait for the second coming? No! A thousand times no! He redeemed us so that we could "receive the promise of the Spirit." Now! So that the kingdom of God could begin in us *right now!* He doesn't save us and then put us on ice. He saves us and wants to ignite us with the holy fire of His Spirit of love indwelling our very being in the present moment! So that we can go out and be Jesus to people!

Well, when it comes to how to receive the Spirit, there you have it, one of the most important texts in all of Scripture on the Holy Spirit. And the whole point of it is, you do not qualify for the baptism of the Holy Spirit by obeying the law or by your own good works and good behavior! Just as you receive eternal life by faith, so you receive the indwelling of the Spirit! You don't have to do anything to qualify for it. You don't have to struggle to earn it. It is not achieved, it is received! It is a gift! You only have to believe Jesus' promise that He would send you the Comforter. (By the way, please note that Jesus did not refer to the Holy Spirit as the "Theology Teacher" or the "Rules Enforcer," Though the Spirit has many roles, His/Her job description is best described as the Comforter! Thank you Jesus! I will take all the heavenly comfort I can get! Comforter is often considered to be a feminine role. I am distressed that we have come to think of the Holy Spirit as somehow somewhat mysteriously vacuous and primarily masculine. We usually refer to the Spirit as "He." But that is so sadly limiting. The Holy Spirit is the most feminine presence in the Trinity and should be regarded and experienced as such. We have a loving father presence in our Abba, we have a brother and bridegroom presence in our marvelous Jesus, but in the Holy Spirit we have the soft, gentle, dove-like, creative, breath-of-life, comforting feminine presence of the Holy Spirit. The Spirit exemplifies all the very best about womanhood and motherhood. One of the gifts of the marvelous book *The Shack* was to present an unforgettable portrayal of the Holy Spirit as an incredibly loving, sustaining, comforting very feminine presence the author chose to call Sarayu (another name for wind). If you haven't read *The Shack*, do so. If you have read it before and are now filled with the Spirit, read it again and enjoy its sweet wonder in the Spirit and you will be greatly blessed. It is one of the most important books of the last 200 years. It is an enduring spiritual classic. It is a powerful book that draws you into the love and presence of God as very few books outside the Scriptures can do. As for those of you that think it is "a work of the devil" because it may take a different view of life after death than your church does … well, I am praying for you! The book is not about the theology of what happens when you die. Remember, Jesus told a much weirder fictional story about the rich man and Lazarus and their very conscious lives after death than this book ever does. He used that story-myth, that fictional parable, as a teaching tool to reveal a greater truth. Are you going to dare to sit in judgment of His theology too? I didn't think so.)

Believe in a God who says that He loves to give good gifts to His children. Believe in a Heavenly Father who says if you ask for the Holy Spirit, you will receive it. There are only two prerequisites for receiving the baptism of the Holy Spirit. 1. You have chosen to surrender your life to Jesus, you are in a personal relationship with Him and as a result you have the assurance by faith of your salvation. 2. You have asked for the baptism of the Spirit. That's it. Period.

I love John best of all the Bible writers. Youngest of the disciples, he was the one closest to Jesus. He bonded with Him with an intimacy that escaped the others. I believe Jesus' greatest truths are best reflected in John's writings. For example it is his gospel that expresses most clearly and profoundly the Divinity of Jesus and the beautiful truth of the Trinity. (By the way, if you are new to reading the Bible, whatever you do, don't start at the front with the book of Genesis, start with the book of John and then run don't walk to the book of 1st John.) One writer said that John, "wrote with a pen dipped in love." Oh, how sometimes I wish that our New Testament ended with the book of 1st John, that book of love, the one that is right there close to the end anyway! Leave it to John to simply and beautifully summarize what we are talking about here. "This is the confidence we have in approaching God: that if we ask anything according to his will, he hears us, whatever we ask, we know that we have what we asked of him." (1 John 5:14,15).

Remember, Jesus commanded His followers to "receive the Holy Spirit" (John 20:21). Obviously then, it is His will that you be baptized with the Spirit. If it is indeed His will, and you have asked for it, then, you can know that it is yours! You can take step C in the simple ABC's of Spirit baptism and claim it! It is just that simple!

Scholars and theologians and preachers and priests and councils and cardinals and committees through the centuries have succeeded in creating a misconception that Christianity is a very complex faith. Not so. Genuine Christianity can be understood by a child. (For hundreds and hundreds of years, the Church leaders were so sublimely egotistical that they were convinced that the average believer could not comprehend the Bible and should not be allowed to read it. It was kept out of the language of the people. Only the priests were allowed to read and interpret it to church members.) As Thoreau said, "Simplify, Simplify, Simplify." The whole truth of Christianity can be summarized in just three sentences: 1. God is love. 2. Jesus saves. 3. The Holy Spirit wants to live in you now. That is all you need to know and you are on your way to glory! Q&A:

Q. If receiving the baptism of the Spirit is as simple as you say it is, why have so many neglected it for so long?

A. *1. Fear.* Fear of the unknown. Fear of change. Fear of stepping outside the crowd, outside the approval of friends or relatives. Fear of being thought of as "different"
or fanatical.

2. Ignorance. Alas, many Christians even today do not even know about the baptism of the Holy Spirit. As I told you, in all my years of theological training there were no courses offered on the Holy Spirit. The subject was scarcely mentioned. However, there was plenty of emphasis on eschatology and the judgment and other complex theological topics which often receive little attention in the New Testament, while the doctrine of the Holy Spirit which is referred to over 250 times in the Bible was ignored! We have put our emphasis on paranoid speculation about last-day events while we have ignored the most important teaching after the Cross.

In the children's and junior's Sunday Schools, I notice that teachers are eager to tell the Old Testament stories some of which can be a bit violent and titillating like David and Goliath and Sampson and Delilah but no one ever says a word to the little ones about the Holy Spirit. Nowadays in Sunday Schools for early-teens and youth there seems to be a lot of discussion about music and movies and dating and wearing jewelry but no one is teaching them about the Holy Spirit. In sixty years of attending church, I can not remember ever hearing a sermon preached on the baptism of the Holy Spirit.

3. Ego. We would all like to think we can do it on our own. Who needs a helper or a counselor or a comforter anyway? To admit that our efforts are insufficient or inadequate is a tremendous blow to that demanding force, the ego. Ego is all about our obsession with ourselves. One writer has called the ego, "the very devil itself!" In fact, the most extreme example of the insane pride of the ego was when Satan asked Jesus, His creator, to bow down and worship him! The ego is completely preoccupied with itself. It tends to shut itself off from God. It is all about our obsession with our self-identity, our work, our education, our material possessions, our beliefs, even our own seductive thinking processes. Ego and its hand-maid, pride, often get in the way of our asking for help or the Helper. *You can either be a hostage to your ego or a host to God.* You decide. You get to choose! Each day. Here is the bottom line; if you can not learn to lose sight of self, you will not know the presence of God. Our mind, our emotions, our ego must be transformed by full surrender to the Holy Spirit. When a person lives only for himself, he is primarily self-conscious, with little consciousness of God. Selfness, ego is what manifests to others. When people receive the Spirit, they become God-conscious and manifest the love of the Father in their lives. Living in the Spirit means living in a state of God-consciousness, God-awareness, God-mindfulness. It means living "in Presence". Living in an atmosphere of unconditional love.

241

When we make the choice to live in this way, others will begin to notice the difference. Even the look on our faces, the way we speak, the tone of our voice, our actions, will reveal that we have come into the presence of God. After Moses had been in the presence of God, he came down from the mountain and there was so much of the light and glory of God in his face that the people asked him to wear a veil so that they would not be blinded! When you have been practicing the presence of God it shows up in your life in many ways. I went to visit with someone the other day and I had only just walked through the door when I could tell he was under the influence. There were two bottles of wine on his coffee table and his eyes were a bit glassy and his speech slower than normal. In the same way, only in a positive way, people can tell when you and I are under the influence of the Holy Spirit! The love will show up! The joy will be evident! "We were all given the one Spirit to drink" (1 Corinthians 12:13).

Death to self, abandoning the ego, death to the ego, surrender, emptying, are necessary before filling, the filling of the Spirit can occur. (Surrendering is the most powerful thing you can do. It is also the easiest. And the hardest.) Surrender is a conscious act on our part. A clear mental decision, and the ego absolutely hates it and vehemently resists it! It is a choice to let go of self totally without any conditions attached. Surrender, emptying is so crucial, because the cup has to be emptied before it can be filled. Any composer can tell you that it is the empty space between the notes that give music its very meaning. Any writer knows that it is the empty space between and surrounding the letters that allows her to form a word and communicate a message. *By surrendering we open the space within so that the Spirit has a temple in which to dwell.* Think about a cup. It is only the empty space within that makes it useful, that allows it to fulfill its true purpose. The walls and roof of a house are what we see when we look at a building, but it is the empty space within that makes it a true home and allows us to live there. Even Jesus had to empty Himself the Bible says. He had to empty Himself of His Divinity so that He could take on humanity and serve and save us. We, on the other hand, must empty ourselves of our humanity, our ego, our self, so that we may take on

Divinity! We must surrender our human nature in order to become partakers of the Divine nature! Total ego unawareness is the goal of the Spirit-filled Christian. "I no longer live for Christ lives within me" is our mantra. I will put it to you as bluntly as I can. The price of fully receiving the baptism of the Holy Spirit is total death to self. Daily. A great Christian lady lay dying. To a distraught friend offering her comfort she said: "It is all right, I died a long time ago." *We are all called to die before we die so that we might fully live!*

There is a cute up-scale little boutique in a trendy Northern California town near where I live. I have to smile every time I walk by it. It is called "All About Me." Each day, you get to decide … who is on the throne of your heart? Ego? Or the Spirit? Is it "all about you"? Or all about Jesus? The ego isolates. It is all about our own small, separated self. The Spirit draws us into connection and oneness, oneness with God and with each other. The Spirit calls us forth on a journey from narcissism to compassion. The Spirit is constantly trying to teach us that everything but love is unimportant.

Getting the ego out of the center, off the throne of the life, prepares us for the Spirit to come in. (Without ego, there is only love.) The saving grace of Jesus allows us to drop our attachment to ego. With ego gone and Jesus on the throne of our lives, we come to realize that we are not good and worthy of ourselves, nor do we any longer condemn ourselves as bad or unworthy. We are at peace. We are "accepted in the beloved"!

It is ego that keeps us so attached to the world of things, of power and possessions. The ego feeds on fear. The soul is nurtured by love. Some denominations teach about a "Great Controversy" between good and evil, between Christ and Satan. While on a grand, universal scale this certainly goes on in the universe, the real "great controversy" that most of us face every day is the war between fear and love. Between ego and surrender.

It is ego that powers the mind and compels it to keep constantly, frantically spinning (monkey-mind!) with our own ideas and plans and fears and anxieties. It is this self-infatuation that blocks us from entering in to the sacred place of quietness and stillness where the Spirit is patiently waiting for us, waiting to connect intimately with us in oneness, waiting to immerse us in love.

Remember the God who was not in the wind or the fire but was in the stillness? Remember that God's language is often silence. Meditative stillness and silence is entering into a place where you no longer are busy reacting to every thing you see or hear or every thing that comes into your mind. When you surrender your ego, when you open your heart, when thought stops and you create this kind of empty space, you are creating a temple for the Holy Spirit to dwell! In rushes the very power and presence of God!

FOOTNOTES CHAPTER 16:

1. Shannon, William H.. *Silence on Fire*,(Crossroad Publishing, Crossroad, NY, l991) p. 22.

2. Manning, Brennan. *The Signature of Jesus*,(Multnomah Books, Sisters, Oregon, 1996) p. 219.

CHAPTER 17:

ARE YOU READY FOR A GROWN-UP'S GOD?
God is Christ-like

When I was a child, there were stories often told to us encouraging us to believe that Christians received special treatment from God. There was the tale of the faithful tithe-paying farmer who had his crops spared when neighbor's on all sides of him had theirs destroyed in a tornado. Or was it grasshoppers that devoured everything in his unfortunate neighbors fields but left his crops untouched? When are we going to let go of our Cradle Roll/Kindergarten concepts of God and move on to some spiritual maturity? Jesus said that God allows the rain to fall on both the just and the unjust. Pain, sickness, death fall on both the just and the unjust also.

At some point we have to address the misconception that the baptism of the Spirit is some kind of panacea for everything that ails a human being. Let's start with the most basic truth of all … God is love. He is pure love. Pure unconditional love. His great love has led Him to arrange for all of us to have what we need most … eternal life through His Son and the gift of the in-dwelling Holy Spirit right now. When you walk into God's restaurant, that is what is on the menu. When you read the sign outside of God's shop, it does not offer plumbing repairs or chiropractic adjustments or cancer cures. God is in the salvation and Holy Spirit business. That is what He offers to you and me. The Scriptures tell us that there are only two prayers God has agreed to always answer immediately and affirmatively: a sincere request for redemption/eternal life and a sincere appeal for the Holy Spirit to come and live within the surrendered heart. To assume that He will provide you with anything beyond those two best of all gifts is pure presumption and speculation. He can and He does offer much more, but all in His own time and in His own way and in His own wisdom.

Some preachers have sold a bill of goods to people that God is committed to making Christians rich, to providing them with an abundance of money and material things. This is simply not true. That is cargo-cult Christianity. Other misguided religious leaders have misled people into thinking that if you are close to God, you are guaranteed good health and freedom from physical or mental illness. Wrong again. Health and wealth are not automatically synonymous with Divine favor. The "prosperity gospel" or the "protectionistic" gospel that some preach is the very antithesis of many of Jesus' teachings.

Let's be very clear. God does not cause pain, sickness or death. He does not cause natural disasters. *So-called "acts of God" are not.* He does not cause floods, earthquakes, fires or car accidents in order to punish atheists, Methodists, Baptists or Democrats or anyone else. He did not cause HIV in order to punish gays. He did not bring down the World Trade Center to punish the USA for allowing abortions. He did not punish Haiti with a mega earthquake because some of the country's founders over 300 years ago made an alleged contract with the forces of evil. The fundamentalist evangelical right wing blamed Katrina on gays, abortion and floozies! Wrong! God does not kill. That is the good news. The bad news: God does not intervene very often in the physical world to save physical lives.

The earthquake that hit Japan in May 2011 was the most powerful to ever strike that country. It was one of the five most powerful earthquakes in the world. It triggered tsunami waves of heights up to an amazing 133 feet. God did not stop the forces that took over 20,000 lives. God did not save six million innocent Jews. He did not intervene in Rwanda to save over one million souls slaughtered and betrayed by their own neighbors. (Sadly, neither did the United States government. Bill Clinton has said that this was the greatest mistake of his presidency.) No, God did not intervene in the Haitian earthquake where 250,000 people perished in a few horrific seconds. Nor did He intervene with the course of events in the Indian Ocean when over 300,000 men women and children were annihilated in an earthquake and tidal wave.

God not only does not usually intervene when natural disasters occur, He also may not intervene when human-caused disasters happen. He did not choose to stop the shooter who executed 20 innocent 6 and 7-year-old grade-school children and six of their teachers in Sandy Hook Connecticut. He did not intervene on 9/11 and 3,000 souls perished. As many or more Christians died on Flight 93 as did atheists.

I am sorry to break the news to you, but there are as many schizophrenic Christians as there are Muslims per capita. If bird flu or swine flu or SARS or Ebola or some other as yet unheard of plague strikes us, Christians will likely die at the same rate as Buddhists or Hindus or non-believers. Christianity, even the Spirit-filled life, is not a magic vaccine against physical or emotional tragedy, illness or death.

GOD'S JOB DESCRIPTION

Stop, think. Countless numbers of sincere Christian men, women and children have physically starved to death through the last 2,000 years. In light of Buchenwald and Sri Lanka, and Sudan do you really want to take time to pray for God to clear up your clogged sink drain or make your bunion go away? I am not saying that God does not care. I just want you to get some perspective. God cares incredibly about the small frustrations of your life. He who notes the fall of the song bird cherishes you and cares about you and what happens to you more than you can imagine. He can provide strength and comfort. He can take the painful, the evil, the hurtful and transform them in to spiritual maturity and blessing and victory for you. (See Calvary.) God cares so much He numbers the very hairs of your head! Go ahead. Stop right now. Pull one out. Someone up in heaven has to change the count! However, to the best of my knowledge He has never performed a hair restoration job on any frustrated bald man!

At this time, God usually chooses not to intervene physically. God is a Spirit. He has not contracted to guarantee your physical safety or comfort on this planet at this time. He does not exist just to make your life physically richer, easier or more pain-free.

Reality check. Consider John the Baptist for a moment. Jesus Himself called him the greatest man ever born of a woman! He was filled with the Holy

Spirit while he was still in his mother's womb! His whole life was dedicated to service to God. He was guided and directed and blessed and led into an incredible ministry of preparing the way for Jesus' work to begin in the world. To top it off, he was the Lord's cousin! If anyone should have been materially blessed and physically protected, you would think it would have been this fine man. At the prime of his life while still in his 30's, at the height of his ministry, he was imprisoned, and then gruesomely executed. If God chose not to give physical protection to this worthy servant, who are we to be so presumptuous as to assume that God has some sort of duty to provide this for us?

Jesus never promised that the Christian life, even the Spirit-filled life, would be easy. To the contrary, He said that following His way could be tough. He said it could bring not peace but the sword, not ease and protection but persecution and suffering. Remember, He said something about "taking up your cross" in order to follow Him? Becoming a Spirit-filled Christian does not include any guarantees that you will escape suffering, pain or illness or physical death. In our culture that focuses so much on cheap and easy happiness, suffering is dreaded; it is something no one wants to even think about. Yet the great Swiss psychiatrist Carl Jung said, "All neurosis is a substitute for legitimate suffering". Spirit-filled Christians will suffer. But they will not deny their suffering. They will not see it as some kind of punishment from God. They will learn to surrender their suffering, to just keep right on putting it in the Divine hands. They will recognize that God is an absolute master at transforming their suffering into, their pain, their grief, their loss, into gifts of wisdom, light and love.

I have seen a nightmare scenario in prayer meetings more than once. It is testimony time and some woman with the spiritual maturity level of a three year-old is going off about how she had been frustrated because she got this new outfit and she really loved it but it was a most unusual color and she had been struggling for weeks to find a pair of shoes that would match it and finally she had prayed for God to help her find those shoes and just a week later she had been back East visiting her sister and she was walking down the street in a little town that you wouldn't expect to have any decent shopping in it and there was a store going out of business and right in the window was the very pair of shoes she needed in the exact color she wanted and God led her to them at 75% OFF! And the "amens" and "praise the Lords" ascend up from the congregation. Meanwhile, sitting quietly in the back row with her head bowed is a mother. A mother whose sweet and kindly sixteen-year-old daughter died of leukemia a month before despite repeated, prolonged agonizing prayers on her behalf. What is the grieving mother to make of a congregation who believes in a God who will answer a neurotic woman's prayer for mauve shoes while her prayer to save her daughter's precious life goes unanswered?

THE SPIRIT TEACHES US HOW TO PRAY

One reason to seek the baptism of the Spirit is because He can teach us to finally learn how to pray with wisdom, reason and maturity! I think it is presumptuous for me to keep telling God what I think I need for a happy life. After all, He is omniscient. I think my energy could be better spent in drawing into oneness, intimacy and closeness with Him, immersing myself continually in conscious awareness of His presence and then trusting Him in His omnipotence to be able to provide for me just what I need, when I need it.

It may come as bad news to some of you, but if you want a new Mercedes SL, putting the request out to God may not be the best place to start. If your neighbor's dog is driving you crazy with its barking in the middle of the night, praying to God to shut up the beast may be a waste of your breath or even a touch blasphemous.

I know people that pray for a good parking spot when they go downtown to shop. I am sorry, being a parking attendant is not in God's job description. However, if you want eternal life, love, joy and peace and patience in your life right now, He is your Man. He is there to provide the strength and courage and wisdom to face any physical or material problem you may encounter, from parking problems, right up to and including death.

How can I explain this without disenchanting some of you? If you have a serious toothache, you don't go to a plumber. Plumbers are not in the business of taking away tooth pain or doing root canals. God is in the love, eternal life and Holy Spirit business. That is what His shingle says. If you want salvation and power and inspiration to lead a life focused on love, joy and peace, He is the one you go to. If you want the power to endure tragedy or pain or loss He is there for you. These are the things and the only things He promises to give you on the spot, just for the asking. Though He can and does occasionally intervene in the physical realm at His discretion and in His mysterious, unfathomable infinite wisdom to bless or guide or protect though this is not His primary role and it is not primarily why we seek Him or the baptism of His Spirit.

Why God allows so much suffering and death in the world is a very great quandary for everyone to deal with. There is no clear cut answer to it. There is no logic to explain it. In spite of the best answers the theologians and philosophers have come up with, we will simply never understand it this side of heaven. And that is okay. It is all right not to know certain things. Also there are some things we are just not intellectually capable of knowing. Our dog Cheyenne is one smart creature. But I don't think I could give him a very good grasp of the way the internet works no matter how hard I tried.

How God chooses to work in the physical world today is a very great mystery and we can not possibly fathom the reasons behind His actions or lack of action. We can only trust Him and know that in the more important world of Spirit, He is always there for us, always available to us. Jesus said, "If you believe in me you will have eternal life." He said, "Ask for the gift of the Holy Spirit and you shall receive it." That's good enough for me.

Are there physical benefits to the Spirit-filled life? You bet. We have already seen that keeping a clear channel open to God, staying connected with Him allows you to receive a kind of guidance in your life that can make all the difference in your fulfilling your purpose day to day and over your lifetime. The wisdom you get from the Spirit can help you make wiser business decisions. The temperance you are inspired to by the Spirit can cause you to take better care of your body and you will then have better health. Notice that the text in Romans 8:11 says something very interesting, "If the Spirit of Him who raised Jesus from the dead dwells in you, he who raised Christ from the dead will also give life to your *mortal* bodies through His Spirit who dwells in you" (emphasis supplied) The word mortal means our physical bodies so it is intriguing to think that there is even a wonderful kind of physical and mental energy that comes from the baptism of the Spirit which can empower body and mind. Just know that such benefits are incidental to the spiritual benefits we receive from our connection to the Spirit. They are not necessarily guaranteed as part of the package and they are not the reason we seek the Spirit-filled life. God is God and there is no limit to how He can choose to work in the world. He certainly can intervene physically, but He is not obligated to do so and usually does not. And that is OK. He has provided us something much more satisfying and essential.

Q and A:

Q. We are told many places in the New Testament that prayer will bring healing to the sick. You seem to be discounting this promise.

A. Being a Spirit-filled Christian is no guarantee of material prosperity or that you will be kept free of illness or pain, physical, mental or emotional. If God routinely did that, people would be drawn to Him for all the wrong reasons. However, God does reserve the right to intervene anytime He chooses in anyone's life and on any level. Sometimes He does. Sometimes He doesn't. We don't understand why. And that is okay.

Q. But one of the gifts of the Spirit is physical healing. Shouldn't we aggressively be claiming our right to possess this gift?

A. No. Gifts are gifts. *They are always at the discretion of the giver.* My wife does not claim or demand a Valentine gift from me. You can rightfully ask for your wages. It is in very poor taste to run around asking for gifts! *There is a great danger that we will be drawn in to seeking the gifts instead of the Giver.* I have seen many eager, earnest, new Spirit-filled Christians get all caught up in the emotion of pursuing the more dramatic spiritual gifts, such as tongues, prophecies, "words of wisdom" for others, physical healings, spiritual warfare and exorcisms. This is always a mistake and a distraction from the true purpose

of Holy Spirit baptism. The filling of the Holy Spirit is given to overflow our hearts with God' best gift; *unconditional love*
(see Romans 5:5).

Being baptized with the Holy Spirit is all about being baptized with love! The Spirit is given in this profound and remarkable experience to draw us into deeper and deeper intimacy and oneness with the Heavenly Father. Its primary purpose is to promote God-consciousness and awareness. It is given to empower us to give the good news of God's outrageous love and salvation to other people, often and usually through simple acts of compassion, kindness and humble, loving service (see Matthew 25).

There is an incredible, often unconscious pull by our egos to lead us to seek spiritual gifts. Ego can be such a subtle trap. Why, if we had one of those gifts … just imagine what we could do! Just think how much good we could do for the Lord! Just think how many people would come to our church if someone was really healed in one of our services! Maybe, but just think how it would be so easily taken by the ego to lead you to regard yourself and your church as "special." Maybe even some kind of "super-Christians!" Tongues have been consistently abused in this way (see the next chapter). Today there are churches that teach unless you have the gift of tongues and can manifest it publicly, you are not Spirit-filled. And even your very salvation may be in question if you don't. This is a travesty. Jesus said, "an evil and adulterous generation seeks for a sign." Remember, a faith that must be supported by physical evidence is not faith. When we are tempted to use any of the spiritual gifts as a sign that we are baptized with the Spirit or that we are somehow more advanced or superior to other Christians, we are on very dangerous ground. There is no entitlement to any of the spiritual gifts.

Q. Then what are we entitled to?

A. That which matters most!

1. The assurance of salvation … eternal life right now.

2. The filling of the Holy spirit, right now, by faith, just for the asking!

3. The *fruits* (as contrasted to the gifts) of the Holy Spirit. The love, the joy, the peace, the gentleness, the forgiveness, the compassion, the self-control! All these splendid, incredible effects of surrendering our heart and souls to God begin *immediately* to be infused into the life and personality of the Christian. Imagine it! Through the Spirit every one of us has the capacity to live on this earth right now, without envying or hating or fighting! When you are living "in-Spirit" there is never criticism of others, only mutual respect and kind words. Forgiveness, gentleness and humility become part of your very nature. And yes, God also wants to give us the gifts of the Spirit to be used in ministry and service to others. These treasurers are given so that we may serve and empower others. However, our energy should not go into pursuing or seeking the spiritual gifts (healings, tongues, prophecy, teaching). Our energy and attention need to go into entering into ever deeper and deeper connection and intimacy with our Heavenly Father. *Then*, out of our focus on this relationship, will come whatever gifts the Father wants us to have, when He knows the time is right. We simply stay close to Him, we put our energy into that, and trust Him to provide whatever He wants to give us when He is ready and we are ready to receive. Our energy is to go into daily surrender of our ego. Into abiding, not trying. Into "snuggling", and not struggling.

CHAPTER 18:

WHAT DO TONGUES GOT TO DO WITH IT?

A wicked and adulterous generation seeketh after a sign.
Matthew 16:4

"Sister, you are going to have to prime the pump," the preacher said. "Just try saying some vowels." "Eeeeeeeee." "Ooooooooooooo." "That should help you get going."

As part of the process of learning about the Holy Spirit, I decided one evening to visit a Pentecostal church. After a lengthy, enthusiastic sermon, a call was made for those who wanted to be "baptized with the Spirit." In that congregation, you were really not considered a total Christian until you were filled with the Spirit. It was also taught that you could not be filled with the Spirit unless you could demonstrate proof of it by speaking in tongues. This was the sign that you were truly baptized with the Spirit. Needless to say, there was a lot of spiritual and psychological pressure put on the people that came forward, to speak in tongues! After kneeling at the front, and with the encouragement of the preacher and some of his assistants, several of the people who had responded to the call began to speak in their new, unknown tongue. Some of them quite softly and others very loudly. There was much praising of the Lord for this. But one poor soul, an older woman, was just not getting it. Everybody else but her seemed to have received "the gift," but nothing came to her. I could feel her struggle and her embarrassment from where I was sitting. That is when the preacher came up to her, put his burly arm around her shoulders and gave her the advice about mouthing the vowels to get her unknown tongue flowing.

I came away from that meeting feeling sorry for the sincere seeking people who so badly wanted something more in their spiritual lives but had been pressured to perform in a certain way. I did not like the idea that somehow the Holy Spirit had to be tricked or manipulated or prompted to deliver the gift of tongues to someone on cue.

254

My further reflection on the subject led me to the clear conclusion that the gift of tongues is not ever given to prove that someone has the baptism of the Holy Spirit. In the previous chapter we saw that the baptism of the Spirit comes by faith. If a physical sign was needed to prove the validity of the experience, then there would be no need for faith would there? It would invalidate the whole concept. Jesus said that "a wicked and adulterous generation" sought for a sign as proof that something has spiritual validity. He said to Thomas, "Blessed are those who have not seen, and still believe." The true presence of God is to be experienced most in the daily, the ordinary rather than in the spectacular. *The truth, the validation of any spiritual experience is not what kind of phenomena it produces but whether or not it changes our hearts.*

It has occurred to me that the gift of tongues may not be as needed today because there is already way too much talk going on in the world. Our generation communicates more and says less than any generation in the history of the world! It seems as if people are constantly talking today. The philosopher-scientist Blaise Pascal understood the hazards of this when he famously said: "All man's miseries derive from not being able to sit quietly in a room alone." What with cell phones and answering machines and voice mail, long distance anywhere in the world for free over the internet, talking heads, talk shows, talk radio, talk, talk, talk! The Buddhists have a word for the incessant spinning of thoughts that run through most people's minds and keep them from stilling themselves and quietly connecting with God; they call that condition "monkey-mind." Such undisciplined thinking can lead to a condition I call monkey-mouth! Overtalk may be the great sin of this generation! After all, it was Jesus who said simply, "Let your conversation be yes, and no."

That reminds me of this little plaque I saw once:

LORD

Please keep

255

your arm

around my shoulder

AND

Your hand

over my

MOUTH!

The great Chinese philosopher Lao-tzu proclaimed:

Open mouth—spirit escapes.

Closed mouth—spirit connection excellent!

When the fine Christian writer Catherine Marshall was led to ask for the baptism of the Holy Spirit in her life, she expected to get a gift of tongues. Instead, much to her surprise ... well, let her tell you what happened:

"The first discipline He gave me was a leash for my tongue. For others the Spirit may give torrents of ecstatic speech; I needed the discipline of not speaking the careless or negative or discouraging word. For weeks I was put through the sharp training of opening my mouth to speak and hearing from the Teacher, Stop! No, Don't say it!! Close the mouth!" 1.

A Spirit-filled Christian should learn to use fewer words. He or she should let go of the need to give advice and absolutely refuse to meddle or participate in gossip. As Eckhart Tolle says, "If your words are less important than the silence, then keep quiet."

I am far more interested in another gift than the gift of tongues. You have met people who are hard of hearing. But stop and think about how many more people today have the problem of being hard of listening! They are so busy talking themselves that they have no time or energy left to really listen to others. They way you begin to show someone your love is to give them your attention. Paul Tournier said, "It is impossible to overemphasize the immense need humans have to be really listened to. Most conversations are dialogues of the deaf." What the world needs most of all is the gift of ears! I would like to see a headline in my next church paper. "Pentecost breaks out in_____. Everyone gets the gift of ears"!

DISTRACTIONS, DISTRACTIONS!

I wish we did not even have to include a chapter on tongues in this book. That is because it is a great big fat distraction! Somebody always brings it up when I am doing a presentation on the Holy Spirit and people can get all worked up about it and lose their focus on what is more important. That and another big distraction: "spiritual warfare". Deliver me! (No pun intended!) Spiritual warfare is often a spiritual trap because all it does is focus people's attention and energy on Satan instead of on Jesus. It can end up empowering Satan. Remember, it is all too easy to empower the demons you fight, to create what you defend against. You become what you contemplate. Whatever commands your attention becomes your master.

Some people, in their religious enthusiasm and paranoia, are eager to sniff out a devil behind every bush. Then they want to show off their power by casting out demons, by rebuking these devils! "I rebuke you devil of the head ache," "I rebuke you devil of the tooth ache." Then there is the ultimate battle of spiritual warfare, the exorcism. As far as I am concerned, most exorcisms are a form of religious abuse practiced against mentally ill people! Or epileptics. Have you ever seen a grand mal seizure? It is not a pretty sight. And when the foaming at the mouth and the eye rolling and the moaning and the violent, un-restrainable thrashing is over, the person collapses in a limp heap. What does that remind you of?

Excuse me. Jesus already took care of the devils. He whipped them at the Cross! He is in charge now. This is His planet. Sure, the devils are still around for awhile, but they are a defeated foe! They are really a pretty sorry bunch of losers. They can't touch you with a ten-foot-pole as long as you are surrendered to Jesus and filled up with the good Spirit! Jesus, the great Judge of the universe issued a restraining order for you against the devil! He can't come near you because you are the Master's cherished child! He even provided you with angel enforcers and protectors to make sure you are safe from evil! So don't put your energy into battling the devil. Put your energy into staying surrendered and practicing oneness with God through the Spirit.

Another distraction can be an over-emphasis on seeking. Sadly it is so easy for us to pursue the gift instead of the Giver! There is a lot of miracle abuse in some churches. Miracles can be dramatic and we all just love drama! We get all worked up about miracles because our ego feeds on anything that in any way might make us look special or powerful or unique. Ego really loves it when it thinks it has something or knows something or can do something that nobody else does. We can easily become miracle-junkies if we don't watch it. No wonder God has to be very careful how He dispenses them. He immediately begins giving all the fruits of the Spirit to everyone who is baptized with the Spirit, and those are what we should be seeking and coveting. But the gifts, which can include some dramatic and attention getting manifestations, that is a whole different matter. To avoid becoming miracle-chasers, to be safe from the thrall of ego, we need to put our energy into practicing the presence of God, into drawing into closeness and intimacy with Him. When we do that, we can then leave the miracles totally up to Him and allow Him to decide if and when He may chose to manifest some special manifestation or gift through us.

A REALLY BIG QUESTION

There is a big question, almost an elephant-in-the-living-room kind of question that most Christians are afraid to ask. I am going to ask it now while not being able to come even close to giving you an answer that might satisfy you: Why did God stop performing miracles on a large scale a short time (weeks, months, and apparently not any more than a few years) after Pentecost?

I can not explain why the dramatic signs and miracles that accompanied the first apostles no longer occur among Christians now as they did then. (At least they are not as frequently occurring in my North American culture.) A lot of us think that our job of giving the gospel to the world would sure be a lot easier if they still happened! (And perhaps they will.) Meanwhile we tend to think it is unfair, that the early believers had a distinct advantage. Of course we forget that they could not practice their religion freely, they did not have the printed Scriptures to pass out, nor did they have satellites that could broadcast the gospel to much of the world simultaneously. (Talk about miracles!) So actually, we may be the ones with the advantages! But there is still a craving on the part of many for the kind of supernatural manifestations that seem to have been almost common in the early church. As a result some people have become so "miracle hungry" that they manifest the opposite dysfunction of those who look for a devil behind every bush. Instead they try to find a miracle behind every bush. They will pilgrimage for miles to see an outline of the virgin Mary burned into a piece of toast! (That piece of toast supposedly sold for $28,000 on eBay!) When I realize I do not have an explanation for the apparent absence of New Testament type miracles among believers today (and some other puzzling religious conundrums like when the Lord will come back), I think of the words of the wise writer Abraham Joshua Heschel who said, "I will not trouble myself with things that are too difficult for me to understand."

While I cannot explain why the signs and miracles do not occur at a level today that they did 2,000 years ago, I do know that Jesus said that "an evil and adulterous generation seeks for a sign." I do know that He said, even if Moses himself came back from the dead, "You would not believe." So signs and miracles may not be all they are cracked up to be. The important point is not to get caught up in putting your spiritual energy into seeking them. Such a practice can be a very great distraction. Don't get me wrong. I believe there are legitimate gifts of tongues and healing that manifest in the world today. I am grateful to God for every one of them. They just do not occur on the scale they did in the New Testament. I also know that if you don't believe a miracle is possible there is no reason to expect one, for we can only have what we believe we can have! (Note to God: I will absolutely take any manifestation or miracle you want to give me!) However it is clear to me that we should not chase after miracles. We should simply stay in intimate connection with the Spirit and trust Him to manifest them in His own time and place. The danger comes in giving too much of our energy and attention to spiritual warfare and the gifts of tongues and healings.

When I see people claiming that it is truly the Spirit of God that has worked in someone speaking in an unknown tongue, or in the healing of a person who was deaf, or had one leg shorter than the other, or whatever the physical problem was, as a realist and as someone who has spent 40 years studying psychology, I am acutely aware that the human potential for self-deception is absolutely enormous. There is the incredibly powerful tendency for people to gullibly create in their mind as a reality, *what they want so badly to believe*. Think hearing the voice of, or feeling the "presence" of a recently departed loved one. (Think Bernie Madoff for that matter.) Think the incredible power of the placebo effect in medicine and how the placebo effect combined with the incredible power of suggestion. Group pressure to please and conform and the desire to please religious authority could factor in to many so-called "faith healings" in the intensely emotional religious services that are conducted in numerous "crusades" every year.

I can promise you this; if you allow the Holy Spirit to fill you and if you stay intimately connected to the Divine, your view of the world will change to one filled with awe and wonder as you receive the greatest gift of all, the miracle gift of unconditional love, for it transforms everything with a heavenly radiance. Remember, it is always love alone that produces miracles. Rather than seeking out specific physical miracles, you will begin to shift to seeing the miraculous in everything and in everyone you encounter! *You will no longer view anything or anyone as ordinary!* You will come to have an intense appreciation for all. Einstein said, "You can view the world in two ways: there are no miracles or …everything is a miracle."

In the magnificent, serenely beautiful book *Gilead*, Marilynne Robinson writes, "Wherever you turn your eyes the world can shine like transfiguration. You don't have to bring a thing to it except a little willingness to see." 2.

It is the Holy Spirit alone who can open the eyes of our heart so we can see with such sacred vision. Isn't it amazing that what exists in the realm of the Spirit is actually far more real than the things that are in the physical dimension! For example, the Spirit alone gives us the awareness to see the Divine essence in every person, not just the outward physical form. Through the eyes of the Spirit you can see beyond appearances. You will be enabled to see into people's hearts and souls and not just to see their physical form. After all, the real person that God would have us to see, and that includes ourselves, is not a body at all, but a soul. A soul created in the image of the Father! The body is, after all, just a container for the soul. Sadly, often all we see is the physical form. The age, the gender, the weight, the sex-appeal or lack-thereof. On these shallow criteria we often make our pre-suppositions and judgments and allow them to determine how we treat people.

Frank Bartleman was one of the leaders of the Azusa Street Pentecostal revival. He understood that nothing must be allowed to supplant the Spirit's greatest work. "Any work that exalts the Holy Ghost or the 'gifts' above Jesus will finally land up in fanaticism. Whatever causes us to exalt and love Jesus is well and safe. The reverse will ruin all." 3.

Jesus Himself said: "When the helper comes …He will testify of Me" (John 15:26) The key in all this is to stay centered on Jesus, surrendered to Jesus, and then trust the Spirit to dispense the appropriate gifts to you as He sees fit in His own good time. Do not concern yourself with the gifts and miracles. Concern yourself with Jesus. Only Jesus is glorified and magnified in the life of a person who is filled with the Holy Spirit.

BAPTIZED WITH LOVE

So much religion … so little love. Jesus came to fix that. Now He sends the Holy Spirit to fix that! Never forget what is truly most important. *The baptism of the Holy Spirit is about being baptized with love*. That is the true and ultimate miracle. The true evidence of one's Spirit baptism is not emotion or tongues or healings or some other gift. It is simply Christ-likeness in the life. It is all about being empowered for a ministry and service of unconditional love. Period. Once you surrender to it, God will take it from there. If you ask for bread, He will not give you a stone. It is up to Him to supply you with whatever gifts of the Spirit you need to carry out your ministry. Trust Him for that and don't obsess or worry about tongues. The really good news? Every Spirit-filled Christian received all the fruits of the Spirit(Galatians 5). The love. The joy. The peace. The patience. The self-control. The gentleness. The whole basket of fruit is yours! I really like it in 1 Corinthians 13, when Paul says, "prophecies will cease, tongues …will be stilled, … knowledge …will pass away" but love will endure and will never fail" (v. 8,13). Now that puts things in perspective!

It is promised in Scripture that every Spirit-filled Christian is supplied not only with eternal life and the wonderful fruits of the Spirit but also with at least one spiritual gift for service. Note however that not everybody gets the same gift and nobody gets them all. And God gets to decide who gets what! (Check it out in 1 Corinthians 12.)

TONGUES: THE BASICS

Point A: once and for all, let's be very clear that speaking in tongues is not required to demonstrate or prove that you have been baptized with the Spirit. Anyone who tells you that you must speak in tongues or pressures you to do it or treats you as a second class Christian because you don't is way out of line.

Point B: There is a legitimate gift of an unknown tongue. 1 Corinthians 14:13, says "For this reason anyone who speaks in a tongue should pray that he may interpret what he says. For if I pray in a tongue my spirit prays but my mind is unfruitful." While it is true that the Spirit at Pentecost also gave another different kind of gift of tongues that allowed the listeners to hear the disciples each in their own language, that does not negate the fact that there is also a gift of an unknown tongue which some may be given largely for their own spiritual edification or devotional use. Which leads us directly to—

Point C: Never, ever judge another Christian because they speak in tongues or exercise some other spiritual gift that you may not accept or be comfortable with. Do not condemn or write off Pentecostals as individuals or as a group. Pentecostalism is not just a denomination. There are "Pentecostal" or charismatic Catholics. Episcopalians. Methodists, Adventists, Baptists and yes maybe even a Presbyterian or two!

PENTECOSTALISM

The year 2006 marked the 100th anniversary of the modern Pentecostal revival that began with a handful of people on Azusa Street in Los Angeles in a 40-by-60-foot woodframe structure called a "tumbledown shack" by one LA newspaper. Today, with more than 600 million adherents (growing by 19 million per year, that's 54,000 per day), the Pentecostal- charismatic movement has become, in just 100 years, the fastest growing and most globally diverse expression of worldwide Christianity. It is the fastest growing Christian movement since the Reformation.

At the current rate of growth, some researchers predict there will be 1 billion Pentecostals by 2025, most located in Asia, Africa, and Latin America. By 2050, most of Africa will be Christian and most of those Christians will be Pentecostals, according to Grant Wacker, professor of Christian history at Duke University. Clearly, Pentecostalism is a major factor driving the explosive growth of Christianity in these three areas of the world. Religious scholar Phillip Jenkins says that the new Pentecostal-influenced churches in Latin America "offer transformations that are both personal and cultural. Converts feel free to speak and think for themselves in a way that was not possible when they were required to show deference to the old hierarchies of church and state."

Pastor E.A. Adeboye, a Pentecostal pastor who *Newsweek* magazine calls "one of the most successful preachers in the world" has started a church that has outposts in 110 countries with 14,000 branches hosting 5 million members. Adeboye, a Nigerian, believes that Pentecostals are growing so fast and are having such an impact in the world because they talk of the here and now, not just the by and by. They believe that God is eager to involve and invest Himself intimately in the daily lives, work and relationships of people right now. .

It is a popular misconception that all Pentecostals speak in tongues. In an October 2006 survey from the Pew Forum on Religion and Public Life, at least 40 percent of Pentecostals in six of the ten countries surveyed said they had never prayed or spoken in tongues. Only half of U.S. Pentecostals had spoken in tongues. 4.

The leader of the Azusa street church was William Joseph Seymour, the African American son of former slaves from Louisiana. He was the driving force behind the earliest Pentecostal revival. He was a gentle man, described as "gracious and soft-spoken." His leadership focused on some important principles largely neglected by main-stream Christianity. He thoroughly believed in the priesthood of all believers and practiced it in his church. His congregation were not spectators come to be entertained, but participants, invited to share in the worship as the Spirit led them. Lay ministers were encouraged and empowered by Seymour. People in his church found many avenues for service. Seymour created (or allowed the Holy Spirit freedom to create) in his church a wonderful sense of community of oneness and support among the members. These principles have infiltrated many churches today and are still serving to revitalize contemporary Christianity.

Grant McLung writes of Seymour:

"The extended prayer sessions he conducted came to be attended by between 300 and 350 people, with many others forced to stand outside. Observers noted that attendees included immigrants, prostitutes, and the poor. Despite the sudden success of his ministry, biographical sketches of William J. Seymour assess him as, 'a meek man' and 'a man of prayer'. Believing that he and the other Azusa Street worshipers had received the promised gift poured out on the early church, Seymour knew they must share this gift with the world. From behind his pulpit of shoebox shipping crates, a new missiological paradigm for the 20th century emerged". 5.

The motto of the Azusa Street Mission was best summed up by Seymour's constant pastoral admonition, "Now do not go from this meeting and talk about tongues, but try to get people saved." This Christ-centered, missionary message of Pentecostals has been highlighted by missiologist Arthur F. Glasser, who wrote: "Many evangelicals have been challenged by the immediacy and reality of God that Pentecostals reflect, along with their freedom and unabashed willingness to confess openly their allegiance to Christ. The achievements of their churches are equally impressive, reflecting their settled conviction that the full experience of the Holy Spirit will not only move the church closer to Jesus at its center, but at the same time, press the church to move out into the world in mission." 6.

Do you really want to take on the Pentecostal movement? Do you really want to condemn it to the lower regions? Do you really want to judge it and say that it is of the devil? I didn't think so.

NEVER, EVER SPEAK AGAINST ANOTHER CHRISTIAN

As long as a person takes the name of Jesus and is doing no harm to you or anyone else, don't you dare say a negative word about him or her. The disciples received a rebuke from Jesus one day. They had witnessed someone exercising a spiritual gift in Christ's name and "because he was not one of us, we told him to stop" (Mark 9:38). "Do not stop him," Jesus said. "No one who does a miracle in my name can in the next moment say anything bad about me, for whoever is not against us is for us" (Mark 9:39).

When I was a young pastor, a renowned evangelist was assigned to my church to hold meetings. One of the persons who faithfully attended these meetings as a visitor was an elder, a lay leader in his own church. I remember him well. He was a gentle man in his seventies with thick white hair and a most pleasant and kindly face. One evening the evangelist and I went to visit him in his home. The evangelist soon got right to the point. He had just presented a particular point of doctrine in his lecture the night before. He was eager to persuade this gentlemen to accept it. They discussed the topic for some time, and much to the frustration of the evangelist, our host kept resisting the evangelist's insistence that he agree with him on this belief. The evangelist persisted to the point of getting irritated. Finally when he could see he was not going to succeed at convincing this man, we took our leave. Our host showed us to the door. I can still see him standing there silhouetted by the lamp behind him. We had walked a few feet up the snowy path leading from the home when the evangelist suddenly spun around. He raised his finger and pointed at the man and said loudly, "I'll see you in the judgment brother."

A few evenings later, in his nightly presentation, the evangelist was warning the congregation about the dangers of Pentecostalism. Earlier that year, the popular singer Pat Boone had been in the news because he had become a Christian and according to his own testimony had been filled with the Holy Spirit. The evangelist announced to the crowd that Pat Boone was "of the devil because he spoke in tongues."

These two incidents were just too much for me and driving the evangelist to his lodging that night, though he was old enough to be my father, I challenged him on both of them. He became highly indignant. The next day he called my boss, the conference president and complained about my insubordination. I still have the conference president's letter of rebuke to me in my file. I was told I should have much more respect for age and experience. Interestingly, the evangelist left the ministry and the church a few years later. Excuse me but when are we ever going to get it? God has not called us to run around negating other people's expression of faith or judging and devaluing their particular religious experience. Remember, a Spirit-filled person will always resist thoughts that condemn or judge and will be learning to extend only thoughts that bless and bring light and love. Judging is such a precarious activity because we do not ever see people as they really are. We see them only as they *appear* to us to be, filtered through the prejudices of our own family and religion and education and conditioning.

THE UNFORGIVABLE SIN

While we are on this subject, let's take a look at a topic from the Bible that scares a lot of people and is often misunderstood. It is often referred to as the "unpardonable sin" or the sin against the Holy Spirit. I have run in to several people in years of counseling that are deeply concerned that they may have committed this sin. They haven't. But here is the text that alarms so many: "Every sin and blasphemy will be forgiven men, but the blasphemy against the Spirit will not be forgiven men, either in this age or in the age to come" (Matthew 12:31,32). Heavy duty stuff. Scary all right. There has been much speculation about what the "unpardonable sin" is. It is simple to understand when you take the text in its context. Before He said what He did about this sin,

Jesus had just finished casting demons out of a demon-possessed man. He had also healed him of some serious physical problems. The people who had gathered around and seen these miracles were astounded. They asked, "Could this be the Son of David"? (v. 23). The church leaders who had observed what had happened had an entirely different explanation for what they had witnessed. They declared adamantly to the crowd, "This fellow does not cast out demons except by Beelzebub, the ruler of demons" (v. 24) Big mistake. Big, big mistake. They were attributing the healing miracles of Jesus to the power of Satan! Every miracle Jesus performed He did by the power of the Holy Spirit within Him. Now these religious leaders dared to blaspheme the Holy Spirit by saying that instead of the Spirit's power accomplishing the miracle, it was actually the infilling of the evil one at work through Jesus. The Lord warned, "He who blasphemes against the Holy Spirit never has forgiveness, but is subject to eternal condemnation" (Mark 3:29.).

It is very simple, the unpardonable sin is attributing to the Devil any miracle that is actually being performed by the power of the Holy Spirit. It is accusing people who are doing the true work of God as being motivated and empowered by Satan. Never, ever put yourself in the position of pointing a finger at someone who does their ministry under the name of Jesus Christ and accuse them of being "of the devil". Paul added this caution: "no one can say that Jesus is Lord except by the Holy Spirit" (1 Corinthians 12:3).

Another helpful perspective on the unpardonable sin is to consider my friend who has a neighbor with a flock of chickens ruled over by a rather arrogant, no-nonsense rooster. This bird insists on proclaiming his authority over his domain every morning at the crack of dawn.
When my friend first moved into that neighborhood I heard him complain frequently about this awful bird. He used some descriptive terms for this fowl that I won't repeat here in front of the innocent women and children who might be reading this book. When I visited him recently, I inquired about the rooster. "What rooster?" he asked. Then he smiled and said, "Oh I don't hear him any more." Was there a wicked gleam in his eye? At that point I immediately suspected the worst. He must have snuck out one night and disappeared the

offending fowl! But then he added, "He is still there and he still crows loudly every morning, but I don't hear him any more! I have gotten used to him."

The Holy Spirit speaks persistently to the heart of every man and woman, always striving to be heard and draw them closer to the Father. If one responds to the voice, it will become more and more clear and consistent. If one ignores, discounts, and rejects it, it will certainly still be there, because the Spirit never stops pleading. But tune it out long enough and you will no longer hear it. That would be the unpardonable sin by default.

BACK TO TONGUES

Speaking of getting in trouble with conference presidents …just recently when I spoke on the topic of the baptism of the Spirit at a week-long campmeeting, the subject of tongues came up as it inevitably seems to in the middle of something far more important. Trying to play it down and get back on track I said, "Don't worry about tongues. Even Baalam's donkey spoke in tongues! Even shoes have tongues! It ain't no big deal. We will discuss it more tomorrow." Well, there was a lady in the audience who became very alarmed. She thought that my remark meant that I was encouraging tongues speaking! She was convinced that on the next day I was going to launch an effort to unloose tongues speaking on the campground. She hurried to the conference president with her fears. First thing next morning he and an equally concerned conference treasurer knocked on my motel room door for a little visit.

I must say that both men were very kind and very polite. After I had explained myself and assured them I did not have promoting speaking in tongues on my agenda, we had prayer together and they left. I learned from that to be more careful about being flip in my comments, to make sure I am making myself clear, and I learned also again how the topic of tongues for some reason carries a great deal of emotional charge and can surely be a great distraction to focusing on the genuine role of the Holy Spirit.

Let me say that in over 30 years of presenting seminars on the topic of the Holy Spirit in the USA, Canada and parts of Europe, I have seen many people come to the assurance of the baptism of the Holy Spirit in their lives. Not one of them has spoken in tongues at any of these meetings. I have never spoken in tongues. I am not saying that that is good or bad or that that is the way it should be or shouldn't be. This is just how it is. What stands out for me at these seminars is the great sense of oneness, community and connectedness that becomes apparent. Such a sense of serenity and peace comes over the group that you could cut it with a knife. When the meetings are concluded, people don't want to leave the room. They don't want to leave that atmosphere.

I do have two close friends who tell me they have received the gift of tongues. Neither of them however uses it in church or any public setting. For them it is a part of their private devotional life. Finally, two important points about tongues ... do not give this gift undue emphasis ... and do not condemn it.

So let us take leave of this topic now, do you mind?

Oh, I almost forgot. *Point D:* Jesus didn't speak in tongues!

Q&A:

Q. How do you know Jesus didn't speak in tongues?

A. You just don't want to let this topic go do you? The gospel writers told us many things about Jesus. We even know what kind of food He ate, what kind of clothes He wore. How He treated children. How He treated women. We know about the people He healed and how He healed them. If He would have done something as unique as speaking in tongues you can be sure Matthew or Mark would not have let it slip by unnoticed. His teachings instruct us about everything important in life. Money, sex, possessions. He instructed us to be baptized. He talked about giving offerings. He taught us how to worship and how to pray. If tongues were an important part of the spiritual agenda, He would have addressed the topic you can be sure and He would have modeled it by His own behavior just as He did water baptism, Spirit baptism and the communion service. The fact that He did not should dis-empower this topic permanently. When He commanded His followers to "Receive the Spirit," He did not say "Receive the Spirit and speak in tongues." The founder of modern Pentecostalism, William Seymour, repeatedly told his congregation at the Azusa Street Church in Los Angeles that their experience with the Spirit was not about speaking in tongues. It was about God's presence in them through the crucified and risen Christ.

I have a theory, and it is just a theory, but I believe that speaking in an unknown tongue as part of a devotional life could be valuable to some people as a healthy form of altered consciousness, as a means of getting outside of their head, their intellect, their belief-based religion and accessing God on a different deeper, more personal level. It could be a way of helping those of us who are terribly intellectual and left-brained to experience God in the emotions and in the sub-conscious or even the unconscious. Romans 8:26 gives a hint of a spiritual communication that is beyond recognizable words: "The Spirit himself intercedes for us with groans that words cannot express."

Jesus would not have needed to speak in tongues because He was already fully-integrated intellectually-emotionally, right-brain-left brain. He was fully in touch with His emotions. He was already fully intimate with God in every level. He was fully aware. Fully conscious. Jesus was fully awake in a world full of people that were asleep! He was fully enlightened. In fact He was not just enlightened, He was the light! Therefore He did not need tongues. He was already in this "altered" state.

(Jesus' state was "altered" only in comparison to our unconscious, regressed and dysfunctional state. Oh that we all should come to be in His "altered" state!)

Q&A:

Q. The evangelist said that people who speak in tongues are of the devil. Don't you think there is a counterfeit gift of speaking in tongues that is from the devil?

A. No. Probably not. The devil gets far too much press, far too much credit and attention today in our churches. The bum was defeated at the cross! "The reason the Son of God appeared was to destroy the devil's work" (1 John 3:8) This pathetic creature was dethroned! Of course Satan is still alive and attempting to do every bit of evil he can in the world today. But he has no power over those who choose to be connected to Jesus. "He who is in you is greater than he who is in the world" (1 John 4:4) The Devil can only harm those who choose to put themselves on his territory. There won't be any room for any evil spirit in you if you keep yourself filled-up with the Holy Spirit!

For centuries, millenniums even, the native peoples of my home state of Alaska and even some from Siberia used to come together in a central village once a year to celebrate a good whaling season or a good harvest of furs by feasting, gift-giving, drumming and dancing. It was a high point of their year in this isolated part of the world. It was a big part of their identity, their culture and likely contributed to the peacefulness and good-will that was generally present among the peoples of the Arctic. Even as late as the 1950's, Protestant pastors were going into the villages and putting a stop to the dancing because they claimed it was a form of devil worship! Many generations of the Eskimo people including those in my own age group were cheated of a meaningful and significant part of their culture because of this busy-body judgmental foolishness. In some cases, missionaries also forbade young people to learn to speak in their own languages and sometimes took children away from their parents and their villages to be raised in "mission schools." Only in the 1990's did some of the native villagers begin to reclaim the right to their culture and revive the old gatherings, dances and drumming. "It is like bringing back our history", said one teen-ager. "It makes us happy."

You see, there is this awful pathological tendency that fundamentalist Christians have to brand everything they do not understand, or do not agree with, or is not part of their culture as "of the devil". Think what the Church did to Galileo, who demonstrated scientifically that the earth is not the center of the universe, that the sun does not revolve around the earth. He was branded by the church as a heretic because his teachings did not agree with the "infallible Holy Scriptures." Think Inquisition. Think Salem Witch Trials. Think how mentally ill people, suffering from what we now realize is a neuro-biological illness just as real and biologically based as cancer or diabetes were branded as demon-possessed because they heard voices! (In regard to Galileo, I love Arthur C. Clark's statement: "Any sufficiently advanced technology is indistinguishable from magic.") Worse, religious people often want to brand any new technology as a tool of the devil. In my own denomination, the first pastor to begin a

271

weekly radio broadcast was accused of using the devil's tool as was the first pastor to begin a television broadcast and as are church leaders today who use YouTube for evangelism.

I do think that there is a "psychological" counterfeit gift of tongues but it has nothing to do with the devil. People are put under such pressure to speak in tongues in some religious settings and there is so much peer pressure to conform to the standard of speaking in tongues in order to demonstrate that they are baptized with the Spirit that some people who are eager to please and highly susceptible to the power of suggestion unconsciously create their own "unknown" tongue in order to fit in and gain approval.

FOOTNOTES CHAPTER 18

1. Marshall, Catherine. *Something More*. (Avon Books, New York, 1974), p. 235.

2. Robinson, Marilynne. *Gilead*. (Picador, New York, 2004), p.245.

3. Bartleman, Frank, quoted in William Menzies, *Anointed to Serve*., (Gospel Publishing   House, Springfield, Mo, 1971), p. 55.

4. *Newsweek*, December 29, 2008, p. 77

5. McLung, Grant, *Christianity Today*. (April 2006).

6. Glasser, Arthur F. *Christianity Today*. (December 2006), p.18.

CHAPTER 19:

PLAN A: THE HOLY SPIRIT, AGENT OF TRANSFORMATION

"I will put my spirit in you, and you shall live."
—Ezekiel 37:14

"But if the spirit of him who raised Jesus from the dead dwells in you
He who raised Christ from the dead will also give life to your mortal bodies
through his spirit
who dwells in you."
—Romans 8:11

Some months ago we had a visiting speaker at our church, the best-selling author, Anne Lamott. There is nobody like Anne Lamott. She is honest. She is hilarious. She is challenging and comforting. God didn't just throw away the mold when He made her: I don't think He even used one! She is one rocky little Christian. A lively, whirling dervish of a Christian! Go ahead, I dare you, read her nonfiction books—*Traveling Mercies, Operating Instructions, Bird by Bird, Grace (Eventually)*. They track her difficult and amazing spiritual journey from barely functioning alcoholic and drug user to a committed Christian writer and speaker who has used her unique experience and personality (and vocabulary!) to touch the lives of hundreds of thousands.

One of Anne's latest books, *Plan B: Further Thoughts on Faith*, is a reminder that the Holy Spirit has many ways to reach people in many different circumstances to draw them into closeness with the Divine. There is not only a Plan B, but a Plan C or D or E, whatever is needed, for God never loses patience with us and His great heart of love longs to bring us into the wholeness that only an intimate connection with Him can provide.

My concern is to make sure that you know about Plan A. Plan A is what this book is all about. It is the quickest, most direct route to a personal encounter with the Divine and to living a transformed Spirit-filled life. Not everyone is ready for Plan A, but if you have read this far in the book you undoubtedly are already doing it or are ready to begin it.

MANY VOICES

There are many voices crying in the wilderness, offering a path to spiritual life and to enlightenment. Some are quite profound, thought-provoking and well-meaning. Take the work of people like Eckhart Tolle or Wayne Dyer or Mary Ann Williamson or Deepak Chopra. By all means, read what these brilliant and dedicated people have to say. They have much to teach you, but while thinkers and writers like those mentioned above can be very helpful and can launch some seekers on the path to truth, their teachings are incomplete. So learn from them but always question them. They do not offer Plan A. To put it bluntly, these teachers and thinkers can be extremely helpful and insightful but are insufficient because they do not present Jesus Christ as Divine. They all have great admiration for Jesus. They quote Him repeatedly as a great spiritual teacher and enlightened thinker but, they do not lift Him up as Lord and Savior from sin. In fact some of these teachers deny the existence of such a thing as sin. That of course brings us to the greatest issue of all … if there is no such thing as sin, then there is no need for a Savior. If Jesus was not Divine, then He was only an enlightened teacher. He could not be the Savior. *The premier task of Christians today is to uphold the full Divinity of Jesus Christ before the world.*

The *Da Vinci Code* set an incredible publishing record by selling over 60 million copies. The movie was a block-buster. It grossed 750 million dollars on opening day. Though nothing more than pure fiction, the book and movie have served to undermine in many people's minds the pivotal teaching of Christianity, the one doctrine upon which the whole structure rests: the full Divinity of Jesus Christ. The objection to the entertaining story Dan Brown invented is that it presents Jesus as only human like you and me. It shows Him to be a wise enlightened man who married and had children with Mary

Magdalene and died a normal death and remained forever in the grave. In one of the brashest and most incorrect statements in the story, Brown has one of his main characters declare that Jesus' own disciples did not see Him as God or as divine, nor did the early Christians. This is completely false. There are many documents from the early years of Christianity's development that show that most followers of Jesus already called him LORD, the Yahweh of the Old Testament. More importantly Jesus Himself made it clear that He was God.

Brown tells his readers that the idea that Jesus was fully God only came into being when the Catholic Church at the Council of Nicea in 325, voted that Christ was to be considered divine! The truth is that church leaders at Nicea rejected the heresy of Arianism (which taught that God created Jesus just like He did Adam). The Council affirmed what was clearly taught in the gospels; that God and Jesus existed together from the beginning in the Trinity.

The plot of Brown's book centers around the efforts of a certain Catholic organization to keep this fact (the fact that Jesus was not divine and was not resurrected) covered up at any cost, even by the use of threats, violence, and murder so that the "myth" of Christianity and the authority of the Catholic Church will not be discredited before the world. Even the heroes of the book and movie are people who also do not believe that Jesus was divine. One of them at the surprise end of the movie even discovers that she is one of the actual physical descendants of Jesus!

LIAR, LUNATIC OR LORD?

The book disregards the most profound fact that Jesus Himself made it abundantly clear that He was God, the Christ, the Messiah. If you take Brown's view that Jesus was an ordinary man, then Jesus' statements and claims about Himself make Him either a pathological liar and deceiver of His gullible followers or a mentally ill person suffering from delusions of grandeur. As C.S. Lewis so famously said, Jesus was either a lunatic or a liar or He was indeed who He said He was. Dan Brown only shows his ignorance (as do many other contemporary spiritual speakers or writers) when he appears to magnanimously portray Jesus as merely a brilliant spiritual teacher. That is not an option open to any thinking, informed person who has taken the time to simply read the New Testament without prejudice.

Such present day fascination with this book and movie and also with some of the non-canonical writings from the early centuries (the Gospel of Judas, the Gospel of Thomas etc.) show that there are many who are looking for a way to justify bringing Jesus down to the level of an ordinary man and discounting Him as Lord and Savior. Why? Because without the full Divinity of Jesus, Christianity is then nothing more than an appealing myth. If Jesus is not truly God, all the moral authority of Scripture crumbles. The church is nothing but a bunch of deluded, well-meaning fools and should close its doors forever. If Jesus is not truly God, then there is no such thing as sin, no need for a Savior and men and women are left on their own to determine right and wrong for themselves and live and behave in any way they wish.

JESUS: FULLY GOD AND SPIRIT BAPTIZER

Plan A avoids these pitfalls and it is very simple. It means acknowledging one's need and one's sinfulness. It means believing in Jesus as fully God and accepting Him as a personal Redeemer and Spirit-baptizer. It is the most direct route of all to eternal life, and to spiritual transformation. A person can grow more spiritually in one day of encounter with the Holy Spirit's baptism then in ten years of reading the best spiritual writers or going to therapy or practicing meditation and yoga.

Having said that, I must clearly acknowledge that there are many people who are not ready or do not know about Plan A. These are people who may need to start their spiritual journey with the well-intentioned counsel of such above-mentioned writers. They may be so full of fear or guilt that they need therapy to heal emotionally before they are ready to hear the gospel, before they can even begin to open their hearts to the world of the Spirit. They may need AA to help rid themselves of an addiction that has been totally blocking their spiritual growth. Plan B, Plan C, Plan D, there are many paths that lead to the Kingdom, though eventually if followed with a pure heart they will all merge in one path, in one Person. But everyone's needs are different. People have to be met where they are. If you came upon a man beside a trail with a broken leg, it would be a crime to try and preach the gospel to him! He has other needs that must be ministered to first.

PLAN A

Some people have been wounded by a bad experience with traditional religion. Others have been badly hurt or abused by someone and must first find healing and support in therapy before they can move on. But while we are making allowances for people and their unique circumstances, their woundedness and dysfunction, I beg of you, never lose sight of the preeminence of Plan A. For most people it is still the best and most direct and most pitfall-free path to an intimate life with God. There may be those who think it is old and trite and just too traditional for them. They may see it as the religion of their grandparents. They are fascinated with the newness of some of the contemporary spiritual teachers who seem to offer an alternative to transformation and enlightenment and connection with God. I want to encourage you if you are able, to stay with the most proven, simple and direct route. Cast your lot with Jesus. Savior. Baptizer with Spirit. Kneel at His feet. Surrender your heart to Him each day. Accept His gift of eternal life. Claim His promise of His Spirit living in you. Worship Him as Lord. Honor Him as God. He is the way, the truth and the life. He is the light of the world. He is the exact representation of the Father. Never settle for second best.

POWER SOURCE

We have seen that while on earth, Jesus made Himself fully dependent on the power of the Holy Spirit. It was the Holy Spirit that "overshadowed" Mary and conceived the Lord in her womb. Jesus did not begin His ministry or start to fulfill His role as Messiah until He was baptized with the Spirit at the Jordan at age 30.

In His death He was equally dependent on the Holy Spirit. It was in fact the power of the Spirit that tore Jesus from the clutches of the devil and death and brought Him forth from the grave. Good news flash… God's love is stronger than death! Physical death and spiritual death! "But if the spirit of him who raised Jesus from the dead dwells in you, He who raised Christ from the dead will also give life to your mortal bodies through his spirit who dwells in you" (Romans 8:11).

The Holy Spirit raised Jesus from the dead and now He wants to resurrect you! (Have I mentioned that you need to die first, before you can be resurrected?!) He is still in the business of raising the dead! Plan A for your life, He wants to resurrect and begin to transform you! Now! He wants to resurrect you from your sins and your powerlessness. Until you allow Him to do this you are still in the tomb. The prison of materialism. The tomb of selfishness, preoccupations and distractions. The prison of addiction. The tomb of religion perhaps! The prison of your own ego.

Without this spiritual resurrection you are numbered among the living dead. The voice of Jesus is calling you out of your personal tomb. He is calling you to wake up. Wake up to reality. Wake up to awareness: moment by moment awareness of the living Presence of the Father with you. He is calling you to a new, high way of life. He is calling you to become an extraordinary creature whose life is centered on love, joy, peace and service. In a sense the kingdom of God begins *right now* for the Christian because the wonderful fruits of the Spirit in the life totally transform the heart.

THE THIRD COMING

Jesus came saying two shocking things: "The kingdom of God is at hand," and, "The kingdom of God is within you." When Jesus said to "take no thought for tomorrow" do you realize that He was not only talking about your physical needs in the future, like we usually think He was, but that *He was telling you not go get too obsessed with worrying about the end of your lives or the end of the world or even the afterlife?*

278

He doesn't want you getting all anxious and distracted and paranoid about the end of days and the time of trouble and the apocalypse and the mark of the beast or what ever negativity you might be prone to focus on. There are way too many apocalaholics in some churches! All that end-times stuff is in God's hands! Worrying about tomorrow or next week or next month or next year or even about the next life *can be a huge distraction to practicing the presence of God and living joyfully in the Spirit right now.* Worry about anything is a badge of our lack of faith. It's been said that worrying is like praying for what you don't want! Directing negative energy at anything, (and that includes fussing and talking about what Satan is up to) only gives it more power and presence in your life. Do you realize that the opposite of peace is anxiety? The third fruit of the Holy Spirit in the life is peace, following love and joy! It is the perfect antidote to worry. Can you accept the fact that you were meant to lead a peaceful, joyful life?

No wonder Jesus said we could have heaven now! What a concept! I love it! God living in us by His Spirit provides us with eternal life right now! His love is stronger than death. Death loses it power and meaning because our God is the God of the living, not the dead! "Dwell in me as I dwell in you", Jesus said. Inherent in that miraculous indwelling is life eternal. "Whoever lives and believe in me will never die" promised our Lord (John 11:26). God has got you covered! God's love is stronger than death! Do you get it? Salvation is not just about what happens after we die. It begins the moment we accept how much God loves and cherishes us.

It is distressing to me that so much emphasis has been placed on the second coming that is in the future while we have neglected the incredible promise of the kingdom coming inside of us now by the filling of the Holy Spirit. You could almost say that heaven is kind of side benefit! Jesus said, "I will pray the Father, and he shall give you another Comforter, that he may abide with you for ever." Then referring to the effect of the Spirit coming to abide *in* and not just *with* the believer, Christ stated, "I will not leave you comfortless: I will come to you" (John 14:16-18) So you see, through the indwelling of the promised Spirit *we already have a second coming!* The kingdom of God truly is at hand and as the Master said, it is now within you and me by the indwelling Spirit! Guess what … *that means forever starts now!* This is not to diminish the hope of what has been called the second coming, when the Lord intervenes again physically in time and space. That will be an outstanding event, but it should be called the third coming! Jesus' birth as a human being in Bethlehem is called "The Advent." That is the first coming. When He is allowed to come into our hearts by His Spirit and set up His kingdom inside us right now, that is the second coming! Thus, His coming in the clouds some day in the future would be "the third coming"! Got it? Kind of neat huh?

A powerful text in 1 Corinthians has been misapplied by believers who seem to think it is a description of something that if we wait long enough and are faithful we can receive after we get to heaven. Wrong! It is an incredible and precious promise for the Spirit-filled Christian right now!   As it is written: "What no eye has seen, what no ear has heard, and what no human mind has conceived—these things God has prepared for those who love him," but God *has* revealed it to us *by his Spirit* (emphasis supplied) (1Corinthians 2:8-10). We need to quit using this text at funerals as a hope for the departed and start using it now as a stunning promise available for fulfillment right now!

Clearly, there are astonishing gifts and experiences and truths available to the Spirit-filled believer right now. They are part of your spiritual inheritance as a son or daughter of God. They are to be enjoyed and celebrated at this very moment in your life. Think about the amazing words of the Master: "I have more to say to you, more than you can now bear. But when he, the Spirit of truth comes, he will guide you into all truth. He will bring glory to me by taking from what is mine and making it known to you" (John 16:12-14). Here is the promise that new and astounding truths, *truths totally in harmony with, but beyond the truths of the Bible, will constantly and continually be revealed to God's Spirit-filled children!* No wonder truth is dynamic and progressive! No wonder we can all be spiritual evolutionists!

"Come forth." He says. Come forth by the power of my Spirit. Come forth to amazing truths and insights and experiences! Come forth to the amazing, abundant, inspired life of spiritual adventure. Come forth, enter into the new kingdom, the new life. The life of love. A life full of sacred adventure and joy. FDR had a sign on the wall of his White House office: "Let unconquerable gladness dwell!" That reminds me of John Wesley's definition of Christianity: "a lifelong love affair with God that produces exquisite joy."

Q&A:

Q. Aren't some of those writers you talked about New Age? How can you say that anything good could come from them?

A. *Oh, stop judging the New Age movement. It is not the Devil's club. It is just a group of people with hungry hearts trying to find their way to God. Yes, some of the ideas are flawed or insufficient. Sometimes people look in the wrong places but most of all shame on us Christians. If we had not kept the gospel all locked up in our pockets and in our churches and buried it under complex doctrines and stale traditions and judgmentalness and legalism, if we had not ignored half the gospel, the exciting news and the exciting energizing, joyful transforming experience of the baptism of the Holy Spirit, a lot of people would not have to be out searching for spiritual life in other places. And yes, praise the Lord, many a person that started out as a "New Age" seeker has now found their way into contemporary Christian churches and found there a home for their heart and the intimacy with God and the filling of the Spirit they were hungering for.*

Speaking of the writers, there is not another human being on the planet I cannot learn something from. Paul, one of the wisest of men, said he was indebted "both to the Greeks, and to the Barbarians" (Romans 1:14 KJV). Jesus said that if His people did not praise Him, the very stones would cry out. Some of these writers are the stones crying out because we Christians have not been doing our job. Think Eckhart Tolle, think Deepak Chopra.

We simply must stop labeling people. We label them "New Age" or "non-believers." or "back-sliders" or "irreligious" or "liberal" or "conservative." Kierkegaard said, "Once you label me you negate me." One of the most common labels is the word "they." Poet C.K. Williams wrote that "there is room for an 'I,' a 'you,' and a 'we,' but there is no 'they'. Walt Whitman in his "Song of the Open Road" wrote:

Not till the sun excludes you, do I
* Exclude you;*
Not till the waters refuse to glisten for
you, and the leaves to rustle for you,
do my words refuse to glisten and
rustle for you.

There are only people on different stages of their journey. Let's just have some compassion for them and stop judging them and learn what we can from them and give them a hand on the way. If you will let the Spirit lead you beyond judgment and learn to see people through the eyes of compassion, you will be able to come into a oneness with them that can draw them toward God as nothing else can.

Q. You talk about the Holy Spirit "transforming" us. What does that mean?

A. We used to talk a lot about the two stages of Christian experience, "justification" and "sanctification." Justification it was said was the work of an instant. It was when God forgave your sins and you received the gift of eternal life. Sanctification it was said, was the work of a lifetime. Sanctification is the ever on-going process of the converted Christian to grow in the image and character of God. It was seen by some as a rather difficult struggle as one attempted to whip the fallen human nature into shape and struggled to become more like God. Paul talks about this in the interesting chapter of Romans 7 where he speaks of his consistent failure to do what he knows to be right and his anguish over his failings. Here is the picture of a person who is a converted Christian yet lacks power and victory in his life and the inability to successfully and consistently keep the law and the will of God. This is a picture of a believer who is converted but has not received the baptism of the Holy Spirit. In Romans 8 Paul moves on to an entirely different scenario. A whole new paradigm! Now he paints the picture of what life can be like for the person who has moved into the Spirit-filled life. What a life of joy, victory and power it is! Solomon had a thing about ants. That's cool, but I say the lowly caterpillar has even more to teach us. For part of its life, the creature crawls around in the dirt in a very small area. Then, one day, it goes for a long nap... and ... transformation! The chubby little grub has become a beautiful butterfly with a slender body and incredible wings. It is gorgeous! It can fly! There is no limit to where it can go. It has been transformed! The Holy Spirit says to us, "don't just be content with change. I am here to transform you into something splendid." By the way, I have a sneaking suspicion that when that little caterpillar lays down for his last nap, it might feel a lot to him like the end, like he is dying. Kind of reminds you of Someone who said: "you must die in order to live."

Q. I think you are misleading us and setting us up for false hopes when you tell us that we can be filled with the Spirit today. The church I belong to teaches that the baptism of the Holy Spirit was given only for a limited time in the apostolic age, in the time of the early Christians to get the church going. Now that the church is firmly established with its organizations and institutions and full-time paid clergy, the Holy Spirit is no longer needed and has been withdrawn from the earth until the end-times when the Latter Rain will fall.

A. Peter replied, "Repent and be baptized every one of you, in the name of Jesus Christ for the forgiveness of your sins. And you will receive the gift of the Holy Spirit. The promise is for you and your children *and for all who are far off* ..." (Acts 2:38,39) (emphasis supplied).

You and I are the "far off"! Praise the Lord! We are included! The gift is for us too!

Jesus Himself promised to believers that the Holy Spirit will "abide with you forever" (John 14:16). He also said, "Ask and it will be given to you .... For everyone who asks receives ... If you then, though you are evil, know how to give good gifts to your children, how much more will your Father in heaven *give the Holy Spirit to those who ask him!* (Luke 11:9-11) (emphasis supplied). I trust my Lord to do what He says He will do for me. He loves me, He cherishes me! And He does not lie.

CHAPTER 20

THE SPIRIT AND I: A PERSONAL ENCOUNTER

There is something I didn't tell you in chapter 12. The same pastor who introduced the concept of the baptism of the Holy Spirit to Pat Boone and who assisted him in asking to receive this gift was present with me when I first asked to be filled with the Spirit. Maybe you can see now why I was a little edgy with the guest speaker in my church who put down Pat and his experience with the Spirit as "of the devil"!

Father Dennis Bennett was the Episcopal priest of whom it has been said he verbally fired the shot that was heard around the world. In April of 1960, Bennett was in the prestigious position of pastor of St. Mark's Church, Van Nuys, California, one of the largest (2,600 members) Episcopal churches in the world. On April 3, he stood in his pulpit and shared with his congregation that he had received the baptism of the Spirit. He was one of the very first main-line Protestant clergyman to publicly share with his church the news of his new spiritual experience. The antagonism and opposition were immediate on the part of many conservative members of the congregation. Dennis was soon asked to resign by some of the more powerful members of his church board. As chief pastor, he did not have to resign, but chose to do so because he did not want to see strife in the church and because he believed his experience was too valuable to fight over. After the explosion in his congregation, the story was carried widely in newspapers, wire services and eventually *Time* and *Newsweek* magazines. Even the *Encyclopedia Britannica Yearbook* had an article which stated that Charismatic renewal may be said to have begun when Pastor Bennett first gave his testimony about his experience with the Holy Spirit to the people of his church in Van Nuys.

Bennett was given what appeared to be a very unappealing option if he wanted to continue to be a pastor. He was told he could leave the ministry or he could move to St. Luke's church in Ballard, Washington, which was a dying congregation, ready to be closed down as hopeless. Dennis made his choice and in his 40's started all over again.

St. Luke's went on to flourish and become a major demonstration of the Holy Spirit's ability to transform an "old-line" congregation. Dennis wrote a book about his experience with the baptism of the Spirit and about what happened at his new church. It was called *Nine O'clock In the Morning*.

About this time, I had just finished my own personal and thorough study of the subject of the Holy Spirit in the New Testament. I knew I desperately needed and wanted the experience of the baptism of the Spirit for myself. As I told you earlier, I had never encountered any teaching on the baptism of the Spirit in college theology training or in three years of graduate study at seminary. I had never heard any of my denomination's preachers speak on the topic or seen articles published on it in our journals. Nonetheless I began to inquire quietly among some of the older ministers in my district and some of my pastor friends. They either showed no interest in the topic or cautioned me to stay away from it to avoid trouble with our church administration.

In my study of the topic, I had found several references in the New Testament about the role of the "laying on of hands" to receive the baptism of the Holy Spirit, played in the early church. It was not always a prerequisite to receiving it and there was clearly nothing "magical" about this simple service. The person who assisted the one asking did not have to be a pastor. After all, they were not the baptizer. Jesus is the only baptizer with the Holy Spirit. However, it was often the case in the early Church that one or more persons, who, had received the Spirit, gathered around the person who wanted the experience and, laying their hands on this individual's head, prayed for him or her to receive it.

I decided that I would like to have the laying on of hands as part of my asking for the baptism of the Spirit. The only trouble was, I could not find anyone in my denomination who believed they had been baptized with the Spirit! One day when I was still pondering what to do, I ran across Dennis Bennett's book. (When the student is ready, the book will appear!) I was encouraged by the assurance that he had of his baptism with the Spirit and delighted to learn of the wonderful things that were happening in the church he was pastoring, which had been on the verge of extinction.

MY JOURNEY

I flew several hundred miles and rented a car to visit a weekday evening service at Dennis' church tucked away in a Seattle suburb. There was a very sweet atmosphere in the room that night. There were probably 50 people present. There was some singing, some poignant testimonies. Then Dennis spoke and when he was finished, invited anyone who wanted to receive the baptism of the Spirit to come forward. Several of us went to the altar. Pastor Bennett came to us one by one and laying his hands on us, prayed that we would receive the great gift Jesus promised we could have. Some who received that night prayed quietly in tongues. Others wept silently, joyfully. Others were just very still and reverent. I remember distinctly a great sense of peace in the room.

My heart was deeply stirred, but I was not overwhelmed with emotion. There were no flashing lights or ringing bells for me. No great ecstasy. (Note: filling does not necessarily imply feeling.) There came flooding over me, a calm assurance that God had heard and honored my request. After the peacefulness, a great feeling of love came over me. I not only felt deeply cherished myself, but I received a powerful feeling of immense love for people. A part of it was this great dose of empathy. I had never felt a love like that before. It was huge and it was transforming. I can truly say that the Spirit baptized me with love! The promise of my favorite text, Romans 5:5, became a living reality for me. "The love of God is shed abroad in our hearts by the Holy Ghost which is given unto us" (KJV).

I received another unexpected and unanticipated gift that night. It clearly came from beyond my self also and that was a deep passion for Scripture. I had studied my Bible dutifully for years. Part of that studying I must admit was done so that I could prove others wrong! (what a motive!) I also studied for my own devotions, for getting ready for Bible classes, for preparing sermons. But I had never had a passion to read the Scriptures before. I often had

286

to force myself to put down a book or a news magazine and make myself pick up the Bible. All of that changed when I asked for the baptism of the Spirit. I realized the next day that I had a great hunger for Scripture. I just couldn't get enough of it. I typed out verses from the New Testament and taped them to the mirror so that I could memorize them when I was shaving. I bought the Bible on tape and listened to it intently as I drove. The gospels of course were especially precious and among those the writings of John were the most inspiring of all. I came to see that the New Testament is a book just full of references to the Holy Spirit. How could I have missed that for so long?

I just want to note here, that by telling you my story of how I received the Spirit, it does not mean that anyone else has to do it in the same way. Though I think it is preferred that you share in the experience of the baptism with other believers, that is certainly not a requirement. Neither of course is being dependent on any other person to receive it. Jesus baptizes you with the Spirit, not any human being. It is entirely possible that you could receive this gift while you are praying completely alone.

After I had asked for the filling of the Spirit, my pastoring and counseling began to take on a whole new emphasis. Little by little I began to let go of my "holier-than-thou" attitude and my man-with-all-the-right-answers stance. I began to let go of a pharisaical and judgmental attitude I had always carried around with me. I also began to realize the vast difference when I was speaking in church or counseling some one when I was in the Spirit and when I was not. And yes, I did and still do fall away from my connection with the Spirit, but now there is a clear distinction for me when this happens. I know when I have blocked or ignored the Spirit or become distracted. When I catch myself operating with ego at the center of my life, I come running back where I belong.

WRITING BEGINS

I had always had an interest in writing but prior to this time I had only produced a few articles for magazines. I soon felt led to begin a book. One of the favorite texts I had discovered in my search for the Spirit was in Romans 5:5: "The love of God is shed abroad in our hearts by the Holy Spirit which is given unto us." The baptism of the Spirit has always been most of all about unconditional love for me. The book naturally then, was about love. In fact it came to be called *Living God's Love*. I know that the Holy Spirit became a great creative force for me as I wrote. I could feel His presence and guidance as I worked on the manuscript day after day. The book came at a critical time for our denomination as it was just beginning the move from an emphasis on law and behavior and legalism to the great freeing truth of salvation by faith. With its emphasis on devotion instead of doctrine, the book helped to open some doors and hearts and was instrumental in ushering in a new era in the church. It sold over 100,000 copies and set some records with the publisher. I know for a fact that book and eight others that have followed since would never have been written without my personal encounter with the Holy Spirit. In the movie *Chariots of Fire*, which tells the remarkable true story of two Olympic runners, the young athlete Eric Liddell says movingly, "When I run, I feel God's pleasure." I can truly say that since I was filled with the Spirit, when I write, I feel God's pleasure. As any writer or musician or artist knows, it is an incredible delight to co-create with Him!

The next adventure the Spirit had for me came up one day when in my new-found love for the Bible I was reading one of Paul's books. In Romans 15:20 he says, "It has always been my ambition to preach the gospel where Christ was not known, so that I would not be building on someone else's foundation." That verse really struck me. By this time I had been pastoring some years. I had been given several nice established churches to serve in that had beautiful buildings already built. They came filled with people who were already Christians. I had certainly been building on other men's foundations! I believe that the Spirit called me that day to reach out and use my energy to build something new for God where nothing existed before.

Within a few months after the poignant moment of reading that challenging text, we had sold almost everything we had, purchased a pickup and camper and were headed up the Alcan Highway. We were headed for the Last

Frontier's fifth largest town, Kodiak, Alaska. My research had shown that our denomination did not have a church there, that in fact the town was under-churched and over-barred! It was a vigorous and boisterous place, the fastest growing town in the state at the time with a prospering fishing industry and a growing military base.

My wife, to her everlasting credit, agreed with and supported this preposterous sacrifice of our security as we set off into the totally unknown. I had always been a salaried pastor before, but our denomination did not have the funds at the time to expand into new areas. We were totally on our own financially. (Self-supporting, I believe you call it.) Since we had two small children, my in-laws were appalled at our decision. I am sure they were quite convinced I had lost my mind.

The remote island of Kodiak was so far out in the North Pacific Ocean that it is due north of Honolulu, Hawaii! It took hours on a ferry (dubbed The Dramamine Express) to get there. The first happy surprise came shortly after we had arrived when a fisherman took a fancy to our pickup and camper and suggested that he would like to take it in trade on his almost-new three- bedroom house. One problem solved without even trying! Then all sorts of opportunities for work started showing up. Within days I had a commercial flying job, both teaching flying and flying charters around the island to outlying communities. I also got a job working in one of the many fish-processing plants and filled in as a longshoreman. I also began selling Christian books in the evening as a way to connect with families in the town.

My wife's skills as a registered nurse were soon put to good use in the island hospital where patients often included men flown in off of Russian and Japanese fishing vessels. Before long, she was in charge of the whole hospital and staff during the night shift. The striking thing was how things just opened up for us without any effort or struggle on our part. I have since learned to describe this with a word I have come to love. Synchronicity.

SYNCHRONICITY

A particularly synchronistic event happened a few weeks after we arrived. It started when I put a small announcement in the local paper. It stated that for the first time church services for our denomination would be held in the town. They were going to be in our home and all were welcome. I was not particularly optimistic about the results this would produce because I had been told by our church office in Anchorage that there were no members of our denomination on the island at all. In fact this was one reason they had tried to discourage me from moving to Kodiak. They said there was another town in the state that had a core of three or four families who were church members. They thought it would make a lot more sense for me to move there to try and establish a new church.

A few days after I had placed the notice in the paper, a man who worked at a satellite tracking station about 20 miles from town got a day off. He decided to go for a long walk on a lonely Pacific Ocean beach nearby. About an hour into his hike, he was walking in the sand near the water's edge when his toe stubbed on something. He looked back and saw a partially buried bottle. He turned around and gave it a kick. When he did, it popped out of the sand. He could see that it had something inside. His curiosity got the best of him and he picked it up and discovered a note sealed in the bottle. The top would not come off so he walked up the beach to a large rock and smashed the glass against it. Out fluttered a piece of paper at his feet. He reached down and picked up a hand-written note. It had been prepared by a lady who over two years before sealed it in the bottle and tossed it in the ocean off the coast of Central California. The note invited whoever found it to consider becoming a Christian. It also suggested that they should enroll in a Bible study course through the mail from an organization called The Voice of Prophecy.

The hiker was stunned. He had graduated some years before from a Christian college. The same school I had. He had been raised as a member of the church which sponsored the college and the Voice of Prophecy. But he had turned his back on Christianity. He had accepted the job at the remote site in Alaska in order to try to get away from a bad experience with the church and from a failed marriage. This "coincidence" (a coincidence is God's way of working a miracle anonymously) of his finding the note in the bottle in such an isolated spot had set his head to spinning. He turned around and began the long walk back to his lodging.

When he arrived he lay down on his bed, and to try and clear his head he picked up the local newspaper. The first thing he saw was my announcement of the beginning of church services. That really got his attention! Bruce attended our first meeting. He came faithfully after that and found his way back to a connection with God. The woman he married eventually became our church pianist.

Through various synchronistic events such as this, within a year and a half we had a good-sized group of people meeting to worship each week. My main task seemed to be just staying out of the way and letting a series of wonderful events happen that kept the group growing. We soon grew large enough to know that we needed a church building. We were already a church family. We just needed the building. In a planning committee meeting someone suggested I contact Maranatha church builders. They were a relatively young organization then whose members donated their vacation time and often flew their own planes to a site to build a new church.

One evening I picked up the phone and summoning up my courage, because I did not know anyone in the Maranatha organization and was sure they had never heard of me, called the President at his home in Michigan. When he answered, I told him that I was Douglas Cooper calling from Kodiak, Alaska. There was a long pause. I was sure I had caught him at a bad time or he was in a bad mood. Finally, he said, "Is this the Douglas Cooper who wrote the book *Way Up North?*" "Yes," I replied, not sure what was coming next. That book had been published just a few months before. It was a series of true adventure stories I had gathered from around Alaska, including several of my own. John Freeman said, "I had that book in my hand when the phone rang. I am right in the middle of reading it. It is one of the most fascinating books I've read in a long time."

Needless to say, the conversation went very well after that. The book had already whetted his appetite to see Alaska and the "coincidence" of my calling out of the blue just as he was reading it was all he needed. That very night before we hung up, John had agreed to bring his whole crew to Kodiak the next summer and build our church.

So it came to be. A beautiful chapel was erected among the tall, green spruce in a very quiet spot overlooking a little lake. It went up in a matter of days, much to the amazement of the town folk and this attracted some more of them to come and worship with us. It was such an attractive building (a talented and generous Christian architect named Don Kirkman had donated his time and travel expenses and drawn up the plans for it, integrating it perfectly into its unique, picturesque setting) that it soon became highly in demand by the residents of the town for weddings and funerals. Soon a Christian grade school occupied the lower level. The church and the building became a great blessing to the community.

Life in the Spirit turned out to be quite an exciting adventure. There have been a total of eight books now, several translated into other languages, all uplifting Jesus in one way or another. I have had the privilege of presenting seminars on Living God's Love and the Baptism of the Spirit in many places in North America and even in Europe. I have been with groups of people during a seminar where the Spirit so filled the place that you could cut the oneness and the peace in the room with a knife. Talk about "a sweet, sweet Spirit in this place." I have felt hundreds of warm, sacred tears of joy splash on the backs of my hands as I have knelt in a circle, holding hands with the group, as men and women prayed with surrendered hearts to receive the gift of the Spirit.

There have been many good times and also some hard times. The Spirit-filled life does not offer freedom from pain and suffering. It does not bring perfection or perfect wisdom. It does offer to all of us, however, the strength we need to meet the challenges of the day that is at hand. Most of all, it brings to us the comforting loving and personal presence of the One who said, "Lo, I am with you always, even unto the end of the earth."

APPENDIX A:

A SPIRITUAL BREATHING EXERCISE

"He breathed on them, and said, 'Receive the Holy Spirit.'"

In this book we have seen that wind and breath are powerful symbols for the Holy Spirit.

It is also humbling and helpful to recognize that every breath we take is on loan from God and to realize that God is never any further away then our next breath! "The Spirit of God has made me: the breath of the Almighty gives me life" (Job 33:4). That means both physical and spiritual life. Not coincidentally, breathing exercises have long been considered a helpful tool for focusing on the spiritual. They can assist a person in stilling the busyness of thought and the frantic activity of the mind (monkey-mind the Buddhists call it!) They can help move one toward stillness, toward being able to quietly practice the presence of God.

Here is an exercise I have developed that assists me if I find myself too caught up in the external world, or if I am lying in bed trying to get to sleep but my mind is spinning with thoughts that won't slow down. You don't have to be in bed to do this. You can do it anytime, in the office, while you are waiting for an appointment, while you are driving (Be careful, it does really calm you!)

Relax your body as much as possible. Let the tensions drain from every muscle.

Exhale slowly.

When you inhale, breathe only through you nose.

Breathe deeply, filling your abdomen, not your chest.

Take your incoming breath in increments and with each increment say to yourself one of the wonderful fruits of the Spirit from Galatians 5 and visualize taking in that part of God's nature:

Love

Joy

Peace

Patience

Kindness

Goodness

Faithfulness

Gentleness

Self-control

Right here and now I am going to take the risk of adding some new fruits of the Spirit that I believe the Spirit Himself/Herself has brought to our consciousness since Galatians 5 was written 2,000 years ago. I know, I know, there are those horrible threats made in the book of Revelation of what will happen to someone who dares to add something new to Scripture. But I believe I will go ahead and take my chances so I can give you this! I feel free to add these fruits of the Spirit because Jesus said that when the Holy Spirit came He/She would lead us into even deeper and greater truths than Jesus Himself could present. This was so because people's hearts were not ready and their consciousness was not yet raised enough to appreciate them! (John 16:13) So here you are!

Sensitivity

Gratitude

Forgiveness

Empathy

Mindfulness

Serenity

Laughter

Humility (Humility is not thinking less of yourself, it's thinking of yourself less)

After you have inhaled, hold your breath and say to yourself a spiritual promise that holds deep spiritual meaning for you. I like to say to myself one of Jesus' beautiful and simple promises that speak of His desire for oneness with us. "Lo, I am with you always," or "I am the vine, you are the branch," or "I no longer live but Christ lives within me." Or state a simple request. "Help me to live in your presence".

Next, begin to exhale. With each increment of exhalation, say to yourself the words that represent the elements you most want to see expelled from your life, such as:

Fear

Guilt

Anger

Selfishness

Judgmentalness

Impatience

This simple exercise can help you stop the racing of your thoughts. It can help you still your busy, hyper-active mind that is either rehashing some drama or problem from the past or pulling you anxiously out into speculating about what is coming in the future. It can bring you into the now, the present moment, the only place where you can encounter God. Repeat this exercise until your body relaxes, your mind stills and you have a sense of connection and inner peace.

THE HOLY SPIRIT AS A POWER SOURCE

You will receive power when the Holy Spirit comes on you (Acts 1:8).

The Holy Spirit is the power source in the entire Bible:

1. It was the Spirit, the holy wind, blowing apart the waters of the Red Sea for Moses.

2. It was the Spirit who overpowered the lions in the den with Daniel.

3. It was the Spirit who sent the walls of Jericho crashing down.

4. It was the Spirit who snatched Elijah up in a fiery chariot.

5. It was the Spirit who turned a shy Carpenter into the powerhouse of a Messiah that could turn the world upside down.

6. It was the Spirit who wrested Christ's body from the clutches of the devil and death.

7. It was the Spirit who ripped apart the curtain in the temple the moment Christ died, allowing every human being access into the intimate presence of God again!

8. It was the Spirit on the day of Pentecost who took a group of mourning, confused, powerless disciples in the upper room and transformed them from very ordinary people into extraordinary people who would found the Christian church.

PREREQUISITES FOR RECEIVING THE BAPTISM OF THE SPIRIT

1. You need the assurance of your salvation by faith in Jesus. You need to have renounced your sins and come to know that He has forgiven you and given you eternal life. Though you do not have to be perfect, this gift - like the gift of salvation - is for people who need it because they are less than perfect; still you cannot be practicing a known sin.

"Repent and be baptized, every one of you, in the name of Jesus Christ for the forgiveness of your sins. And you will receive the gift of the Holy Spirit" (Romans 2:38).

2. Only total, absolute surrender will open the door to the Spirit. Acts 5:32 says, "We are witnesses of these things, and so is the Holy Spirit, whom God has given to those who obey him." R. A. Torrey said that the heart of obedience is in the will; the essence of obedience is the full surrender of the will to God. In his years of teaching about the Spirit, Torrey says that people who prayed something like "Heavenly Father, here I am. I am your property," were the ones who came to receive the filling of the Spirit. This reminds me of Brennan Manning's habit of praying each morning as soon as he wakes up, "Abba, I belong to you! You have bought me with a price. I acknowledge your ownership and surrender myself and all that I am absolutely to you. Send me where you will; do with me as you will; use me as your will."

Torrey stated that he often saw this kind of prayer as the decisive step in a person receiving the baptism of the Holy Spirit. He said, "When we can truly say, 'my all is on the altar,' then we will not have long to wait for the fire!" (Torrey, C.A. *The Person and Work of the Holy Spirit*. (Whitaker House, New Kensington, Pa, 1996) p.242, 243)

3. There needs to be a specific, definite, personal, "real time" asking for the baptism of the Holy Spirit. The Holy Spirit has been available to every Christian since Pentecost, but you simply must appropriate it for yourself. "If you then being evil, know how to give good gifts to your children, *how much*

more shall your heavenly Father give the Holy Spirit to them that ask him?" (Luke 11:13 (emphasis supplied).

    4. By faith, believe you have the gift that Jesus promised and it will be yours. "He redeemed us … so that by faith we might receive the promise of the Spirit" (Galatians 3:14). "This is the confidence we have in approaching God: that if we ask anything according to his will, he hears us. And if we know that he hears us – whatever we ask- we know that we have whatever we asked of him" (1 John 5:14).

APPENDIX D

GUIDELINES FOR SPIRIT-FILLED CHRISTIANS

1. Since this experience is by faith, do not seek a sign to confirm it. God will confirm it for you in his own way and in his own time.

2. Do not be proud because you are Spirit-filled. Being Spirit-filled does not make you a super-Christian. You will not be perfect, you will still make mistakes, look at Peter and Paul!
The bad news? You will not get a higher IQ, and you will still need daily forgiveness!

3. It is the opposite of bragging to say you are filled with the Spirit. It is an acknowledgement of your need. You didn't have the love, you didn't have the power, so you chose to ask for something more.

4. The Spirit is given for both sanctification and service. It is to equip you for your own ministry.

5. You may not feel different after receiving the baptism of the Spirit. It is a matter of choice, of setting the will to ask for it and receive it. It is not primarily about a feeling. It is a matter of sitting down and writing a check on your spiritual bank account, of deciding to draw on your inheritance. You may feel very unspiritual some days, but you can still be filled with the Spirit.
Hannah Whitehall Smith wrote:

The baptism of the Spirit means far more than emotion. It means to be immersed or dipped into the Spirit of God into His character and nature. The real evidence of one's baptism is neither emotion nor any single gift, like tongues, rather there must be Christ-likeness in life and character; by fruits in the life we shall know whether or not we have the Spirit.

6. The baptism of the Spirit will get you into trouble. Jesus said He did not come to bring peace but the sword. "All those who live godly in Christ Jesus will suffer persecution." The trouble will come from where you least expect. Usually not from the world, but from your own church, or perhaps from your own family.

7. The filling of the Spirit is not "once filled always filled." It is a daily dying to self, a daily surrender of the will and of the ego. A daily filling is needed. Dwight L. Moody said: " I have to be filled with the Spirit every day because I leak!" The baptism of the Spirit is a journey not a destination, it is a process, not a single experience.

8. The cross is still central. Nothing will even replace that as the center of your spiritual life. The role of the Spirit is always to uplift Jesus, not Himself. "He shall glorify me" (John 16:14). "…He shall testify of me" (John 15:6).

9. Read John, Luke and Acts. Underline every passage you find about the Holy Spirit.

10. Get in a small group of Spirit- filled Christians. Share, pray, praise, teach and admonish one another, tell your story. We need each other.

11. God will not give you a false gift or a false Spirit. Not to worry. If you ask for bread, you will not be given a stone. God will not allow Satan to counterfeit an experience of the Holy Spirit in you if you have asked for the Spirit with a surrendered heart.

12. The Sprit will give you at least one gift for ministry, but you start getting *all* the fruits right now—love, joy, peace, serenity, self-control. This means that in a very real sense the kingdom of heaven begins for you now! Paul said the Holy Spirit is a down-payment on what we are going to get in heaven! Jesus came saying, "the kingdom of God is at hand," "the kingdom of God is within you." This promise has been sadly neglected. There has been so much emphasis on the second coming in the future that we have ignored the very real "coming of the kingdom" here and now. Jesus promised, "I will pray the Father, and He shall give you another Comforter … I will not leave you comfortless. I will come to you" (John 14:16-18). In a very real sense, the second coming has already happened! The much heralded "second coming" that is going to happen in the future should really be called the third coming!

13. When the Spirit fills you, your ordinary life will start to become extraordinary, you will become a great and extraordinary person, not great in power or money or sex appeal, but great in service, great in compassion, great in love. Like Jesus was.

14. There are three great essentials for maintaining the Spirit-filled life. Without any one of the three it is very difficult or impossible. They are so simple and basic they are often over-looked:

A. Prayer, both alone and with others. This is how connection with God and oneness with others is best enabled … the two absolutely essential pieces of the Spirit-filled Christian life.

B. Bible reading. *Not* Bible study. After you become a Spirit-filled Christian you will never "study" your Bible again. You will *meditate* on the word of God. Study is an intellectual activity. Remember, the Bible is a love-letter. You must learn to read it with your heart as well as with your head. You would not "study" a love-letter you received from your beloved like it was some kind of homework assignment. You would take it in to your soul, contemplate it, reflect on it, meditate on it, ponder it and treasure it.

It is through this incarnation of the Word in us that we enter eternal life, "Heaven and earth will pass away," Jesus says, "but my words will never pass away." Jesus is the Word and his words are everlasting life. His Word is the bread that takes our hunger away, the light that dispels our darkness, and the life that allows us to face death without fear … Reading the Word as a word of God for us is a sacramental event, an event by which the Word becomes present and transforms us into itself." Nowen, Henri. *The Selfless Way of Christ*. (Orbis Books, Maryknoll, NY 2007) p.80.

Remember, while the Bible is always the foundation, particularly the life and teachings of Jesus, the enlightening "Word" of God still comes to us through contemporary spiritual teachers, writers and speakers. Read as many spiritual books as you can. Spiritual reading is capable of giving great meaning and depth to your life. It is essential to your spiritual growth that you are fed regularly by other servants of God. Always have your Bible and a spiritual book beside your bed and read from each daily. *The Spirit still inspires!* The Spirit is still eagerly teaching new truth that the church has never heard before! He/She is constantly providing new, deep insights into the things of the kingdom of God! Always offering a deeper, more precious and personal experience with the presence of God! The last prophet did not die in AD 70! The last mystic did not wither away in a cave in France in 1300! Truth and spiritual experience are

301

oh so excitingly progressive and are being constantly and loving revealed! You are invited to this party!

C. Fellowship in both a small, intimate sharing prayer and support group and the larger church body. A burning, live red coal taken out of the fireplace will quickly lose its heat, color and energy if it is taken out of the fire and placed on the hearth by itself. We *need* each other to maintain our spiritual life, energy and balance. Even the perfect Jesus needed the intimacy, support and prayers of His close friends and His disciples to maintain His spiritual well-being. How much more then can we not afford to ignore this precious and essential spiritual resource. Go ahead. Just do it. Go to church even when you don't feel like it. Just show up. Showing up is a real big part of the Christian walk. Go with an open heart. Check in your judgmentalness at the door and you will be blessed regardless of the preacher or the sermon or some of your fellow parishioners that you find less than adorable!

APPENDIX E

THE LAYING ON OF HANDS

Theology professor Leo Van Dolson, a former missionary to Japan tells of an encounter he had there with someone who was questioning him about his Christian beliefs.

We were comparing our respective beliefs when suddenly he asked me a simple question but one I had never thought of and couldn't answer. 'You claim to follow all the practices of the apostolic church,' he said, 'why then don't you practice the laying on of hands as the New Testament tells us the apostles did?'

In Hebrews 6:2 immediately after referring to baptism, the writer lists the laying on of hands as one of the foundation principles of the early church.

Van Dolson went on to say:

"It is because many young people with whom I have come in contact in my classroom could easily be described as being ignorant of the Holy Spirit's work upon the heart even though they are believers that I am convinced that a return to the New Testament practice (of the laying on of hands) is *essential* in our church today. Our young people and our converts need to be impressed in a holy and solemn way with the fact that God bestows upon us, as He did upon Christ at His baptism, the gift of the Holy Spirit.

Also, in a time when the church is expecting a new outpouring of the Spirit as at Pentecost, it seems to me that such an emphasis would in a signal way make people aware of the bestowal of Christ's great and precious gift to the church. The practice of laying on of hands associated with baptism continued into the time of the development of the Catholic Church as attested to in the patristic writings. However, even as baptism was gradually changed by the church, this rite gradually changed from its original simple form until it has become the confirmation ceremony of the Roman Catholic Church. Most Protestants have rejected its current form as mere empty ceremonialism.

Calvin is said to have acknowledged that the custom of praying for converts to be filled with the Spirit was derived from the apostles. He stated, 'Wherefore the pure institution at this day ought to be retained.'

Acts 8 seems to indicate a precedent for believers who have already been baptized taking part in a special service of laying on of hands for the reception of the Holy Spirit, with remarkable manifestation following.

I cannot help wondering whether such a practice instituted in our churches today, in order to bring us fully into line with our own claim that we are following New Testament practice, might not also serve to bring our church not only a new insight in the beauty and significance of the spiritual gifts but also some of the power that we know is to be manifested in a remarkable way among God's people." (*Ministry Magazine*, Jan. 1969, pp. 37, 38.)

APPENDIX F

Statement of purpose for a small group focused on learning about and experiencing the gift of the Holy Spirit:

MISSION STATEMENT

After the cross, the most important doctrine in all of Christendom is the doctrine of the baptism or in-filling of the Holy Spirit. Yet, it is the most neglected and misunderstood of Christian beliefs.

The purpose of this group is to demonstrate that the filling of the Spirit is not merely a teaching to believe in but an enlightening, empowering encounter to be experienced each day. It is the throbbing heart of a vital, dynamic Christianity. Its result is the establishment of a precious moment-by-moment intimacy with God through Jesus Christ as we learn to become more God-conscious and to practice His loving presence.

This mystical, marvelous gift, won for you and me by the sacrifice of Jesus on the cross as certainly as He won eternal life for us, is available to every believer right now, solely by faith in the One who promised it to us and who commanded us to receive it.

The gift of the filling of the Holy Spirit is the true seal of God on the Christian. It is a "down-payment" on heaven. It is an identifying sign that the kingdom of God is indeed here now, and inside of you and me just as Jesus said it could be. It brings with it the sacred gifts of love, joy, peace, patience, kindness and forgiveness. It empowers one for a life of loving service to others.

Goal: To move from a traditional doctrinal paradigm as the foundation of one's religious experience to a new, relational-spiritual paradigm which recognizes that connection, moment-by moment connection, with the Divine through the in-dwelling presence of the Holy Spirit, is everything.

THE COMING OF THE KINGDOM OF GOD AND THE SECOND COMING:
TWO DISTINCTLY DIFFERENT EVENTS
LUKE 17:20,21

THE SECOND COMING	THE COMING OF THE KINGDOM
1. A physical, historical event	A spiritual event
2. It happens in the world, external	It happens in the heart, internal
3. It is an event	It is an experience
4. Everyone sees it with their eyes	It is unseen
5. Seeing ("every eye shall see Him")	Believing
6. Faith not necessary to experience it	Experience it only by faith
7. It will occur in the future	It is here now
8. No one knows when it will occur	You decide when it will occur
9. God makes it happen when He is ready	You make it happen when you are ready
10. You can't ignore it	You can ignore it
11. It is about justice	It is about transformation
12. It is historical	It is mystical
13. Jesus mentioned it a few times	Jesus talked about it constantly
14. It is about re-organization	It is about incarnation
15. Jesus does it physically	The Holy Spirit does it spiritually

APPENDIX H

RELIGION / SPIRITUALITY: THE DIFFERENCES

RELIGION IS MORE ABOUT MORE ABOUT	SPIRITUALITY IS
Fear	Awe
Coercion	Choice
Change	Transformation
Believing	Knowing
A Creed	A Person
What I Believe	Whom I Believe In
Rules	Principles
Exclusive	Inclusive
Unchanging Traditions	Expanding Truths
Force	Power
Christ is our Example	He is our substitute
Trying	Abiding
Struggling	Surrendering
Salvation by Works (Behavior)	Salvation by Faith
Imitation	Incarnation
Romans 7	Romans 8
Answers	Questions
Reason	Faith
Thinking	Feeling
Understanding	Experiencing
Platonic	Passionate

The Map	The Journey
The Menu	The Meal
A Committee	A Party
Conformity	Individuality
Closed	Open
Exclusivistic	Pluralistic
Talking	Listening
The Mouth	The Ears
Martha	Mary
Fund-raising TV Evangelists	Mother Teresa
Judging	Accepting
Institutionalized	Individualized
Hierarchical System	The Individual
Patriarchal	Gender Blind
Past or Future Focused	Present Focused
Heaven Above	Heaven Within
Heaven Comes Later	Heaven Now
Pushing	Pulling
Grasping	Releasing
The Law	Grace
The Truth	Love
Doing	Communing

APPENDIX I

THE SPIRITUAL DISCIPLINES

1. Silence --- stillness --- solitude "Be still and know that I am God" (Ps. 46:10).

2. Meditation: personal prayer, heart-prayer, soul-prayer

"I will meditate on all your works and consider all your mighty deeds" (Psalms 77:12).   "To pray is to descend with the mind into the heart and there to stand before the face of the Lord."

3. Group and public prayer

4. Fasting … from food, or from rich food or from excess food or from electronics, the media and social networks, or from words and even from thinking so much! Perhaps the most powerful fast of all.is to fast from words and even thoughts, while inwardly communing with God.

5. Fellowship --- oneness --- communion, vulnerability, intimacy, small groups "Confess your faults one to another and pray for each another" (James 5:16).

6. Immersing oneself in the love letters, the Bible and other spiritual enlightening books, tapes, CDs, DVDs, blogs, podcasts, audio files and other ways God expresses His living, progressive, dynamic truth in the world today

7. Assembling to worship with other people

8. Giving: money, time, attention, loving, unconditional service, sacrifice

9. Confession

10. Working for peace, freedom, justice and dignity for other human beings

11. Continually expressing gratitude and praise and adoration to the Father

12. Practicing the presence of God

13. Surrender

APPENDIX J

THE THREE GREAT TRUTHS

1. GOD IS LOVE

2. JESUS SAVES

3. THE HOLY SPIRIT WANTS TO FILL YOU NOW

APPENDIX K:

THE FRUITS OF THE EGO

(To be contrasted with the Characteristics of the Spirit-Filled Life at the beginning of the book)

1. SELFISHNESS
2. FEAR
3. RAGE
4. GREED
5. LUST
6. ENVY
7. POWER-HUNGER
8. ARROGANCE
9. ANXIETY
10. BITTERNESS
11. JUDGMENTALNESS
12. CYNICISM
13. RESENTMENT
14. JEALOUSY
15. SELF-RIGHTEOUSNESS
16. EXCESSIVE AMBITION
17. MATERIALISM
18. PRIDE
19. DECEIT
20. ISOLATION
21. LONELINESS
22. DESPAIR
23. NEEDINESS
24. NARCISSISM
25. LAZINESS
26. COMPULSIONS
27. ADDICTIONS
28. GLUTTONY
29. DEATH

APPENDIX L

FEELINGS: A PATH TO CONNECTION

Note: Communicating on a "feeling" level instead of just on an information or ideal level allows us to move more directly into a place of connection and closeness. The goal is to be able to freely express our feelings to others as one way to draw deeper into an intimate fellowship and oneness. It is this kind of oneness that helps create the atmosphere where the Spirit can be present and bring healing and comfort and new insight and truth.

Feelings are not good or bad. They are just feelings. We can learn to be aware of them in ourselves and others without judging them. As we become more conscious of them, we will be able to acknowledge them as valid, to "feel" them and express and share them where appropriate. Then, we can either release and surrender them to God if they are negative or celebrate and enjoy them if they are positive. Like music or prayer, feelings can be a portal to the soul, to connection to each other and to God.

I FEEL:

AFRAID
ANGRY
LEFT OUT
REJECTED
BETRAYED
WRONGED
INSULTED
HOPELESS
ANXIOUS
FRUSTRATED
GUILTY
LONELY
EMPTY
SAD
EMBARRASSED
OVERWHELEMED
HUMILILATED
(Warning: Marianne Williamson says that, unless acknowledged, negative feelings translate easily into… "I feel hungry". Then, people tend to eat to block out their negative feelings or emotional pain)

I FEEL:

CHERISHED
LOVED
CARED ABOUT
HEARD

VALUED
HONORED
JOYFUL
EXCITED
ENTHUSIASTIC
PASSIONATE
ENERGIZED
BLESSED
SATISFIED
SERENE
PEACEFUL
GRATEFUL

APPENDIX M

CONSCIOUSNESS RAISERS!

1. God is love
2. You can only have what you believe you can have
3. Why be normal?
4. Jesus is not a religion
5. Without God, democracy can not endure
6. Live in a state of ecstatic gratitude
7. Inspired = in-Spirit
8. You are a habitation for God
9. Detach from the outcome
10. Your highest purpose is service
11. Infinite patience produces immediate results!
12. You are love
13. Make a somersault into the inconceivable
14. Go on a rampage of appreciation.
15. Life is service
16. Kindness is everything
17. Nothing matters but Him
18. Never take yourself seriously
19. You are peace and joy
20. Be thankful
21. Act "as if"
22. You are not your stuff
23. You are free
24. It will all work out
25. He who has the most toys… is distracted
26. Forgiveness… the only path out of hell
27. See the light in people
28. Be at peace
29. Fear not
30. Show mercy
31. Dwell in love
32. Give your life away
33. Start now
34. Listen to your heart
35. What is essential is invisible to the eye
36. Giving: a way of life
37. Don't die with your music still inside you
38. Miracles happen
39. Believe in miracles
40. Open the door
41. Reach out
42. Live your passion

43. Raise your frequency of vibration
44. Align yourself with beauty
45. Instill calmness
46. Let go of your need to have more
47. Die daily
48. Peace is of God
49. Stop being offended
50. Angels are present
51. Stay connected
52. Renew your mind
53. Be love
54. Sufficient unto the day...
55. Extend kindness
56. Surrender
57. Truth is expanding
58. Live in the light
59. Banish doubt
60. Away with fear
61. Someone is knocking
62. Don't do stress
63. Now is the portal to God
64. Things are getting better
65. Stop talking so much
66. No evil will triumph in the end
67. I'm here on purpose
68. Abiding, not trying
69. It will all work out in the end
70. The present moment is all there is
71. Truth is progressive
72. Live in wonder
73. Take the first step
74. Stop offering resistance
75. There is a Power within you but not of you
76. Snuggling, not struggling
77. The solidity of matter is an illusion
78. Transcend your ego
79. Practice the Presence
80. The only time is now
81. See the big picture
82. Honor everyone
83. The Kingdom is within you
84. The Kingdom is here now
85. You are not your feelings
86. God is an is
87. The past and the future veil God from our sight
88. The secret of life is to die before you die
89. Let go of your pain
90. Let go of your fear

91. Question all authority…especially all religious authority
92. The time is now
93. Learn from a child
94. It's up to you
95. Bloom where you are planted
96. Practice forgiveness
97. Consciousness is rising
100. I am
101. God is beyond and within
102. Without ego there is only love
103. Feel your legitimate pain
104. Just ask
105. Become love
106. Choice is everything
107. The curtain was torn
108. Detach
109. Suffering …the path to enlightenment
110. The past does not exist
111. Worry doesn't work
112. Speak softly
113. Yield to overcome
114. Surrender … the key to the spiritual
115. Accept what is
116. Accept what isn't
117. You are not your mind
118. Jesus saves. Really
119. Refuse to be a victim
120. Get over it
121. Blaming doesn't help
122. Eat slowly
123. What is, is.
124. Higher consciousness wants to manifest in you
125. Create no further pain
126. Become joy
127. Be where you are
128. Stop comparing
129. Underneath the anger there is always fear and pain
130. Love the one you are with
131. Darkness can not survive the presence of light
132. Be where you are
133. Become joy
134. Just admit it
135. Stop comparing
136. Get your dying out of the way now
137. Let go
138. You are cherished
139. Just do it
140. The choice is yours

141. Nothing is ever missing
142. Want what you have
143. Become peace
144. Don't wait
145. Live in a state of alert presence
146. Normal is overrated
147. Favor the bold
148. The future is not here
149. Surrender your pain
150. Show up as you
151. Life is now
152. Be fearless
153. Breathe
154. Be His love
155. Surrender your fear
156. Start where you are
157. Love is a synonym for God
158. Give to receive
159. Die to live
160. Lose to find
161. Release to keep
162. I no longer live
163. Speak your truth
164. Simplify
165 De-accumulate
166. Walk in love
167. Surrender all
168. Still yourself
169. Start out
170. Rejoice
171. Be here now
172. Judge not
173. Consider the lilies
174. Listen
175. It's not all about you
176. It is always now
177. Be your word
178. Own it
179. The two most powerful words …"I surrender"
180. Live to serve
181. Let it go
182. God is Christ-like
183. Turn the other cheek
184. Suspend disbelief
185. Connection is everything
186. Love is doing
187. Be the light
188. Love mercy

189. The Holy Spirit wants to fill you now
190. Angels light the way
191. Death is just a sleep
192. Now is the day of salvation
193. Jesus paid it all
194. Sing the song of life in the key of love
195. Every breath is on loan from God
196. He is coming back
197. The only limits on your spiritual growth are self-imposed
198. Beware of arriving
199. The only good ego is a dead ego
200. Normal is just a dryer setting
201. Don't get caught up in the results
202. Do one thing at a time
203. People who are afraid of the dark are not the problem; it's the people who are afraid of the light
204. Two ways to view life … there are no such thing as miracles: Everything is a miracle!
205. The whole purpose of life is to become God-conscious
206. Are you connected?
207. Your very consciousness is a supreme gift form God
208. Be Jesus to people
209. Be kind
210. You are not your thoughts
211. The mind is to be a tool for the soul
212. Everything is connected
213. Everyone is connected
214. Stop thinking so much … It is a mystery!
215. God is nowhere and everywhere
216. Transcend judgment
217. Life is a dream … you do not wake up until you die
218. Become the observer of you
219. Be a spiritual evolutionist
220. You are either living in ego… or living in Spirit. Choose
221. You can't think your way to heaven
222. Be love to people
223. You are His arms
224. Ask and you will receive
225. Enter into Presence
226. Be humble
227. Bear one another's burdens
228. It's a process
229. Be grateful
230. Listen with ears of love (I hear you)
231. I see you
232. God manifests through people
233. God has you on backup
234. Violence breeds violence

235. Resist not evil
236. Living an egocentric life only creates more misery in the world
237. Become the space where God can dwell
238. If God is omnipresent... then everywhere is sacred
239. No self ...No problems
240. Be on time
241. The Journey ... is from egoism to unconditional love
242. Whatever commands your attention is your master
243. What you love, you will become
244. Without dying, the soul cannot come to life
245. The child of God is sustained by the Father within
246. Pray for everyone you meet
247. When the phone rings, pray to be love to whoever is calling
248. True prayer is nothing but love
249. Send people loving thoughts
250. Love outrageously! Extravagantly!
251. What we love, we will become
252. Help me to live in your Presence
253. Adore God
254. Rest in God
255. Listen to God
256. Love wins

ABOUT THE AUTHOR

A wilderness lake, surrounded by snow-capped mountains, was the setting for Douglas Cooper's childhood. He spent his time skiing, ice-skating, hiking, and fishing. There was no electricity or roads in the remote native village in western Alaska where he lived. Doug's parents were commercial fishermen and tug boat operators. He grew up fishing for salmon with nets and hauling freight on barges. No cars where he grew up led him to begin learning to fly before he learned to drive.

Hiking is his favorite pastime, whether it is in Alaska where he spends every summer commercial fishing, or in the mountains and valleys of Northern California where his home is the rest of the year. Currently Doug lives in the Napa Valley with his wife Pamela. He is the father of four children: Scott, Shana, Vanessa and Dan.

Doug has enjoyed numerous and varied occupations including longshoreman, taxi driver, deckhand, salesman, cannery worker, fishing boat captain, tour guide, pastor, hospital chaplain, family counselor, commercial pilot and flight instructor. He holds flight ratings for land and seaplanes and multi-engine planes.

Currently, Dr. Cooper is president and owner of The Alpha Corporation, a wholesale distributing firm, and a part-time family counselor. His writing career includes publication in many magazines including *Good Housekeeping, Plane & Pilot, Yachting, Ministry, Signs of the Times,* and *Life and Health*. He has had eight books published: *Way Up North, Living God's Love* (over 100,00 copies sold), *Living God's Joy, Living in our Finest Hour, Living We Have Just Begun, Living the Spirit-filled Life, Stranger to the World, Living in the Light* and *Gentle Dove, The Holy Spirit, God's Greatest Gift*.

Doug is a graduate of Walla Walla University (B.A. Theology, 1964), Andrews University (Master's degree in Theology, 1967), and the California Graduate School of Family Psychology (now Argosy University), (Ph.D. in Marriage, Family and Child Counseling 1992).

Dr. Cooper is a spiritual teacher and lecturer who leads retreats and seminars for churches and other groups.

His favorite themes are "Living God's Love," "Living in the Spirit," and "The Truth about God."

You can contact him by phoning Alpha Communication at 1-800-289-2025 or by emailing douglascooper12@gmail.com.

This book is available on line to download to your computer, tablet, or phone, or to your electronic reader at www.amazon.com, www.barnesandnoble.com,   and other locations. To order it on eBay go to www.stores.ebay.com/thealphacorporation. To order additional printed and signed copies of this book, go to www.thegentledove.com which is also Douglas Cooper's website.